Battle of the Little Bighorn Series
Volume Four

The ABCs of Custer's Last Stand

Arrogance, Betrayal and Cowardice

by
Arthur C. Unger

Upton & Sons, Publishers
El Segundo, California
2004

TABLE OF CONTENTS

ILLUSTRATIONS

EXHIBITS & MAPS

PREFACE

This study is an in depth review of the Battle of the Little Bighorn, based upon the premise that the course and conduct of the battle were well known to the Army survivors and rescuers immediately after the battle. Diligent forensic studies were made of the battlefield, in the days immediately following the battle, by the survivors and rescuers. Letters, journals, telegrams, reports and maps were prepared, by the Army survivors and rescuers that were sent to loved ones back home, Superior Officers in the East or later published. These documents recorded precisely where the bodies of men and horses were found and how it appeared that the battle was fought. These documents were later augmented by the statements of the Indians who fought in and were the victors of the battle. The facts are presented in a straight forward, undiluted manner, with excerpts given showing exactly what each person said. Analysis is then performed and conclusions reached based upon these known facts. The interrelationships of the main protagonists, their personality flaws and the effects they had upon each other and the outcome of the battle are superimposed on the conclusions drawn from the known facts, thereby generating a true and realistic description of what transpired.

One purpose of this writing is to refute the popular images and Hollywood myths which have long surrounded the battle and been accepted as truisms. The known facts prove that the outcome of the battle was an inglorious event caused by the failings of the surviving Army Officers to obey the orders of their commander and to properly execute and perform their duty. It will show that Custer relied on his subalterns, Major Reno and Captain Benteen, to perform their duty and obey his orders. When they failed to do so, Custer was annihilated due to a lack of support and a reticence on the part of more than half his command to come forward to the sound of the guns and engage the enemy, even when there was neither enemy nor resistance in their front. Custer relied on the proper performance of his subalterns but he was denied their obedience, prompt and proper compliance to his orders and dutiful execution and performance of their duties as officers of the United States Army.

The text will show that the course and conduct of the battle, as it is generally believed to have occurred, are the culminations of more than 125 years of distortions, manipulations, concealing of documents, government alterations and changes to original documents, suppression of the truth and overt lying on the part of certain survivors, for the sole purpose of protecting their self images and the alleged good of the Army.

This book will provide, to the public for the first time ever, the long suppressed and hidden **original map of the battlefield as drawn by Lieutenant Edward Maguire, signed by him, in his own handwriting.** This map was hidden from the public for more than one hundred years by Edward W. Smith and his descendants. Edward W. Smith was a Captain in the Army, he served as Adjutant to General Alfred Terry and was General Terry's brother-in-law. The map was kept from public examination and scrutiny until the early 1990's when it was sold at a public auction by the heirs of Edward Smith. It was subsequently sold at auction two more times before it became the property of the author, who now, for the first time, opens it to the light of public scrutiny. The map conclusively shows Custer's trails and routing to Last Stand Hill via Medicine Tail Ford. It indicates that General Custer did in fact attempt to ford the river and attack the village. It also shows the true size and location of the village. All of the foregoing were known facts of the battle, prior to 1879, and have been needlessly debated these many years afterwards. This original map and its conclusions will be strongly supported by undistorted written documents and oral statements made prior to 1879. These facts existed prior to the United States Army's attempt at a broad brush whitewash of the battle, utilizing a sham event called the Reno Court of Inquiry.

June 25, 1876, was a day whose events have inspired more debate and controversy than any other day in United States Military History. More has been written about this single, relatively insignificant battle than any other battle in our nation's military history. The Battle of the Little Bighorn lasted two days, June 25, 1876 and June 26, 1876. The Indians besieging the surviving elements of United States Army's vaunted Seventh Cavalry withdrew, at approximately 3:00 P.M. on June 26, 1876. This was nearly a day prior to the arrival of a relief column commanded by General Terry and Colonel Gibbon, but neither Reno nor Benteen made any attempt to find or assist their commander. During the course of the battle, approximately 260 officers, men, scouts and civilians assigned to the Seventh Cavalry perished. Both Reno and Benteen failed to advance their troops toward the sound of the guns, when it was obvious to all present, save them, that Custer was hotly engaged and was in need of reinforcements and ammunition which he had requested with a written order. Reno abandoned his command for nearly an hour on a fool's errand. In his absence Benteen made no effort to fulfill his duty as a subaltern and send assistance to his commanding officer. It was only when they were shamed by the unilateral action of Captain Weir that a feeble attempt to go to Custer's assistance was made. This effort was quickly withdrawn when it encountered light resistance. Thereafter, both Reno and Benteen disavowed any knowledge of Custer's possible whereabouts or his status; even though they were both under a duty as subalterns to report to their commanding officer as quickly as feasible after performing their ordered actions. Their failures were a betrayal of their oath, commander and comrades and showed cowardice in the face of an enemy who was no longer offering resistance in their front.

The battle was not significant because it determined the outcome of the war, as the victors of the battle were the eventual losers of the war. The battle did not cause a change or betterment of government policy, if anything the outcome hardened the already intransigent stand of the government on a socially negative position. The more famous last stand segment of the battle did not yield to history glorious acts of great courage, as there were no soldier survivors from this segment of the engagement to retell their stories. The acts of bravery committed by soldiers during the secondary or siege phase of the battle were performed, by a few, in a defensive stand necessitated by a cowardly leader's refusal to act or fulfill his duty. Custer's last stand and the siege of the Seventh Cavalry by Sioux and Cheyenne Indians was not a battle which caused major social or economic change. There were not any great new military innovations or strategies advanced, if anything it was a resounding defeat of a modern army by Northern Plains Indian opponents. When the true insignificance of the battle is understood, then one can readily see that the original debate was generated not by real issues but personal and political motivations. An Army which hoped to whitewash the embarrassing story of reluctance, disobedience, drunkenness and cow-

ardice; the desire of a grieving widow to buy a glorious page in history for her departed husband; a pro Democratic press which was grateful for any excuse to torment a Republican President; all combined to provide the fertile ground for the legend of a man to grow into an icon which symbolizes all that was good and all that was evil, in the dealings of two races. Thus has ensued a debate which has lasted for more than one hundred twenty-five years.

Most, if not all, the texts previously written, focus on: why did Custer do this, or what did Custer intend to do when he went there, or how did Custer plan on accomplishing this, etc.? These questions were usually augmented with: what if Reno continued, what if Benteen arrived earlier, what if Reno and Benteen went to Custer's assistance earlier, what if Custer arrived the next day, what if Custer took the Gatling guns or the Second Cavalry troops, etc. The simple fact, which is greatly overlooked by these scholars, is that the truth of how the battle was fought was well known prior to the Army whitewash of 1879. That all one need do is study the available documents created between June 25, 1876 and January 1, 1879 and overlay upon them the interviews of the Indians who fought in the battle, and the picture becomes clear as to what occurred.

An arrogant Army, with inadequate numbers of ill equipped and poorly trained soldiers, believed it could overcome large numbers of primitive natives. This was based upon the premise that Indians as a whole would not stand and fight, but merely scatter and flee, while at most fighting a rear guard action. Lieutenant Colonel George A. Custer, who believed his objective was containment of the Indians, and that he would have failed in meeting his objective if he allowed the Indians to escape by running away and scattering, was a commander who relied on his orders being obeyed and fulfilled to the best of his subalterns' abilities. Custer relied on the belief that all of the men under his command would fight the enemy as ordered and be willing to make the ultimate sacrifice if called upon to do so, as readily as he would. Major Marcus A. Reno was a drunken, cowardly second in command who might have had a limited amount of courage and ability to follow, but was totally devoid of any courage or ability with which to lead men. Captain Frederick W. Benteen was a malcontent, vindictive third in command. He allowed his repressed hatred for his commander to effect his thoughts and actions. This caused him to act in an unprofessional and nonmilitary manner on June 25, 1876, thereby, forever leaving his hands partially stained with the blood of 212 of his needlessly slaughtered comrades in arms. A commander, no matter how gifted he is, in the leadership of men and military strategy, simply cannot achieve victory when seven twelfths of the men under his command either refuse to fight or are not ordered to do so by their immediate commanders.

The core elements necessary for a disaster to occur, Arrogance, Betrayal and Cowardice, were present and flourished on June 25, 1876. The defeat of a modern army by an overwhelming multitude of Indians, who for the first time in their history, chose to stand and fight, rather than run and scatter in all directions, as the **Arrogant** Army Staff had anticipated. Captain Benteen **Betrayed** his commander when he allowed his hatred to overrule his natural tendency toward obedience, causing him to perform in an unprofessional and nonmilitary manner. He did not obey his commander's orders by hiding behind the pretense that he was under the command of a sniveling, drunk, coward. He, thus, betrayed and endangered the entire command, by placating Reno. Major Reno failed to perform his duty, obey his orders and act in a professional military manner. He was drunk, unable to perform his duty and abandoned his command at a time when it was in dire need of leadership. When he was faced with the complexities and burdens of command, a level to which he aspired, his sole reaction was **Cowardice** in the face of the enemy. He jeopardized his entire command and caused the annihilation of his commanding officer and 212 other officers and men, who died, looking east wondering where the requested relief was and when it would arrive!

Arthur C. Unger
2004

DEDICATION

To: Aunt Sue.

CHAPTER 1
Washita: The Seeds of Disaster

The seeds of disaster may well have been planted on the field of the Battle of the Washita, fought on November 27, 1868. In the freezing pre dawn of this winter morning, Custer attacked the sleeping village of Black Kettle from multiple directions. The 7th Cavalry killed 17 warriors and 105 women and children in the course of this attack. The results of this battle were much distorted and puffed up by the Army, for it sorely needed a "great victory" against the Plains Indians. It was this action that gained for George Custer the reputation of being a great Indian fighter. It also was the cause of internal strife and conflict within the 7th Regiment United States Cavalry that was to haunt the regiment, until it met its date with infamy and forever thereafter.

Captain Benteen was a victim of his own malcontent personality, and he was extremely jealous of Custer. He resented that Custer, who was much younger than he, had achieved far higher rank during the Civil War. Benteen felt that because he was a Southerner by birth, he was not given full and ample recognition for his performance in the Civil War. Benteen testified against Custer during Custer's Court Martial in 1867. By the time of the Battle of Washita, the jealousy had festered into animosity, and post Washita it grew into overt hatred.

Prior to the commencement of the battle, Custer had given orders that no one was to leave their units and go off independently. Major Joel Elliott had his own agenda, as he was looking for glory and promotion. These are the acts and traits normally attributed, negatively, to Custer. During the battle, a small group of Cheyenne fled the village perimeter and headed downstream toward the nearby Indian villages. Major Elliott took off in pursuit with some eighteen men, in direct contradiction of Custer's pre battle orders. When Elliott rode off in pursuit of the escaping Cheyennes, he turned in the saddle, waved to Lt. Owen Hale, and delivered a line which almost sounded theatrical: *"Here goes for a brevet or a coffin!"*[1] Over the course of time, variations of this quote have often been

---

[1]Connell, *Son of the Morning Star*, 195.

erroneously attributed to Custer, to serve as evidence to condemn him for being an overzealous fool.

Custer, much like at the Little Big Horn eight years later, had attacked Black Kettle's village with limited prior reconnaissance. Had a more extensive reconnaissance been performed, it would have been known before the attack that Black Kettle's village was merely one circle of a semi contiguous group of Indian circles, extending in length for nearly twelve miles. There was a mixed population of plains tribes present, including Comanches, Kiowas, Apaches, and Arapahos, camped along the Washita River. The difference between Washita and Little Big Horn was that Black Kettle's circle was isolated from the rest of the circles. Had the attack been closer to the heart of the village, the results might well have resembled the debacle at the Little Big Horn, instead of being hailed as a great victory for the Army. It was only after the initial successful attack on Black Kettle's camp that Custer became aware of the imminent danger of thousands of Indians being nearby, massing to come to Black Kettle's aid.

Custer had the immediate area searched for Elliott and his party, but to no avail. Elliott disobeyed orders by leaving the village area in pursuit of a few fleeing Indians. As commander, Custer had to weigh the value of a prolonged search to find Elliott against the risk posed to the entire regiment of a counterattack from the large numbers of warriors rushing to Black Kettle's aid from downstream villages. Custer made the prudent decision, unfortunately, it was one for which Benteen never forgave him.

There was a seasonal difference between the battles which yielded a great advantage to the Army. It was this seasonal difference that allowed Custer to commit a similar blunder to one he later committed at Little Big Horn, but this time he was rewarded with victory instead of disaster. Custer attacked at Washita, without thorough reconnaissance beforehand, much as he did at Little Big Horn. At Washita, he wound up attacking a single isolated circle beyond the immediate supporting range of the other circles camped along the river. Custer achieved victory. The seasonal differences required great distances between the camps because of the lack of grass for grazing, sanitary purposes, and the inability of the Indians to be mobile in the winter.

As Washita was a winter battle, the Indian circles were much farther apart and not in supporting distance of each other. Estimates of the combined population of the multiple villages strung out along the Washita River that day run from 5,000 to 9,000 souls. If the warriors present represented only twenty percent of the combined population, there would have been from 1,000 to 1800 warriors in the many villages, far more than the number of soldiers present and comparable to the original Army estimates of the number of warriors who would be found near the Little Big Horn.

It was perhaps the impression that Custer gained from Washita that allowed him to attack the Indian village at Little Big Horn with bravado and no prior scouting. Washita may have planted a seed in his brain that grew to a theory, no matter how many Indians there are, they are never close enough to each other to assist themselves. The large disjointed far-flung village at Washita was a far cry from the immense contiguous village at Little Big Horn. The memory of a large sprawling village may have prompted Custer's ordering of Benteen's scout to the left and Reno's valley charge. Benteen being sent to "find" the other villages and Reno being sent to attack a part of the whole. Memory told Custer he had sufficient time to attack a single village, capture many prisoners, destroy large quantities of valuables and depart with his forces intact prior to the other Indians in the supporting villages being able to arrive and counterattack. It was perhaps the tainted memories of good results from questionable acts that prompted Custer to repeat these poor acts at Little Big Horn. Unfortunately for him and his men, the law of averages caught up to him, and Custer's Luck took a holiday on June 25, 1876.

Elliott was ordered not to leave the village on his own, as were all other officers. He disobeyed orders and left the vicinity of the village to chase a few Indians. His disobedience was in blatant violation of direct orders, supported by his statement, "Here goes for a brevet or a coffin." Elliott was the true glory seeker who knowingly disobeyed orders and irresponsibly put his regiment at risk. Custer could not further jeopardize the regiment with a prolonged search for Elliott. Warriors were already strafing the village with a sniping fire, and a large force of Indians downstream were massing for a counter attack. Custer, rightly so, was forced to abandon the search for Elliott, enabling Custer to leave the battlefield before the counterattack could be accomplished.

Benteen was a close friend of Major Elliott, and he felt the search should have been continued until Elliott and his command were found. Benteen's thought process was adversely affected by his acerbic personality and myopia. He demonstrated a gross inability to see reality in any situation that put him at odds with Custer. Subsequent to Washita, Benteen's hatred of Custer became more open, as Benteen would forever blame "Custer's desertion of Elliott" as the cause of Elliott's death. Benteen could not accept that Elliott's foolhardy actions caused his own demise and Custer had acted prudently in the best interests of the majority of his command.

This hatred grew within Benteen, and it is well possible that it adversely affected his thought processes and actions at the Little Big Horn. It was Benteen's belief during the battle of the Little Big Horn that Custer had deserted Reno and Benteen, just as Benteen felt Custer had deserted Elliott at Washita. This is supported by a conversation held between Benteen and General Terry on the morning of June 27, 1876, as retold by Charles Roe to Walter Mason Camp, on December 8, 1910:

...when Terry came up on the morning of June 27 the first thing Benteen said was to ask Gen. Terry if he knew where Custer had gone. Terry said: "To the best of my knowledge and belief he lies on this ridge about 4 miles below here with all of his command killed." Benteen

said: "I can hardly believe it. I think he is somewhere down the Big Horn grazing his horses. At the Battle of Washita he went off and left part of his command, and I think he would do it again." Gen. Terry said: "I think you are mistaken, and you will take your company and go down where the dead are lying and investigate for yourself." Benteen did this, Capt. Weir going along. When Benteen came back he was pale, and looked troubled and said: "We found them, but I did not expect that we would."[2]

When Benteen returned from the battlefield, he had a pale and ghastly look about him, much as if the ghosts of 212 of his comrades were sitting on his back and his hands were red with their blood. Benteen may not have done all that he could have at the Little Big Horn to assist Custer and follow the orders given to him. The longer the battle endured the more he felt that his portion of the regiment was deserted by Custer, this was exacerbated by his hatred for Custer and his acerbic malcontent personality. Benteen's feelings that Custer had abandoned the rest of the command at the Little Big Horn may well have been the driving force behind his unwillingness to urge Reno to march to Custer's aid long before he did, and while such an action might achieve a positive result.

---

[2]Hammer, *Custer in 76*, 248-249.

CHAPTER 2
The Grand Plan

The government of the United States had decided in late 1875 to confine the Sioux and Cheyenne Nations to reservations, in order to open their lands to settlement. This was the reason outwardly given, but the additional unstated motivations included the Government's desire to gain possession of the Black Hills from the Sioux, to allow exploitation of its natural resources and the completion of the trans-continental railroad without further Indian interference. The Fort Laramie Treaty of 1868[3] ceded the Black Hills to the Sioux for "as long as the waters flowed and the grass grew."

The discovery of gold in the Black Hills, in 1874, by an expeditionary force commanded by Lt. Colonel George A. Custer, caused the Government to reach the conclusion that the water was no longer flowing and the grass had stopped growing. Thus, the United States Government, utilizing the principles of Manifest Destiny, felt justified in forcing the Sioux to live on new reservations. This would allow white prospectors to legally ravage the Black Hills in search of gold, mining and lumber interests, to exploit the vast natural resources there, and the railroad magnates back east to complete the transcontinental railroad thereby reaping enormous profits.

The Indians were given an ultimatum in the fall of 1875, either surrender to a reservation by January 31, 1876 or be declared hostile. Most copies of the ultimatum that were sent to Indian Chiefs were not even delivered by the deadline. The Indian Chiefs who received the ultimatum did not believe or understand it, as they relied on the provisions of the Fort Laramie Treaty. On February 1, 1876, most if not all Sioux and Cheyenne were declared hostile, and the matter was transferred to the War Department for resolution. To accomplish the task, a most formidable, for the day, grouping of troops was assembled. The troops committed to the confining of the Indians to reservations consisted of three

---

[3]Exhibit 16.

columns, aggregating in excess of 2200 officers and men. This was one of the largest convergence of United States troops in the thirty- three year period between the Civil War and the Spanish American War. It was also the Army's most dismal failure in the same period.

The southern, or Wyoming, column was the strongest of the three columns consisting of more than 1100 officers and men, augmented by approximately 300 Crow and Shoshone Indian Scouts. The column was commanded by Brigadier General George Crook. Crook preferred to use his military expertise to amass supplies and outfit his troops, rather than to actually fight in battles. Over the course of his career, he perfected the art of supplying his troops while others actually fought the battles intended for him. Crook's column was proceeding on a northerly march and was intended to be one of the three convergent forces that was to overwhelm the Sioux, publicly estimated to have a strength of between 800 and 1500 warriors. Lieutenant General Sheridan, who had overall command of the operation and was the formulator of the plan, believed that any one of the three columns, individually, could defeat the enemy.

Consistent with his record, Crook never made it to where the Indians were believed to be. The only reason Crook was engaged, was that the Sioux came to him and attacked his column. Crook met less than half of the same hostile forces, which later annihilated Custer. Crook's engagement was fought in the valley of the Rosebud River, on June 17, 1876, and he was nearly defeated, though the battle was officially declared a draw. His inability to subdue the Indians, who were essentially equal in number to his force, was mostly due to the ineptitude of his subordinate officers and his personal unwillingness to join the battle. It further dealt a severe blow to Sheridan's theory that the Army could engage huge numbers of Indians, many times the Army's numbers, and win decisive victories. It also voided the premise that the Indians would scatter and flee and not stand and fight. The reason the battle was deemed a draw was that near the end, when the outcome appeared dire, Crook's Crow Scouts attacked and drove off the Sioux. This saved Crook from a debacle of the magnitude which Custer would suffer eight days hence.

Foolish Elk, in a September 22, 1908 interview, described the Battle of the Rosebud in this manner:

"Before the battle of the Rosebud started, they were in doubt as to the intentions of the soldiers, not knowing whether they wished to fight or make a treaty. The Indians therefore got all ready to fight and waited to see what the soldiers would do. As the soldiers started firing, the Indians concluded that they desired to fight, and so they gave them what they appeared to want. In this fight the Indians thought they had won a victory, but it was understood that other troops were in the Indian country, and they concluded to go to the big village with Sitting Bull on the Greasy

Grass Creek (Little Bighorn) without further loss of men and ammunition."[4]

On July 10, 1910, He Dog related the following regarding the Battle of the Rosebud:

"Indian in lone tepee was a Sans Arc, a brother of Turning Bear. He was shot through bowels in Crook fight. We started out to fight Crook the second time but did not see Crows around and afraid Crows would get at our village, and we turned back. The reason did not pursue Crook was that we were far from our villages which were not only a long distance off but were strung out over much country. Did not pursue Crook because afraid Crows and Shoshones would get at our village. We saw Crook had a good many Indians. We knew that we had defeated him because he turned back."[5]

The Sioux felt they had defeated Crook as he abandoned the field of battle. They intended to come forward and engage him a second time. As they could not ascertain the whereabouts of Crook's Indian Scouts, who were more feared than the soldiers, they returned to their villages. The Battle of the Rosebud was perhaps a tactical draw as both sides departed from the field of battle and returned to their respective camps. However, the battle allowed the Sioux to test their mettle against the soldiers, and they found them not to be invincible. The Sioux had a strong resolve to stand and fight as they came forward to meet Crook and determine if he wanted to talk or fight.

The Sioux considered the battle a victory. All of this toughened and strengthened the resolve of the Sioux to stand and fight when Custer attacked them at the Little Bighorn. They had been tested in battle by this enemy and achieved victory. The "long knives" were no longer feared as invincible, and the Sioux that fought at the Rosebud, felt they could defeat these soldiers. When Custer attacked, many thought it was Crook returning. Thus, Custer would face an Indian enemy with a resolve and will to fight never before seen on the Great Plains.

After the engagement, Crook did what he did best, he retreated from the field, returned to his base camp in Goose Creek, Wyoming and set about resupplying his troops. While at Goose Creek, even though he was fully aware that two other columns were in the field searching for the same hostiles which he had fought, Crook took a sabbatical and went fishing. He did not bother to send word of his debacle to the remaining two columns in the field and he waited until June 23, 1876 before he sent a telegram to General Sheridan, informing him of the battle and its outcome. He concluded the telegram to General Sheridan with "I expect to find those Indians in rough places all the time and so have ordered five [5] companies of Infantry and ***shall not probably make any extended movements until they arrive."***[6] What Crook was saying, was that he had no desire to take to the field for a long time and that Sheridan

[4]Hammer, *Custer in 76*, 197.
[5]Ibid., 205.
[6]Exhibit10.

would only have two small swords to swing at the enemy.

As a result of his engagement, Crook was aware of a heretofore never seen willingness to stand and fight in the Sioux. He had stated in his telegram to Sheridan "that it is impossible to correctly estimate their numbers the attack however showed that they anticipated that they were strong enough to [thoroughly - crossed out] defeat the command during the engagement."[7] The intelligence he could have provided, may well have been all that was necessary to change the outcome of the Battle of the Little Bighorn. Crook knew his troops were engaged by approximately 1,200 warriors, a force of Indians within the parameters officially expected by the Army, but well below the numbers Sheridan knew had been massed. The Sioux had a willingness to fight that was not previously encountered. He knew his counterparts were unaware of the enemies' strength and willingness to fight. Crook allowed them to remain unaware until it was too late.

Why he did not make an effort to inform the other columns of the strength and aggressive attitude of the enemy and his own defeat is an unresolved mystery and may well have been a reasonable topic for a Court of Inquiry to investigate. Instead it has become an ignored by-product of the Custer defeat, and Crook's reputation did not gain the well-deserved tarnish it should have.

The western, or Montana, column was under the overall command of General Alfred Terry who was also tactical but not field commander of both the Montana and Dakota columns. The western, or Montana, column consisted of approximately 450 men, under the field command of Colonel John Gibbon. It was by far the weakest of the three columns consisting of approximately 300 infantry soldiers and four troops, 150 men of the Second Cavalry under the command of Major James S. Brisbin. It was this puny column, the smallest and weakest of the three, which rescued the remaining troops of the Seventh Cavalry on June 27, 1876. The remaining troops of the 7th Cavalry numbered 387 men and was essentially equal to Terry's column in manpower. However, while the Seventh Cavalry force was by far a more superior tactical fighting unit, it was hampered by a large number of wounded.

The northern, or Dakota, column that approached the Valley of the Little Bighorn under a southerly march was under the command of Lieutenant Colonel George A. Custer. The official regimental roster shows that the Regiment had a battle strength of 31 Officers, 567 Enlisted Men and 54 Indian Scouts and Civilians, on June 25, 1876. When the Battle of the Little Bighorn was over, the dead and missing aggregated 264 including, 16 Officers, 238 enlisted Men, and 10 Civilians. [See Exhibit 11]

The Dakota column, which was exclusively the Seventh Cavalry, was perhaps the tactically strongest column of the three as it numbered 652 men and was an all cavalry force. It was

---

[7]Ibid.

not, at Custer's specific design, hampered by pack wagons, infantry, or Gatling guns. It thus could and did move quickly and well at night.

Lieutenant General Philip H. Sheridan, though he knew full well the approximate strength of the Indians his three swords might face was in the thousands, let all three columns go into battle believing that the Sioux strength was between 800 and 1500 warriors. On June 8, 1876, a telegram was sent to Sheridan's Chicago Headquarters, informing him that there were "twelve hundred and seventy-three (1273) lodges under Sitting Bull, Crazy Horse and others on their way to Powder River to fight General Crook."[8] Sheridan did absolutely nothing about this telegram and made only the most feeble of attempts to advise his Field Commanders of the magnitude of the danger they faced. Twelve hundred and seventy lodges could contain from five to seven people and three to four warriors per lodge. This would indicate that the approximate number of Indians roaming the plains, on June 8, 1876, under Sitting Bull and Crazy Horse were between 6,500 and 8,500, with a warrior density ranging between 3,500 and 5,000. The question arises, what did Sheridan do with this intelligence and how did he try to inform his Field Commanders that they faced overwhelming odds? Sheridan made a very feeble and perhaps token attempt to disseminate this information by sending General Terry a letter. It is not known if a similar letter was sent to General Crook as well. Lieutenant Charles Varnum, Custer's Chief of Scouts, wrote in a July 4, 1876, letter to his parents:

*"When we got mail yesterday by a carrier from Fort Ellis, we received a letter from Sheridan, **a month old,** [effects added] cautioning Terry not to split his command as he had information that at least five thousand warriors were assembled, and I don't think there is any doubt but that we fought four thousand of them."*[9]

Sheridan greatly overestimated the ability of his three columns to fight the Indians. He was also an avowed Indian hater who coined the expression "the only good Indian is a dead Indian." Sheridan arrogantly believed that any of his three columns could defeat any enemy force that it might meet and engage. Sheridan, in part, based this belief on the knowledge that the Plains Indians had never previously stood and fought a major engagement. The Plains Indians had only stood and fought when they had prepared a trap and had a vast superiority in numbers, as demonstrated in the Fetterman Massacre. Captain Fetterman was lured into a trap by Crazy Horse who was fighting under Red Cloud. Red Cloud's warriors numbered more than one thousand, and three hundred of them, under Crazy Horse, lured Captain Fetterman and his eighty men into a trap, where they were annihilated.

Sheridan did not believe the Sioux would stand and fight against any of

---

[8]Exhibit 6.
[9]Graham, *The Custer Myth*, 343.

his three columns, he feared greatly that the Indians would do as they had historically done, scatter and flee the field, while fighting a rear guard action to allow their civilian population time to escape. Sheridan had an unwarranted and greatly exaggerated opinion of his troop's ability to engage large numbers of Indian warriors. As Crook had the largest force with approximately 1100 men, Custer the middle range force of approximately 650 men and Terry and Gibbon the small force of 450 men, Sheridan committed these units against a known Indian count of up to 5,000 warriors. Accordingly, Sheridan was willing to commit his forces against negative odds of from four to one against, to ten to one against them. He believed his forces would prevail against any group of Indians they might encounter, as he believed they would run and not fight.

So while Sheridan was personally aware that approximately five thousand Indians had massed to meet his three swords, he made only a feeble attempt to inform his Field Commanders. Sheridan wanted to change his plan from having three columns converge on the Indians to two columns. He notified Terry of this change in plans by a letter that was delivered nine [9] days after the Battle of the Little Big Horn. How and if he tried to notify General Crook of his desire to make a change in the plan is unknown. Sheridan allowed his Field Commanders to proceed, believing they would face from eight hundred to fifteen hundred warriors and any one of the columns could handle what it

might meet. Sheridan did this while he was in possession of information that told him there was upwards of five thousand warriors massed, and the two smaller columns, on their own, would be insufficient to handle what they might find massed against them.

Sheridan made a most feeble and futile attempt to change the plan, *by sending a letter*, apparently neither marked urgent nor delivered expeditiously to General Terry, that arrived after the debacle. If Sheridan had a true desire to change his plan, he could have and should have used an expeditious means of communication. Supplies were continually being ferried to Terry by the river steamer Far West. A dispatch rider or telegram could have been sent to Terry via the Far West. Sheridan had until June 22, 1876 to reach Terry with the news. That gave him a window of fourteen days, starting from when he received the June 8, 1876 telegram, which informed him of Sitting Bull and Crazy Horse's joint strength. Terry had a united force on the night of June 21, 1876 and it wasn't until noon June 22, 1876 that Custer departed for his date with infamy. If Sheridan had used an expeditious form of delivery for his change of plans and it had reached Terry prior to June 22, 1876, while Terry was still in command of a united force, the outcome at the Little Bighorn surely would have been different.

Sheridan feared escape by the Indians and desired to converge multiple columns against them, from different directions, in the belief that whatever column met the Indians, it could successfully engage them and in whichever direction the Indians fled to, there would be another column to meet and stop them. He allowed his arrogance and contempt for the Indians as fighters to influence his plan by originally committing inadequate forces against them. When he became aware of the true number of warriors arrayed against his troops, he feebly attempted to change his plan and consolidate his assets but did so in a most inadequate manner. Sheridan's arrogance produced a plan which reeked of overconfidence and was destined to produce disaster. Sheridan from prior to the Battle of the Little Bighorn, through the public announcements of the debacle, after the battle, was in Philadelphia enjoying the country's centennial celebrations. Perhaps that is why communications were so slow and devoid of useful information between his headquarters in Chicago and the troops in the field. Sheridan, by not supplying his field commanders with accurate information in a timely manner, was a primary cause for the debacle at the Little Bighorn. Had Sheridan acted properly and in a timely manner, Custer would not have been on his own in command of the 7th Cavalry, but merely serving as a commander of a unit, under the overall and present command of General Terry. The results of June 25, 1876 would most assuredly have been entirely different from what did occur had the change of plans reached Terry in a timely manner.

CHAPTER 3

Sheridan Knew How Many Indians Had Massed

A review of the numerous telegrams exchanged between the Army personnel in the field and Headquarters staff, in Chicago and Saint Paul, during the month of June 1876 indicates there was sufficient intelligence available for the Army to have formulated an accurate but perhaps not precise opinion as to the number of warriors opposing the troops in the field and the hostile attitude of those which had left the reservations.

The incriminating volume of correspondence during June of 1876 includes:

June 2, 1876, a telegram from Merritt to Sheridan[10] *"the post commander here has sent to the post commander at Robinson for all information as to Indians who have left agencies up to this time. I will await instructions from headquarters here."*

June 2, 1876, a telegram from W. H. Jordan, Capt 9th Infantry Camp Robinson to Major E.F.

Townsend 9th Infantry commanding Fort Laramie, W. T.[11] *"I have the honor to acknowledge the receipt of your communication of the 29th ultimo asking for information as to **the number of Indians that have left Red Cloud and Spotted Tail agencies...and from my own knowledge I believe that at least 2000 Indians [1500 Sioux and 500 Cheyennes] men women and children have left the Agency here and gone north since the 10th ultimo, containing among the number at least 500 warriors.** I would report further that the Agent here claims that 12,000 Indians men, women, and children belong to this Agency."*

June 2, 1876, a telegram from Major E. F. Townsend to Lieut. Gen. Sheridan[12] *"...**it is safe to say that a great many Indians have left the Red Cloud Agency. It is***

---

[10]Exhibit 1.
[11]Exhibit 2.
[12]Exhibit 3.

said there are not five hundred warriors remaining there. Some families have gone. It is hard to tell how many as the Indian agents are themselves but poorly informed and are interested in understating the number. *The Indians now on reservations are bitter against all who took part in last winter's expedition and there was no chance of Crook inducing any of them to go with him this time.* Captain Egan whose report you have seems positive that from seven hundred to one thousand warriors have left the two agencies. He also says some have gone from Missouri River Agencies..."

June 4, 1876, a telegram from Capt Poland 9th Infantry, to Assistant Adjutant General Department of Dakota, St. Paul Minn.[13] "... *that Chief Kill Eagle a prominent chief of the Blackfeet Sioux at this Agency who lately left with 20 lodges, ostensibly to hunt, has certainly joined the hostile Sitting Bull...and that the camp is drawing rations for over 7,000 Indians... but there are only 4,500 present."*

June 7, 1876, a telegram from Merritt to Sheridan[14] "*It is thought that from 1500 to 2000 Indians have left the reservation since the tenth of May a large proportion of those that have gone are warriors. The Agent is inclined to underestimate those who have gone...when he admitted*

reluctantly that Red Cloud had informed him that some of his and other prominent families had gone... Some of the sons of principal chiefs are absent. The Indians here are not friendly in their feelings in fact they are generally hostile, the feeling at Spotted Tail is better though some Indians have left there."

June 8, 1876 a telegram from R. Williams Fort Robinson to Sheridan, "Commanding Officer at Laramie reports[15] *Hand Indian Courier from Red Cloud brings report that just before he left an Indian arrived from the mouth of the Tongue River. Found there 1273 lodges under Sitting Bull Crazy Horse and others on their way to Powder River to fight Gen. Crook.* On his return he met some band that Egan saw May seventeenth they told him that they had met Custer's troops and had fought them all day. Many killed on both sides no result reported. This occurred about eight days ago. He also reports *Spotted Tail at Laramie yesterday who says his people are at home and will not go out and that many have left Red Cloud and other agencies on the Missouri River.*

June 15, 1876, a telegram from Crook to Sheridan[16] "*I think their*

---

[13]Exhibit 4.
[14]Exhibit 5.
[15]Exhibit 6.
[16]Exhibit 7.

main camp is on little Rosebud or Tongue River and probably attack to cover movements of the main body will you please direct such disposition and movement of the fifth cavalry as circumstances require it being impossible for me to know what is necessary in time to direct movements."

June 19, 1876, a telegram from General Alfred Terry by Ruggles Assistant Adjutant General to Adjutant General Division of Missouri Chicago,[17] "*Reno Companies seventh Cavalry is now well up the River on his way to the forks whence he will cross to come down Mispah Creek and thence by Powder Creek to Tongue River where I expect to meet him with rest of the Cavalry fresh supplies. I intend then if nothing new is developed to send Custer with nine companies of his regiment up on the Tongue and thence across to and down the Rosebud. While the rest of the seventh will join Gibbons who will move up the Rosebud. Have met Gibbon and concerted movements with him. Troops and animals in fine condition.*"

June 23, 1876, a telegram from Crook to Sheridan,[18] "*We had a sharp fight on Rosebud Creek Monday morning seventeenth instant lasting several hours. Our loss nine men killed and twenty-one wounded... We won the fight and camped on the field. The* Indians made the attack and had a force they no doubt believed sufficient to whip the command.*"

June 23, 1876, a telegram from Crook to Sheridan,[19] "*Scouts report Indians in vicinity and within a few minutes we were attacked in force the fight lasting several hours. We were near the mouth of a deep canyon through which the creek run. The sides were very steep covered with pine and apparently impregnable the village supposed to be at the other end about eight miles off...They displayed strong force at all points occupying many and such covered places that it is impossible to correctly estimate their numbers the attack however showed that they anticipated that they were strong enough to defeat the command during the engagement...the* command finally drove the Indians back in great confusion following them several miles the scouts killing a good many during the retreat our casualties were nine men killed and fifteen wounded of Third Cavalry three men wounded Fourth Infantry... It is impossible to correctly estimate the loss of the Indians many being killed in attacks others being gotten off before we got possession of that part of the field thirteen dead bodies being left. We remained on

---

[17]Exhibit 8.
[18]Exhibit 9.
[19]Exhibit 10.

15

*the field that night and having nothing but what each man carried himself we were obliged to return to the train to properly care for our wounded who were transported here on mule litters...**I expect to find those Indians in rough places all the time and so have ordered five [5] companies of infantry and shall not probably make any extended movements until they arrive.** Officers and men behaved with marked gallantry during the engagement.*"

The question now arises, what did Sheridan do with this wealth of information he had available. He should have known that thousands of hostile Indians, a high percentage of whom were warriors, had commenced jumping the reservations, beginning in mid May 1876 and were continuing to do so. He had very good reason to believe that there was an immense gathering of tribes occurring under the very hostile leadership of Sitting Bull and Crazy Horse. In early June 1876 he was advised that Sitting Bull's village numbered at least 1273 lodges. This very critical number of lodges represents the low end of most sets of parameters used to quantify the size of the village that Custer attacked. The range generally used is from a low of 1200 lodges to a high of 1800. It is quite reasonable to interpolate from the 1273 lodges reported on June 8 to the much larger number of 1800 lodges and 400 wickyups found on June 25 to June 29.

It appears all that Sheridan did was write a letter to Terry advising

him not to split his forces, and then he left for Philadelphia to enjoy the Centennial! There is no evidence of any telegrams being sent by him with urgent messages redeploying his troops or changing his strategy, nor any other form of expeditious communication, only a mere letter sent through the U. S. Mail. The contents of the letter shows clearly that Sheridan knew the strength of the Indians opposing his troops, and that he was trying, half heartedly, to change plans and strategy, but he incompetently failed to disseminate his knowledge to his field commanders in a timely manner. If there is one single cause for the debacle at Little Big Horn it is none other than Sheridan's absolute failure as a Headquarters Commander to keep his Field Commanders timely informed of the ever increasing strength of the enemy.

As it is quite evident that the Field Commanders had little trouble getting their information to Sheridan, by expeditious telegrams, the unanswered question stands as to why Sheridan failed to reply in kind, with an expeditious telegram and opted instead for the intolerably slow United States Mail. It is perhaps unfortunately too true that probably his mind was more occupied with the festivities of the Centennial Celebrations in Philadelphia. His arrogance had convinced him that any of the units in the field could handle whatever they encountered, therefore the troops in the field were in no danger.

He overconfidently believed that the columns he had deployed against the Sioux were, each within themselves, capable of handling whatever they might run into. The actual deficiency within this plan was that none of the three columns put in the field were adequate to handle the large number of Indians known to be massed against them, either individually or in concert.

He attempted to change his plan by ordering that Terry should proceed with Gibbon and Custer, as a unified command. This change made the revised battle plan be a pincer movement with Terry coming down from the north while Crook advances from the south. He confidently assumed that his order sent by the U.S. Mail would be timely delivered before his troops in the field engaged the enemy. There was no need for further action on his part, as he believed his revised forces would be more than sufficient to hold their own against any force of hostile Indians they might encounter. The Army's arrogant concept that it could handle any force it might encounter is demonstrated by a June 24, 1876 entry in Lieutenant Bradley's diary:

"We are now fairly en route to the Indian Village, which is supposed to be on the Little Bighorn. It is undoubtedly a large one, and should Custer's command and ours unite, we, too, will have a large force numbering all told about one thousand men, armed with the splendid breech-loading Springfield rifles and carbines, caliber forty-five, and strengthened by the presence of Low's battery of three Gatling Guns.

Should we come to blows it will be one of the biggest Indian battles ever fought on this continent, and the most decisive in its results, for such a force as we shall have if united will be invincible, and the utter destruction of the Indian village, and overthrow of Sioux power will be the certain result. There is not much glory in Indian wars, but it will be worth while to have been present at such an affair as this."[20]

It is reasonable to assume that the field commanders Terry, Gibbon and Custer had amassed knowledge, on their own, as to the size of the Indian force opposing them. They had a realistic anticipation of engaging thousands of hostile Indians. Brisbin states, in his letter to Godfrey of January 1, 1892:

"That Custer knew the strength of the Indians, I know, for at the mouth of the Rosebud, Gibbon and I had laid for days with our commands, and had picketed one side of the Yellowstone, while they had picketed the other. They had even crossed over and killed three of my men. Gibbon had sent Bradley over in the night, with scouts, to count them or get some idea of the strength of their camp, and Bradley had done so, being chased in and nearly captured by them. Bradley said their camp was seven (some) miles long, up Rosebud, and we all put them at

---

[20]Bradley, *The March of the Montana Column*, 148.

1000 to the mile, or 5000 souls, with 3000 fighting men, as they did not seem to have many squaws or children with them."[21]

Bradley describes[22] the linkage with Reno on June 18 in his diary. He talks of Reno following a trail that contained 360 lodge fires, plus enough excess to make 400 fires, all of which was heading toward the Little Big Horn. Certainly, if they could estimate 400 lodges on June 18 when they first found the trail, it should have been obvious to them on June 22, when the trail is again found, that size of the village and the number of Indians had greatly increased in the ensuing four days. Custer did have specific knowledge of how big the village was, from the size of the trail and the information related to him by Gibbon and Brisbin. He should have known that the trail he was following was far greater in size than the village represented by the trail that Reno found, and that either Reno's trail had merged into this one, or that he was now following a different village.

Lt. Charles Varnum retold some of the events of the morning of June 24 in his July 4, 1876 letter to his parents[23]

"The signs indicated an immense force, and we were in a hurry to take them by surprise."

It thus appears that even without relayed intelligence from Sheridan, when Custer struck the trail on the 24th he knew the approximate size of the village from the magnitude of the trail, and Varnum conveys inference of this knowledge through the use of the word "immense" in describing the village. It is quite possible that the trail he was originally following on June 22 was a smaller band of perhaps 400 lodges, but then on June 24 that trail merged into the trail of the larger village, the one created by Sitting Bull's village migrating from the Rosebud to the Little Big Horn campsites. The magnitude of the increase had to be quite evident. This is supported by a December 16, 1893 letter from then Captain Luther R. Hare to Colonel Robert Hughes. Hare was Custer's second in command of the Indian scouts at the battle and Hughes was General Terry's brother-in-law and Aide de Camp at the time of the battle. Hare adequately demonstrates that the entire command was well aware of the size of the hostile force they were about to engage:

"Referring to General Fry's comments on Captain Godfrey's article it seems singular, at this day, that any one should allow the idea to creep into an article, of this kind, that any one there thought that there were only 500 or 800 warriors in the village.

*I heard Mitch Boyer tell General Custer myself that it was the largest village that had ever been collected in the Northwest and that he, Boyer had been with those Indians for many years (over 30 I think he said.) The size of the trail we were following and the additions to it after crossing the divide **were proof conclusive***

---

[21]Brininstool, *Troopers With Custer*, 278.

[22]Bradley, James H., *The March of the Montana Column*, 141.

[23]Graham, W. A., *The Custer Myth*, 342-344.

that there were at least three times the larger number, and any argument founded on the supposition that something near the size of the village was not known is worthless because founded on a false basis."[24]

Hare's contentions that Custer was aware of the size of the village and was informed of the number of Indians estimated to be there by Mitch Boyer is reinforced by Varnum.

Varnum wrote, in an April 14, 1909 letter to Walter Camp that

"Custer listened to Boyer awhile he gazed long and hard at the valley. He then said, 'Well, I've got about as good eyes as anybody and I can't see any village, Indians or anything else,' or words to that effect. Boyer said, 'Well, General, if you don't find more Indians in that valley than you ever saw together you can hang me.' Custer sprang to his feet, saying 'It would do a damned sight of good to hang you, wouldn't it' and he and I went down the hill together. I recall the remark particularly because the word 'damn' was the nearest to swearing I ever heard him come...."[25]

Custer, though he was aware of the village size, may have repeated one of his Washita mistakes here, and assumed based on Washita, that the village was spread out over many miles with each circle out of cooperating distance from the others. It is quite conceivable that his initial attack was, in his mind, merely an attack against a single circle and that the other circles were further up river and not within supporting proximity.

---

[24]Urwin, *Custer and His Times-Book Three*, 210.
[25]Hardorff, *On The Little Bighorn With Walter Camp*, 53.

CHAPTER 4
Why the Army Plan Failed

Did the Army have a plan for the Summer Campaign of 1876? The answer is yes, if stating the number of troops taking the field and the direction they would be marching suffices as a plan. The Army would state that its plan was to put three columns in the field and hope to trap Sitting Bull's bands between these converging forces. Alternatively, if one of the forces found and engaged the warriors, each force was deemed sufficient in its own right to handle anything it might encounter. Unfortunately, this plan was compromised by the failure of Sheridan's Headquarters to disseminate to the field commanders of his three pronged attack, the intelligence being assembled in Chicago. The various telegrams received described the location and size of the Indian gatherings, but this vital information was not relayed to the troops in the field.

The Army of 1876 was not a place for independent thinking, the mind set of the top general, Sherman, was passed down through the ranks and became the modus operandi of all units. Custer was merely complying with the mind set of the upper echelon Army Generals: if you find them-fight them before they scatter.[26] Sherman's prediction was both ominous and accurate, "Unless they are caught before early spring, they cannot be caught at all."[27] While Sherman implied that knowledge of their true numbers would have altered military plans and dispositions and averted disaster,[28] "The truth is that the generals worried much less about the enemy's strength than about his traditional reluctance to stand and fight. Campaigns usually failed because the Indians could not be caught and engaged in battle. Besides, chances of encountering any significant portion of the warrior strength at one time were remote. Grass and game could not long support large gatherings of Indians."[29] Herein lay the fallacy upon

---

[26]Robert M. Utley's, *The Frontier Regulars-The United States Army and the Indian*, 1866-1890, 258-259.

[27]Ibid., 255.

[28]Ibid., 260.

[29]Ibid., 260-261.

which the Army based its Grand Plan for the Summer Campaign of 1876 - The Indians will not stand and fight - they will instead scatter and run. This paranoia was passed down through the ranks from Sherman to Sheridan, Sheridan to Crook and Terry, Terry to Gibbon and Custer. If you find the Indians, you must do everything possible to bring them to battle, for if you do not, they will not stand and fight and will instead scatter and run, causing the search to begin anew.

If there was a set of general operating guidelines handed down from the chief of staff, it was "if you find them, fight them and that is the plan." The theory behind this was the paranoia that the Indians would not stand and fight. They had to be caught when they were at a disadvantage, poor weather conditions, a dawn attack or a surprise attack. Any other type of engagement when the Army's intent to attack was known to the Indians would lead to their breaking camp and running. A replay of Washita would be ideal - find the hostile camp, don't waste time with reconnaissance, hit it hard, hit them fast and hit them from multiple directions at once. It worked before why wouldn't it work again? If there were a battle plan for the Seventh Cavalry the script would read quite similar to the following:

Custer would take the trail at once, with the Seventh Cavalry more than 800 strong, with no knowledge of enemy strength, he would hasten to the attack, buglers would sound the charge, the band would play Garryowen, in four attack groups the cavalry would sweep into the valley, from as many as four directions they would come, within ten minutes the troops would have possession of the village.[30]

Unfortunately, that was taken from a description of the Battle of Washita and not a prospective plan for the Battle of the Little Big Horn, but from the seeds of a victory previously achieved, came the fruit of a subsequent failure. If a strategy worked once before against a similar enemy, why wouldn't it work again, for that matter why wouldn't it work against all such similar enemies? One can be almost certain that as Custer entered the Valley of the Little Big Horn, the vision of Washita replayed itself over and over in his mind.

On March 30, 1876, Colonel John Gibbon and a force of 450 men left Fort Ellis, it was thus that the Montana Column became the first of the "three swords" of Sheridan's Grand Plan to take the field. By far Gibbon's column was the puniest of the three, it consisted of only 450 men, a combined force of six companies of the Seventh Infantry and four troops of the Second Cavalry. Major James S. Brisbin commanded the cavalry troops, while Captain Freeman commanded the infantry, with both being under the overall command of Colonel Gibbon. Gibbon augmented the size of his column by the addition of 25 Crow Scouts. This column was commanded by officers in poor health. Gibbon was severely afflicted with arthritis which

---

[30]Ibid., 155-156.

caused him to walk with a limp and generated his Indian nickname of "No Hip." He also suffered from colic and colitis for much of the campaign, and this may have well slowed his participation. Brisbin was nearly crippled by rheumatism and could barely sit on a horse, though he commanded the cavalry battalion.

Terry and Custer were the second of the two swords to take the field, departing Fort Abraham Lincoln on May 17, 1876 to the tunes of *"The Girl I Left Behind Me."* The Dakota Column must have presented a truly impressive sight as it departed Fort Lincoln. Nearly a thousand men in total, consisting of all twelve troops of the Seventh Cavalry and three companies of Infantry to guard the Supply Train [two from the Seventeenth and one from the Sixth], a detachment from the Twentieth Infantry to man the Gatling Guns and approximately 40 Arikara Scouts.

The final sword of the plan to take the field was Crook's Wyoming Column, which consisted of fifteen troops of Cavalry [ten from the Third Cavalry and five from the Second Cavalry] and five companies of Infantry [two and three from the Fourth and Ninth Infantry regiments, respectively], aggregating nearly 1000 officers and men. On June 14, 1876, the force increased by the addition of 176 Crow and 86 Shoshone Scouts.

Thus the stage was set, with all three of Sheridan's swords finally in the field to commence the Grand Plan. It cannot be over emphasized that the consensus of opinion was that **whichever** of the three swords eventually

found and engaged the Sioux had sufficient strength to be victorious, as the great concern was that they would not stand and fight but scatter and run. This concept included and applied to Gibbon's Montana Column even though it was less than half the strength, in manpower, of each of the other two columns and mostly Infantry. There was perhaps a small equalizer that was applied to Gibbon's column, as it was predominantly Infantry it held a slight edge, because Plains Indians were confused and fearful of "soldiers that walk" and had difficulty fighting infantry and counter attacking infantry tactics. Subsequently, this became more readily apparent, as the most successful campaigner against the Plains Indians became General Nelson A. Miles and his vaunted Fifth Infantry.

On June 17, 1876, Crook thought the Indian Village was near, specifically Crazy Horse's, and he sent Captain Anson Mills and his battalion of the Third Cavalry forward to attack, without reconnaissance or scouting, actions for which Custer received severe criticism and blame for his defeat at the Little Big Horn. Crook was merely complying with the mind set of the of Army as manifested in the persona of Sheridan, if you find the Indians you attack them immediately. Custer did the same at the Little Big Horn, and many chastise him for it.

Terry's own views of the "plan" and his words forever render moot any suggestion of a rendezvous and coordinated attack on June 26, 1876 or on any date for that matter. Terry's version of his plan, couched in well crafted language derived from his civilian career as a lawyer, states, "I had no idea where I would find the Hostiles, which of my two forces, if any would engage them, and how we would fight them if we did in fact find and engage the Hostiles." Terry states that:

> *"This plan was founded on the belief that at **some** point on the Little Big Horn a body of hostile Sioux would be found; and that although it was **impossible** to make movements in perfect concert, as might have been done had there been a **known** fixed objective point to be reached, yet, by the judicious use of guides and scouts which we possessed, the two columns **might** be brought within cooperating distance of each other, so that **either** of them which should be **first** engaged might be a waiting fight - give time for the other to come up. At the same time it was thought that a double attack would very much diminish the chances of a successful retreat by the Sioux, should they be disinclined to fight."*

A. H. Terry
November 21, 1876[31].

Terry did not have a clue as to which of his two columns would find the Sioux, or where and when it would happen. All that he hoped was that if one column found the Sioux, it could keep them engaged until the other column could come up and join it.

Gibbon's writings on the topic of a plan of joint operation are no more informative than Terry's and indicate that if anything were expected to occur, that it was anticipated that Custer's column would be the first to meet the Indians. If Custer followed the modus operandi of the Army, he must then engage them as soon as they were found, to prevent their running and scattering.

The concept of a joint operation may well be summed up and rendered moot for all time by a June 20, 1876 entry in the diary of Lieutenant Bradley of the Second Cavalry, Gibbon's Chief of Scouts:

> *"with reference to a combined movement between the two columns in the neighborhood of the Sioux village about the same time and assist each other in the attack, it is understood that if Custer arrives first, he is at liberty to attack at once if he deems prudent. We have little hope of being in on the death, as Custer will undoubtedly exert himself to the utmost to get there first and win laurels for himself and his regiment"[32]*

General Gibbon's report number 3 A dated October 17, 1876 which is included as part of the Secretary of War's report, contained in "House of Representatives, Executive Document No.1, Part 2, 44th congress, 2nd

---

[31]Carroll, John M., *General Custer and the Battle of the Little Big Horn The Federal View*, 87.
[32]Bradley, *The March of the Montana Column*, 143.

Session."[33] "As it would take my command three days to reach the mouth of the Big Horn, and probably a day to cross it over the Yellowstone, besides two more to reach the mouth of the Little Big Horn, and Lieutenant Colonel Custer had the shorter line over which to operate, the department commander strongly impressed upon him the propriety of not pressing his march too rapidly. He got off with his regiment at 12 o'clock the next day [22]." Gibbon's math is somewhat suspect as to how he derives the conclusion that Custer had the shorter line of march, as Gibbon had 100 miles to march versus Custer's 125. However, Gibbon's inference that Custer had the shorter march suggests that it was expected that Custer would arrive first and be the first to engage the Sioux.

Gibbon, whether with the benefit of hindsight or not, estimated that his march would take six days, and six days it did take. Thus, it is impossible to infer that his column could be in the vicinity of the Little Big Horn before June 28, 1876, based upon his starting date of June 22, 1876. If, and as Custer had 125 miles to cover, with slow marching of 25 to 30 miles per day, his force would be at the Little Big Horn in 4 to 5 days, one or two days before Gibbon. Thus, by Gibbon's own words, there was an anticipated two day gap between the arrival of Custer's Column and the arrival of Gibbon's Column. Accordingly there could not have been any possible discussion or plan of a coordinated attack by the two columns, even if they had a clue as to where the Indians were.

Of course, the location of the Sioux wasn't known till they were found. The sooner they would be found, the greater the disparity in days there would be, before the two columns would be in supporting distance of each other. On the assumption that Custer found the Sioux after marching 73 miles in two and a half days, Gibbon would now need, at the least, two more days to get in place for a joint action, creating a four day differential before the two columns could support each other. Do those who berate Custer for taking independent action suggest that under this scenario, he was to take the ridiculous action of staring at the Indians for four days, while waiting for Gibbon and his foot sore troops to arrive, to enable a joint action. That would be as ludicrous a concept as is the intimation of a joint action being anticipated for June 26, 1876! There was no prior definitive knowledge of the whereabouts of the Sioux between the two converging forces. The two columns had to traverse a line of march 250 miles long to unite. The impossibility of predicting a rendezvous point for such a joint action should be self evident. All that was hoped was that if Custer found the Sioux and caused them to flee, Gibbon would be close enough to close the back door.

Simply stated, the Grand Plan was the concept that whichever unit found the Sioux, it could handle them, and should handle them, then and there! This is exactly what Custer did. He

---

[33]Carroll, John M., *General Custer and the Battle of the Little Big Horn The Federal View*, 99.

acted according to the main principles of the Grand Plan, he found the Indians and attacked before they could scatter and flee.

CHAPTER 5
Orders, Suggestions, or Carte Blanche

On June 22, 1876, Brigadier-General Alfred H. Terry delivered the following document to Lieutenant George Armstrong Custer, the debate has ensued ever since, was it an Order, a series of Suggestions, or Carte Blanche to Custer to do as he saw fit from that moment on.

HEADQUARTERS DEPARTMENT OF DAKOTA, (IN THE FIELD) Camp at Mouth of Rosebud River, Montana, June 22, 1876

COLONEL: The brigadier-general commanding directs that as soon as your regiment can be made ready for the march, you proceed up the Rosebud in pursuit of the Indians whose trail was discovered by Major Reno a few days since. It is, of course, impossible to give you any definite instructions in regard to this movement; and were it not impossible to do so, the department commander places too much confidence in your zeal, energy, and ability to wish to impose upon you precise orders, which might hamper your action when nearly in contact with the enemy. He will, however, indicate to you his own views of what your action should be, and he desires that you should conform to them unless you shall see sufficient reason for departing from them. He thinks that you should proceed up the Rosebud until you ascertain definitely the direction in which the trail above spoken of leads. Should it be found (as it appears to be almost certain that it will be found) to turn toward the Little Horn, he thinks that you should still proceed southward, perhaps as far as the headwaters of the Tongue, and then turn toward the Little Horn, feeling constantly, however, to your left, so as to preclude the possibility of the escape of the Indians to the south or southeast by passing around your left flank.

The column of Colonel Gibbon is now in motion for the mouth of the Big Horn. As soon as it reaches that point it will cross the

Yellowstone and move up at least as far as the forks of the Little and Big Horns. Of course its future movements must be controlled by circumstances as they arise; but it is hoped that the Indians, if upon the Little Horn, may be so nearly inclosed by the two columns that their escape will be impossible. The department commander desires that on your way up the Rosebud you should thoroughly examine the upper part of Tullock's Creek; and that you should endeavor to send a scout through to Colonel Gibbon's column with information of the result of your examination. The lower part of this creek will be examined by a detachment from Colonel Gibbon's command.

The supply-steamer will be pushed up the Big Horn as far as the forks, if the river is found to be navigable for that distance; and the department commander (who will accompany the column of Colonel Gibbon) desires you to report to him there not later than the expiration of the time for which your troops are rationed, unless in the mean time you receive further orders.

*Very respectfully,
your obedient servant,*

*ED. W. Smith
Captain, Eighteenth Infantry,
A. A.A.G.*

*Lieut. Col. G. A. Custer,
Seventh Cavalry.* [34]

As so much has been written about this document and its very substance debated so vitriolically a complete dissection appears appropriate. The very contents of this document answers the question of whether or not Custer disobeyed orders, because contained within contents is the comment that Terry does **"not wish to impose upon you precise orders."** Accordingly there were no specific orders to disobey, merely suggestions to follow or not follow depending on whether or not Custer should **"see sufficient reason for departing from them."** Whether the attack by Custer on June 25, 1876 was premature or not, it was within his discretion as granted by Terry. As there never was, nor could there have been a joint attack contemplated, by the two columns, not waiting for Gibbon, is just one more aspect of the battle that Custer has been unjustly maligned about in the years ensuing the battle.

The brigadier-general commanding directs that as soon as your regiment can be made ready for the march, you proceed up the Rosebud in pursuit of the Indians whose trail was discovered by Major Reno a few days since.

• The first sentence tells Custer to follow the trail of the Indians discovered by Major Reno's scout of June 10, 1876 and to move forward with alacrity.

It is, of course, impossible to give you any definite instructions in

---

[34]Terry, Alfred H., *Field Diary of General Alfred H. Terry 1876*, 4-5.

regard to this movement; and were it not impossible to do so, the department commander places too much confidence in your zeal, energy, and ability to wish to impose upon you precise orders, which might hamper your action when nearly in contact with the enemy.

• The second sentence, should for all time, answer the question of whether there were or were not orders given. This sentence emphatically states that **"it is impossible to give you any definite instructions..."** Therefore anything that follows can only be described as suggestions, or less. Terry further propounds the looseness of the document with **"It is, of course, impossible to give you any definite instructions in regard to this movement"** and **"wish to impose upon you precise orders"** phrases. These words, Terry's own words, definitively state that he is not giving Custer orders, he is giving him suggestion, desires, and hopes **but** not orders. Therefore Custer had the latitude as field commander to deviate from them, whenever he felt that the then current circumstances necessitated that he do so.

He will, however, indicate to you his own views of what your action should be, and he desires that you should conform to them unless you shall see sufficient reason for departing from them.

• In the third sentence, Terry now states that he is merely giving Custer, Terry's view of what might occur and that Custer has full and complete latitude to deviate should he have

sufficient reason to do so. Sufficient reason includes no longer being necessary, actions which have unwarranted risk, or actions which through the passage of time would then have a negative effect on the overall goal of the mission.

He thinks that you should proceed up the Rosebud until you ascertain definitely the direction in which the trail above spoken of leads.

• In the fourth sentence, Terry wants Custer to proceed up the Rosebud until Custer finds the trail. He infers, because he is not certain of what Custer will find, that should the trail be on the Rosebud, Custer should not directly follow it but go past it and then turn in an effort to contain the Indians. Custer on finding the trail on the Rosebud finds a much larger trail than was expected. This constituted sufficient reason for him not to go past the trail and to turn then and there in pursuit of the Indians. The growth in the size of the trail created an urgency, as the larger the gathering the more limited the ability of any campsite to support the inhabitants with the necessities of life. The larger the gathering the quicker it must split and scatter to find new camp grounds capable of sustaining life. The growth in the size of the trail mandated that Custer take up direct pursuit immediately, before the large gathering splits into smaller groups.

Should it be found (as it appears to be almost certain that it will be found) to turn toward the Little Horn, he thinks that you should still

proceed southward, perhaps as far as the headwaters of the Tongue, and then turn toward the Little Horn, feeling constantly, however, to your left, so as to preclude the possibility of the escape of the Indians to the south or southeast by passing around your left flank.

- The fifth sentence contains another seed of disaster, as it plants the thought in Custer's head that it is of the upmost importance to protect the left flank and prevent the Indians from passing around him by this flank. It is these words, almost assuredly, that contributed to Custer sending Benteen on the scout to the left.

The column of Colonel Gibbon is now in motion for the mouth of the Big Horn.

- The sixth sentence indicates that Colonel Gibbon was sent forward already, as if this were a contest to see which column would reach the Indians first and Gibbon was given a head start.

As soon as it reaches that point it will cross the Yellowstone and move up at least as far as the forks of the Little and Big Horns.

- The seventh sentence shows that it is contemplated that Gibbon's force will go as far as the forks of the Little and Big Horns but does not give a date or time as to when they might reach this point. This negates the thought of a joint action at the Little Big Horn at any point in time.

Of course its future movements must be controlled by circumstances as they arise; but it is hoped that the Indians, if upon the Little Horn, may be so nearly inclosed by the two columns that their escape will be impossible.

- The eighth sentence states that "future events must be controlled by circumstances as they arise." It infers both the thought that Gibbon's time of arrival is uncertain and there is a question as to whether or not he will ever get there. This phrase suggests that should the Gibbon column find a trail going in a different direction it will follow it and not head towards the Little Big Horn. Or if some other situation arises that gives Terry sufficient reason to deviate from the stated objective he will. It does express Terry's hope that whichever of the columns first finds the Indians, it will drive the Indians towards the second column and thus trap them between the two forces. He talks of trapping the Indians between the two columns, not of jointly attacking the Indians with the two columns.

The department commander desires that on your way up the Rosebud you should thoroughly examine the upper part of Tullock's Creek; and that you should endeavor to send a scout through to Colonel Gibbon's column with information of the result of your examination. The lower part of this creek will be examined by a detachment from Colonel Gibbon's command.

- Much has been made of the ninth and tenth sentences as concrete proof of Custer disobeying orders. We must first and foremost remember that the entire document, in Terry's own words, were not orders because Terry felt it impossible to impose orders upon Custer and had too much confidence in Custer to impose orders upon him, if he could. Therefore, there cannot be a disobedience of orders if no orders were ever given. Custer on deciding to follow the ever growing trail down the Rosebud, when passing Tullock's Creek both saw no sign of Indian movement into or in Tullock's Creek and realized no part of the trail entered the Tullock's Creek area. The events surrounding Tullock's Creek were summarized by Frederic F. Gerard in his interviews with Walter Camp on January 22 and April 3, 1909:

> *"I have heard General Custer criticized for not sending Herendeen to scout Tullock's Fork. General Custer did not overlook this, and the subject came up for discussion while we were on the divide. From the Crow's Nest we had a good view of the valley of Tullock's Creek, which takes its rise not far from where we were. We could see all over that part of the country, and as no trail led that way we concluded there were no Indians in that part of the Country."*[35]

Custer thus had sufficient reason not to undertake the scout. Custer on realizing that the trail proceeded down the Rosebud only, with no part of the trail extending into the Tullock's Creek area, properly concluded that to scout the area constituted unwarranted delay of the operation and would produce no useful results. It further appeared to be an unwarranted risk to the life of a messenger, to try and send

a messenger through, with this meaningless information. This information could be obtained by Terry as a result of Gibbon's examination of the lower portion of Tullock's Creek, and it served no purpose to be ratified by Custer.

The supply-steamer will be pushed up the Big Horn as far as the forks, if the river is found to be navigable for that distance; and the department commander (who will accompany the column of Colonel Gibbon) desires you to report to him there not later than the expiration of the time for which your troops are rationed, unless in the mean time you receive further orders.

• The eleventh sentence clearly states that Terry does not expect to or desire to see Custer until such time as Custer had exhausted his rations. Custer's troops were rationed for fifteen days, Terry therefore was giving Custer an independent command for fifteen days to go forward, using his own discretion as to how to accomplish the task of finding and engaging the Indians. If there was any preconceived rendezvous, it was on July 10, 1876 at the farthest point up the river that the steamer Far West could achieve.

The analysis clearly shows that Terry gave Custer Carte Blanche on how to find the Indians and what to do when they were found. Terry specifically states, both, that he is not giving orders and he feels it would be impossible to give precise orders.

---

[35]Hammer, Kenneth, *Custer In 76*, 231.

Thus, any "directions" contained in the document from Terry are nothing more than mere suggestions. Terry gives Custer specific permission to deviate from any of the suggestions or directions should Custer find sufficient reason to do so. Terry further states that Custer is rationed for fifteen days and Custer is not to report back to Terry until the expiration of time for which his troops are rationed, unless he receives further orders. In effect, Terry gave Custer an independent command for fifteen days to find and engage the Indians.

What was Custer's impression of the scope and latitude of the document given him by Terry? Even though Custer was killed in the battle, from the grave, he left a mechanism to express his understanding of Terry's suggestions. Custer's views and understanding of Terry's suggestions are contained in a letter Custer wrote to his wife Libbie just before the regiment moved out. It is appropriate, at this time, that the letter be reproduced in its entirety[36]

June 22, 1876

My Darling-I have but few moments to write as we start at twelve, and I have my hands full of preparations for the scout. Do not be anxious about me. You would be surprised how closely I obey your instructions about keeping with the column. I hope to have a good report to send you by next mail. A success will start us all toward Lincoln.

I send you an extract from

General Terry's official order, knowing how keenly you appreciate words of commendation and confidence in your dear Bo: "It is of course impossible to give you any definite instructions in regard to this movement, and, were it not impossible to do so, the Department Commander places too much confidence in your zeal, energy and ability to impose upon you precise orders which might hamper your action when nearly in contact with the enemy."

Your devoted boy Autie

There are two statements that literally jump out from this letter. Custer is in all his glory because Terry has given him an independent command and that the operation is a scout. Custer conveys with the words, **" I have my hands full of preparations for the scout,"** that the mission he is embarking on is a scout, a reconnaissance in force, an effort to find the enemy and then if warranted engage them. The use of the word scout negates in Custer's mind the concept of a planned attack against the Indians. It further eliminates the concept that Custer had received orders pertaining to a planned joint attack, on a specific date. Custer telling Libbie that, **"I send you an extract from General Terry's official**

---

[36]Merington, Marguerite, Editor, *The Custer Story-The Life and Intimate Letters of General George A. Custer and His Wife Elizabeth*, 307-308.

order, knowing how keenly you appreciate words of commendation and confidence in your dear Bo," that he views Terry's document as a complete vindication of him, a resounding compliment of his abilities to command a scout and carte blanche to proceed as he sees fit. He expresses confidence with his, "hope to have a good report in the next mail." Custer adeptly defends himself from the grave – he was beaming that Terry gave him carte blanche to do as he saw fit when in contact with the enemy. It was his command, he had been given a free reign, and he was proud of it.

Boston Custer in a letter to his mother dated June 21, 1876[37], states that the regiment leaves the next day and Custer will be in command with the hope of overtaking the Indians.

"My Darling Mother-The mail leaves to-morrow. I have no news to write. I am feeling first rate. Armstrong takes the whole command and starts up the Sweet Briar on an Indian trail with the full hope and belief of overhauling them- which I think he probably will, with a little hard riding. They will be much entertained.

I hope to catch one or two Indian ponies with a buffalo robe for Nev, but he must not be disappointed if I don't. Judging by the number of lodges counted by the scouts who saw the trail there are something like eight hundred Indians and probably more. But the number great or small, I hope I can truthfully

say when I get back, that one or more were sent to the happy hunting ground...

Good-bye my darling Mother. This will probably be the last letter you will get till we reach Lincoln...We leave in the morning with sixteen days rations with pack mules."

Both Custer and his brother Boston sounded confident, Boston expected a buffalo hunt and a mere 800 Indians, some long days in the saddle, to return to Lincoln, and possibly being on the trail for 16 days. Boston's comments indicate that the command would be covering many miles per day - "some long days in the saddle," so those who contend that Custer engaged in forced marches for some ulterior motive are proved wrong by the prospective knowledge of these marches, expressed by Boston.

Neither of the Custer brothers mentioned or inferred that there was an impending rendezvous with Terry contemplated for the 26th, or for any other day. Neither mentioned a planned attack on the anticipated 800 Indians by the two forces, because one was not planned or even discussed. McClernand's version of the plan was "The plan seems to be for us to move up the latter and thus get below the Indian Village supposed to be on that stream, while Gen. Custer strikes them from above."[38] Dr. Holmes Paulding noted in his journal, "Started to move up Tullock's Fork to strike the

[37]Ibid., 306-307.
[38]Koury, *Diaries of the Little Bighorn*, 60.

33

mouth of the Tongue River where we are to meet Custer on the 27th."[39]

It may well be that the concept of Custer being given an independent command had been lingering before the troops for some time. On June 8, 1876, Boston Custer wrote to his mother:

"I do hope this campaign will be a success, and if Armstrong could have his way I think it would be, but unfortunately there are men along whose campaign experience is very limited, but, having an exalted opinion of themselves, feel their advice would be valuable in the field.. But I think before this trip is over they will be thoroughly understood by those who should know."[40]

Who exactly these unnamed men are is unknown but it is possible to make logical guesses. The words, "if Armstrong could have his way," infer that someone in a position senior to him, or someone with the ear of a superior, was preventing him from leading the operation in what he perceived to be the right way. Possibly it was already known to the command that Reno would be leading the scout that commenced on June 10, 1876, only two days after the letter was written.

Terry professed that he had limited field command experience and had requested that Custer have an independent command.

Brisbin had Terry's ear and later suggested to Terry to combine the cavalry forces into one unit. Brisbin intensely disliked Custer and would insist that if the cavalry units be combined, Terry should command.

Brisbin however was not around at the time Boston wrote the letter.

Was Gibbon trying to plan an infantry orientated operation, which would hamper Custer's mobility or chance to fight the winning battle? This is highly doubtful as Gibbon already had an independent command and knew whoever found the Indians first would have the honor of first blood. As the reference appears to be towards men who are either senior to Custer [Gibbon, Terry], or high enough in rank that they could have Terry's ear [Brisbin, Reno, Benteen], the field narrows to Reno and Benteen. It is doubtful that it is Benteen, as he is too low in rank, has had campaign experience and was not known for offering advise.

That leaves Reno as the lone and likely possibility. Reno had command of the Seventh Cavalry in Custer's absence and had requested that he be given permanent field command of it. Reno was at odds with most of the officers present, as Reno believed that the Indians were on the Powder River. This was not the belief of Custer and most other officers present. Reno did get the independent scout of June 10, 1876. He disobeyed his orders, extended the area scouted, in an attempt to prove his Powder River theory. Upon Reno's return from his scout, he received a severe reprimand from Terry. This act of disobedience by Reno narrowed the number of field officers that Terry could trust, and may have contributed to Terry

---

[39]Ibid., 76.
[40]Ibid., 301.

granting Custer an independent field command.

The logical question would now arise, that if Custer acted independently, following his orders as given to him by General Terry, why then was there not a plan of joint operation. The answer appears to be the health of the other senior officers and their ability to perform their duties. Brisbin suffered greatly from rheumatism and though he was the officer in charge of Gibbon's cavalry, he spent much of his time in an ambulance being unable to sit on a horse. Gibbon suffered from severe arthritis, and he too had great difficulty in riding a horse. Gibbon was also prone to sever attacks of colic and colitis. Terry was generally infirm at the time as well. "It would seem that, of the senior officers present, only Custer was in good health. Terry is reported quite ill in several entries of various diaries. Brisbin was in poor health, and Carroll tells us Gibbon is sick."[41] Gibbon must have been the sickest of the group, as he has the most of the notations in diaries indicating that he was sick. Additionally, they show that he did not finally leave the Far West and rejoin his command until June 25, 1876.

Lieutenant Bradley notes in his dairy on June 24,1876 that "General Gibbon has been quite sick and is still on the boat, but is expected to join tomorrow."[42]

Matthew Carroll, Gibbon's master in charge of transportation, had in his June 24, 1876 entry "General Gibbon, I am sorry to say, is very sick"[43]

General Terry, whose diary is noted for its brevity, lack of detail and scarcity of significant events, noted on June 24, 1876, "Gen. Gibbon sick on boat and unable to move. Started in person with staff, orderlies & H. Qrs pack train at 6 o'clk P.M."[44]

Gibbon, himself, described his condition in his article The American Catholic Quarterly Review of April, 1877, on June 24, 1876 as, "I had been attacked with very severe illness the night before, had remained in bed all day and was unable to move. General accompanied the command in person, leaving me on board to meet the column at the mouth of the Little Big Horn."[45]

To say that this group of Officers was too ill to lead a force into battle is an understatement. They were so infirm, that they were barely able to move at all, and in Gibbon's case he was unable to do that.

Custer is often criticized for pushing his command and his horses too hard and too fast, but there are no diary entries to sustain this. In fact the opposite is quite apparent, the troops and horses of the 7th Cavalry were well maintained and in good condition.

Colonel Gibbon described the 7th Cavalry on June 22, 1876 in this manner, "The regiment presented a fine appearance, and as the various companies passed us we had a good

[41]Koury, *The Diaries of the Little Bighorn*, 71.

[42]Bradley, *The March of the Montana Column*, 147.

[43]Koury, *The Diaries of the Little Bighorn*, 71.

[44]Terry, *The Field Diary of Alfred H. Terry*, 23.

[45]Gibbon, *Gibbon on the Sioux Campaign of 1876*, 24.

opportunity to note the number of fine horses in the ranks, many of them being part-blooded horses from Kentucky, and I was told there was not a single sore-backed horse amongst them"[46]

The 7th Cavalry appears to be in fine shape on June 22, 1876 and they were not put to any extremes between that point and the attack on June 25, 1876, with 30 to 35 miles per day being accepted as a normal day's march. In his 1874 narrative, *My Life On the Plains*, Custer commented on the cavalry's ability to perform rapid marches, over great distances, in short periods of time, with specific reference to his having just marched elements of the Seventh Cavalry **one hundred fifty miles in fifty-five hours**, in 1867:

*"Some may regard this as a rapid rate of marching; in fact, a few officers of the army who themselves have made many and long marches (principally in ambulances and railroad cars) are of the same opinion. It was far above the leisurely made march, but during the same season and with a larger command I marched sixty miles in fifteen hours. This was officially reported, but occasioned no remark. During the war, and at the time the enemy's cavalry under General J. E. B. Stuart made its famous raid around the Army of Potomac in Maryland, **a portion of our cavalry, accompanied by horse artillery, in attempting to overtake them, marched over ninety miles in twenty four***

***hours.** A year subsequent to the events narrated in this chapter **I marched a small detachment eighty miles in seventeen hours,** every horse accompanying the detachment completing the march in as fresh condition apparently as when the march began."[47]*

For Custer to be criticized for marching his force too fast to arrive at the enemy's position prior to Gibbon and Terry's arrival, to usurp the glory, two points must be unequivocally proven:

1 - That Custer knew the location of the enemy and thus had a specific target that he was seeking.

2 - That Custer marched his force at a far greater rate than that which was considered acceptable and his rate of march could be construed as extreme and excessive when compared to other marches that he or others had led.

Neither of these elements are present and in fact the opposite is quite true. Custer had no specific knowledge of the whereabouts of the enemy and his rate of march was quite comparable to a standard rate of march. His rate of march was nowhere near what could be construed as excessive, certainly when compared to that which had been previously accomplished both by Custer and others under extreme conditions.

Still if there was to be a joint operation, was Custer early or was Gibbon late? Custer, from all

---

[46]Ibid., 23.

[47]Custer, *My Life On The Plains*, 82.

previously noted comments, was free to act on finding the Indians, so clearly he can only be judged as being on time. Gibbon on the other hand was bed ridden until June 25, 1876, Brisbin spent most of his time in an ambulance, and Terry is noted as being ill a good part of time, but what about the condition of Gibbon's men?

Bradley's diary on June 25, 1876 contains, "The men had emptied their canteens of the wretched alkali water they started with and were parched with thirst as well as greatly fatigued and clambering over such ground. *A worse route could not have been chosen,* but destitute of a guide as we are, it is not to be wondered that we entangled ourselves in such a mesh of physical obstacles."[48]

Brisbin states, *"The condition of the footmen was distressing, their feet being blistered, and every caisson and Gatling gun that came in was loaded down with exhausted men. I put my cavalrymen in the timber and went back to see what could be done. On the road I met Doc Paulding coming up to see me. He said the infantry was plumb played out, the men's feet blistered, and they - or many of them - could not walk further. He ordered them to bathe their feet in the Big Horn."[49]*

Captain Freeman, the senior captain in charge of Gibbon's infantry, noted in his diary on June 25, 1876, "Very hot. No water. Men played out when we reached the river"[50]

Gibbon's analysis of the condition of his Infantry, upon finally joining with his command is "that they had a terrible march the day before over the rough mountainous region lying between the Big Horn and Tullock's Fork, during which the men suffered very much from exhaustion and want of water."[51]

McClernand notes in his diary on June 25, 1876, "the cavalry reached the Big Horn where troopers and their mounts first quenched their intense thirst, after which many canteens were filled and sent back to the weary and even more thirsty foot troops."[52]

Thus, contrary to what the revisionist writers and anti-Custer protagonists would have the public believe, it was not the 7th Cavalry that suffered exhausting marches, over poor terrain affecting its ability to fight, it was Gibbon's 7th Infantry that was parched, foot sore, exhausted and played out by the night of June 25, 1876, as a result of lengthy marches over intolerable terrain. To the extent there was a contemplation of a joint effort on June 26, 1876, against which there is overwhelming evidence refuting such a concept, Gibbon's Infantry was played out and incapable of participating in such a joint effort. It was devoid of healthy commanding officers and the enlisted men were footsore, thoroughly exhausted and completely played out.

---

[48]Bradley, *The March of the Montana Column,* 149.
[49]Brininstool, *Troopers with Custer,* 281.
[50]Freeman, *The Freeman Journal,* 57.
[51]Gibbon, *Gibbon on the Sioux Campaign of 1876,* 24.
[52]McClernand, *On Time For Disaster,* 49-50.

There is further doubt that if Gibbon did locate the Indians he would engage them. Gibbon had located a large camp of Sioux on May 27, 1876 and did nothing but observe them for ten days. On June 14, 1876, Dr. Holmes O. Paulding, Gibbon's Chief Medical Officer, wrote the following in a letter to his mother:

"A large camp was found up the Rosebud [on May 27, 1876] 18 miles off, but our genial C.O. did not deem it advisable to attack it, a chance any other commander would give any price for, and after laying there for ten days with the Indians showing themselves everyday in plain sight, as though they knew what a harmless concern they were dealing with, he at last began to do something, not to cross the command in boats & attack - but to go away, and this we did, keeping on down the river till we met Terry.

Our C.O.'s excuse was that he had rec'd orders...to guard this side of the Yellowstone. There's literal obedience for you! This whole trip has been a miserable farce and everything has been as disagreeable as idiotic, pig headed stupidity could make it."[53]

Captain Freeman expresses his frustration with the situation with this May 28, 1876 notation in his diary:

"Am afraid our work will be for naught unless the different columns co-operate more intelligently than heretofore."[54]

Bradley has this notation in his diary on May 28, 1876:

"Everybody wondered why we were not ordered over to attack the village; but the General probably had good reasons. The village was only eighteen miles distant, we had half a day to cross in, and by leaving the horses behind, could have been over the river ready to begin the march at dark. The absence of Lieutenant English's company left us with an available force of only about 350 men, and whether that was enough to have attacked successfully is uncertain. It was subsequently ascertained that the village contained about 400 lodges, representing a fighting force of between 800 and 1,000 warriors. It was pretty big odds, but I imagine the majority of our officers would not have hesitated to give them a trial, and there are some who assert confidently that we would have gained a rousing victory, dispersed the village, and prevented that tremendous aggregation of force a month later that made the massacre of Custer's command possible. On the other hand, we might ourselves have been massacred."[55]

General Terry has two terse comments in his diary for June 9 and June 10, 1876, respectively:

---

[53]Urwin, *Custer and His Times-Book Three*, 184-185.

[54]Freeman, *The Freeman Journal*, 50.

[55]Bradley, *The March of the Montana Column*, 126.

"Met General Gibbon some distance below his camp at 11 o'clk" and *"Gibbon did nothing."*[56]

Notwithstanding the arrogant belief of the Army's Officer Corps from Sherman at the very top to Bradley near the bottom, that any of the three forces put in the field could handle whatever opposing force of Indians it might encounter, Gibbon found a village and did nothing but observe it for ten days and move away without firing a shot. It can be well assumed that this incident was a topic of discussion on the Far West the night of June 21, 1876. Custer may well have noted Gibbon's lack of desire to engage the Indians and developed the belief that this was designed to be a **"Let George and the 7th do it campaign."** Custer would certainly have developed doubts as to what support Gibbon would supply, if he were put in a situation where support was necessary.

In 1896, General Nelson A. Miles published his autobiography, *"The Personal Observations of General Nelson A. Miles."* In this work, he claimed to have an affidavit from a witness to General Terry's last meeting with Lt. Colonel Custer. For various reasons, Miles refused to release the name of the person who gave the affidavit.

The affidavit became the subject of debate, ridicule and challenge. In 1953, Colonel William A. Graham included the full text of the affidavit in his work, *"The Custer Myth,"* and the document became known as the "Mary Adams Affidavit." Graham also included copies of letters and documents challenging the credibility of the

document. It was Graham's conclusion that, "The affidavit is fraudulent, and the conversation Miles refers to between Terry and Custer never took place."[57]

In 2000 a second edition of John S. Manion's 1983 work, *"General Terry's Last Statement to Custer"* was published by Upton and Sons. Manion's research conclusively shows that there were in fact two women, Mary Adams and her sister Maria Adams. One of them did in fact accompany Custer on the Little Big Horn Expedition. It is likely that she was present on the night of June 21, 1876 when Terry gave Custer his final verbal instructions, and that the affidavit does appear to be legitimate, true and accurate. The final conversation as related in the affidavit was:

"Mary Adams ... and was present in the said General Custer's tent on the Rosebud River in Montana Territory when General Terry came into said tent, and then Terry said to General Custer, 'Custer, I don't know what to say for the last.' Custer replied, 'Say whatever you want to say.' Terry then said, 'Use your judgement and do what you think best if you strike the trail. And whatever you do, Custer, hold on to your wounded,' and further saith not."[58]

Custer then proceeded to do just as Terry instructed him to do.

---

[56]Terry, *The Field Diary of General Alfred H. Terry,* 21.
[57]Graham, *The Custer Myth,* 282.
[58]Manion, *General Terry's Last Statement to Custer,* 62.

CHAPTER 6
Custer's Plan

George Armstrong Custer was a Civil War hero of great renown. He was the youngest major general in the country's history, the leader of a great many successful cavalry charges during the Civil War, and the man who accepted the flag of truce at Appomattox. In 1876, he was still the fair-haired boy of Lieutenant General Philip H. Sheridan, who was the field commander of the entire United States Army and second in command to General William T. Sherman. Sherman answered directly to President Grant.

Custer had stagnated in the small Army that existed subsequent to the Civil War. It was an Army where promotions took ten years or more to occur, unless there was a death on the seniority list in front of your name. By 1876, Custer had spent 10 years at the rank of Lieutenant Colonel of the 7th Cavalry. When he was originally given that rank, it involved much back door maneuvering as it placed him ahead of many other more senior officers. Many of those that he jumped ahead of joined the list of junior officers who

were jealous of him or bore him animosity.

In May, 1876, Custer was freshly smarting over a recent rebuke from President Grant which had temporarily cost him his command of the Seventh Cavalry. It was his sobbing, bent knee pleas to General Terry which caused Terry to intercede on Custer's behalf with Sheridan, who in turn pleaded Custer's cause with Sherman and President Grant.

As much as Grant despised Custer and wanted to publicly defrock him of his command and ego, Grant acquiesced and allowed Custer field command of the Seventh as long as he served under the overall command of General Terry. This was largely due to the overwhelming pleas from all concerned that Custer's presence was essential to the success of the impending action. Custer was essential, it was argued, because of his vast experience as an Indian fighter and the lack of similar experience among the other commanding officers assigned to the mission. The extremely important point too often overlooked at this juncture is that Custer's vast experience merely consisted of one prior major attack on a sleeping Indian village, in the middle of winter. It is probable that Custer never killed an Indian, anywhere but at Washita and the Little Bighorn. Grant gave in to the pleas and paranoia of Terry, Sheridan and Sherman and allowed Custer to go. Grant insisted, however, that Terry remain in overall command of the expedition, and that Terry keep a tight rein on Custer.

Custer may have sensed that his military career was in jeopardy absent a major victory by troops under his command. The glory and notoriety of such a victory would be the only event that would allow his military career to go forward and gain him a promotion to general. The Army was quite small in 1876, and the number of generals allowed for on staff was limited by Congress to fifteen. The Army Generals then held their commission until they retired or died. Thus, it took dozens of years, if at all, for an officer to rise to the rank of general through the seniority system. Custer's impasse with Grant combined with his low status on the seniority list virtually insured he would leave the Army a Lieutenant Colonel without the major victory which could earn him a field promotion. He further believed, that for the victory to earn him a field promotion, it must be a victory of the Seventh Cavalry and only the Seventh Cavalry.

For Custer and the 7th Cavalry a victory, on June 25, 1876, would have consisted of the accomplishment of any or all of the following objectives:

• Driving a substantial number of Indians back to their reservations

• For those not driven back to their reservations, the destruction of their ability to make war, roam and sustain life away from the reservation - by the destruction of the pony herd, confiscation or destruction of their weapons and limiting the number escaping to an ineffective few.

• For those Indians who did scatter and escape, elimination of their ability to survive as an independent group by the destruction of as much of the life sustaining material (buffalo skins, lodge poles, stored foods etc.) within the camp, as possible, thereby making them incapable of sustaining life on their own, totally dependent on the government for sustenance and forcing them of their own volition to turn themselves in to reservations.

•Victory would have been the destruction of the infrastructure, essential to the maintenance of their way of life, of a substantial number of the Indians assembled.

The Army was operating under the direction of General of the Army William T. Sherman, formulator of and very strong proponent of the "Concept of Total War" for waging war. His theory of total war included the concept of carrying the war to the civilian population and thereby destroying their ability to maintain a war effort. The destruction of the infrastructure of the enemy's society would depress the morale of the fighting forces and take away their will to fight and win. From late 1875, the Indians were under an ultimatum from the Government to either return to the reservations or be deemed hostile and be subject to punishment by the Army. As long as the Indians could be brought back to the reservation in such a manner as to not further interfere with the westward expansion condoned by the government of the railroads, lumber and mining interests, gold miners in particular and settlers of the new lands, the Army would be able to claim victory.

As the Indians were nomads, totally dependent upon their pony herds for transportation, obtaining food and making war, the primary objective in any engagement would be the capture or destruction of the pony herd. Lakota Indians, on foot, would pose no further threat to the United States and be forced to surrender to reservation life. Keeping this objective in mind Custer formulated his plan of attack. He intended to assault the village with two waves of troops, a basic frontal assault across favoring level terrain. He ordered Reno to attack, as the vanguard, with the first wave and it was his intent to follow close behind him. Reno was ordered to take the Arikara Scouts with his vanguard wave and the scouts' objective was to capture or drive off as much of the pony herds as possible. Their success in obtaining this objective would leave the Sioux on foot and force them to surrender to the

attacking troops. Custer committed Reno and his battalion to attack the main village, it was not ordered to chase a small band of Indians fleeing in the direction of the village. Such a group if it existed would be dealt with in the total onslaught that was contemplated against the main village. A small group of Indians fleeing would have been deemed, by Custer, a decoy force attempting to lure the Cavalry into a trap. Custer was well aware of this favorite tactic of the Plains Indians and described it, in this manner:

> *"The latter [Indians], as usual, were merely practising their ordinary **ruse de guerre**, which was to display a very small venturesome force in the expectation of tempting pursuit by an equal or slightly superior force, and, after having led the pursuing force well away from the main body, to surround and destroy it by the aid of overwhelming numbers, previously concealed in a ravine or ambush until the proper moment."*[59]

Such was the methodology employed in the Fetterman Massacre and most likely how Major Elliott and his troops met their demise at Washita. These events and others were firmly imbedded in the thought process of every Army Officer on the plains and would prevent them from committing the folly of taking the bait and chasing small groups of Indians, having the appearance of decoys, when a much larger and more important target was

---

[59]Custer, *My Life On The Plains*, 126.

within their sights.

There is a great deal of support for this premise that Custer's original plan was to hit the village with two waves of troops, Reno's battalion followed by his own. That support comes from the testimony of the survivors who were privy to hearing the order delivered.

Major Marcus Reno, commanding a battalion consisting of Troops A, G, and M.

Q. *"I would like you to repeat that order again."*

A. *"General Custer directs you to move forward at as rapid a gait as you think prudent, and to charge afterwards, and you will be supported by the whole outfit." I think these were the exact words.*[60]

Q. *"State at the time you received the order from General Custer, through Lieutenant Cooke, what your reply was to that order, if you made any."*

A. *"I made no reply whatever, I proceeded to carry it out."*

Q. *"Did you ask any questions of Lieutenant Cooke as to whether you would be supported or not?"*

A. *"No, sir, I had official information that I would be supported by the whole outfit."*[61]

H. R. Porter, acting assistant surgeon, *"I heard his adjutant give an order, I think about 1 o'clock . It was right near where they struck the first tepee where the dead Indians were. The adjutant came over and*

told him the Indians were just ahead and General Custer directed him to charge them. He turned around and asked the adjutant if General Custer was going to support him. He said Custer would support him. He asked him if the General was coming along and he told him, 'Yes', the General would support him."[62]

Q. *"How close were you to Major Reno when he made that remark to the adjutant?"*

A. *"Within hearing distance"*...

Q. *"How close was the adjutant to Major Reno at that time?"*

A. *"Close enough to speak to him."*[63]

First Lieutenant George D. Wallace, assigned to G Troop on June 25, 1876: Lieutenant Cooke, the adjutant of the regiment, came from General Custer to Major Reno and said to him, "The Indians are about two miles and a half ahead, on the jump, go forward as fast as you think proper and charge them wherever you find them and he will support you." "My mind is not exactly clear. I know he was to be supported." "Yes, sir. I understood that General Custer was to support him."[64]

---

[60]Nichols, *Reno Court of Inquiry*, 580.
[61]Ibid., 584.
[62]Ibid., 188.
[63]Ibid., 199.
[64]Ibid., 44.

First Lieutenant Charles De Rudio.

Q. *"Had Captain Benteen parted from Major Reno or the main column before that order was given by Adjutant Cooke?"*

A. *"Yes, sir"...*

Q. *"Repeat in what way the order was given."*

A. *"Girard comes and reports the Indian village three miles ahead and moving. The General directs you to take your three companies and drive everything before you. Colonel Benteen will be on your left and will have the same instructions..."*

Q. *"After adjutant Cooke gave that order to Major Reno where did he go?"*

A. *"I don't know where he went immediately after. A short time after, as the command started out, I saw him and Captain Keogh both with Major Reno."*[65]

Sergeant Edward Davern, F Troop serving as orderly to Major Reno on June 25, 1876.

Q. *"State whether you heard Adjutant Cooke give any orders to Major Reno when he was moving towards the Little big Horn River."*

A. *"I heard Adjutant Cooke give him an order."*

Q. *"Tell what that order was and where you were when it was given."*

A. *"The order was, 'Girard comes back and reports the Indian village three miles ahead and moving. The General directs you to take your three companies and drive everything before you.' Those I believe were the exact words."*

Q. *"Was anything else said?"*

A. *"Yes, sir: 'Colonel Benteen will be on your left and will have the same instructions."*[66]

George Herendeen, civilian scout and courier. *"I heard General Custer tell Major Reno to lead out and he would be with him. Those were about the words I understood him to use, That is all I heard."*[67]...

Q. *"Might not Lieutenant Cooke have given an order to Major Reno and you not know it?"*

A. *"He could have done it."*[68]

Captain Myles Moylan, *"I know nothing about it excepting by hearsay."*[69]

First Lieutenant Charles Varnum.

Q. *"Do you know what orders were given by General Custer or his adjutant to Major Reno on the 25th of June 1876, with reference to attacking or pursuing the hostile Indians."*

A. *"I did not hear any. I was not present."*[70]

Captain Frederick Benteen, First

---

[65]Ibid., 359-360.
[66]Ibid., 332.
[67]Ibid., 251.
[68]Ibid., 270.
[69]Ibid., 215.
[70]Ibid., 139.

Lieutenant Edward Godfrey, and Second Lieutenant Winfield Scott Edgerly, though present and testifying at the Inquiry were not asked any questions regarding who delivered Custer's orders to Reno as their battalion had separated from the command prior to the order being issued and it was assumed they hence had no direct knowledge about its method of delivery.

F. F. Girard, civilian interpreter. *"The General hallooed over to major Reno and beckoned to him with his finger and the Major rode over and he told Major Reno, 'You will take your battalion and try and overtake and bring them to battle and I will support you.' And as the Major was going off he said, 'And take the scouts along with you.' He gave him orders to take the scouts along and that is how I heard it."*[71] *"... Then I rode to the command, we went but a short distance before General Custer called Major Reno who was then to his left. He beckoned to him with his finger and Major Reno rode over. That being my first trip with troops I was very anxious to know what was going on and hear the orders... 'Major Reno, you will take your battalion and try to overtake the Indians and bring them to battle and I will support you.' And as Major Reno was moving off and had got 6 or 8 or 10 feet, General Custer said, 'and take the scouts with you.'"*[72]

The testimony clearly indicates that Lieutenant Cooke the Regimental Adjutant delivered one and perhaps two orders to Major Marcus Reno. The

essence of the orders were the same, with the second order having an embellishment. It is not that we are dealing with distortion as to what the order was, its substance is clear, the confusion arises from the embellishment which suggests a second order was sent via Cooke. Reno, Porter and Wallace mention only that Reno was directed to charge the village. De Rudio and Davern add that the village is three miles ahead and moving, with the embellishment that "Girard reports that the village is moving." Only Herendeen uncertainly acknowledged it might have been Cooke who delivered the order, supported Girard that Custer delivered the order in person to Reno after beckoning him across the River. The problem here may be sequential and not factual. Custer issued his orders to Benteen and then supplemented them with messengers. It is not unlikely that Custer first issued the order to Reno after calling him to come across the river and then augmented it once by Cooke and Keogh before receiving Girard's information and a second time with Cooke after receiving Girard's information. In all cases the essence of the order was the same, Reno was to charge the village and Custer would support him, to this moment the inferred support is a second wave of a frontal assault by all of the remaining command.

Cooke's report of Girard's information that the village is moving, causes Custer to become the victim of misinformation. He reacts rashly by

[71]Ibid., 86.
[72]Ibid., 112.

altering his plan on the fly, based upon the misinformation and changes his plan of attack. This is something he had done all through his career, especially during the Civil War, effectively directing his troops from his saddle. In most cases he met with great successes like Hanover, Winchester and Yellow Tavern, but he did have prior disasters like Trevelyan Station. The altered plan of attack can only be theorized, as there was no survivor from Custer's battalion who was privy to his thoughts. However, he left an adequate trail, post battle forensics and the positions of his dead all lead to a general hypothesis of what his continuing plan was and how he attempted to carry it out.

Lt. Cooke, the Regimental Adjutant and Captain Keogh second in command of Custer's battalion, had ridden part of the way with Reno during his advance to attack, probably the end result of delivering a follow up order to Reno. Keogh was with Cooke because he would be leading the second wave of the attack, and he was there finalizing the battle plan with Reno.

They had left Reno and were on their way to rejoin Custer and the contemplated second wave charge up the valley to support Reno's attack. Lt. Cooke had stopped at a small knoll, when F. F. Girard, a white civilian serving as an interpreter, saw a dust cloud created by the Indians driving a pony herd and assumed the Indians were coming up to meet Reno. Girard first reported this sighting to Major Reno and then went to report it to Custer. On his way to Custer he met

Lt. Cooke at the small knoll and told him that his intention was to inform Custer that "the Indians were coming up the valley to meet us." Lt. Cooke ordered Girard to return to Reno, informing him that he would relay the information to Custer.[73]

When Cooke informed Custer that the Indians were coming up the valley to meet Reno, Custer wrongly, without making any attempt to confirm this information, changed his plan. He now concluded that Reno's force alone was adequate to act as a blocking force, creating in effect an anvil, upon which he could drive the Indians with a hammer in the form of a rear or flank attack. Custer reached this conclusion based upon the Girard information, for if "all the Indians are coming up the valley to meet Reno," then there must be no Indians in the rear to protect against another attack from a different direction. Custer immediately ordered his battalion to the right and proceeded to seek a place where he could ford and attack the Indian rear. If his plan would succeed, he would trap the Indians between two converging forces and compel their surrender.

If Girard had not misinformed Cooke and indirectly Custer, there would have been eight troops chagrining down the valley in two waves, soon to become eleven in three waves, when Benteen reached the valley. Custer's original plan was nothing more fancy than a plain old frontal assault, by as much of the regiment as he could possibly put into the effort. The likely effect would have

---

[73]Ibid., 87.

been a full surprise attack on an unprepared opponent leading to a success that would have allowed the Army to claim a victory under the objectives previously set forth.

The bad information became further exacerbated when Custer went to the top of Weir Point. At that time he saw a big dust cloud in the valley heading towards Squaw Creek Coulee, a coulee north and west of Medicine Tail Coulee on the opposite side of the river, which was being created by the women and children rushing there to seek shelter from the attack. He wrongly assumed that Reno was continuing in his charge, and the Indians were fleeing and about to scatter. As his greatest fear, that the Indians would scatter and escape, was being confirmed in his mind, he ordered Benteen to come up and support him because he would need more troops than he had with him to contain and capture the scattering Indians, Custer, then theorized that, as the Indians were fleeing, he would have to cross the river, pursue and capture them immediately.

He decided to lead Captain Yates' battalion down Medicine Tail Coulee to ford, cross and attack the village. Custer intended to drive straight across the village and capture the non-combatants he saw gathering at Squaw Creek. If successful in doing so, he would achieve a quick and complete victory with minimal losses. He left Captain Keogh, the senior captain in the battalion, with an independent command. Keogh was instructed to position his battalion on ridges west of Medicine Tail Coulee and wait for Captain Benteen, holding further orders for Benteen, as well as for himself. Keogh was now to simultaneously serve as cover for Custer's attack, be a union point for Benteen to come to and act as a rear guard and reserve for his advance. His attack would prevent the non-combatants from fleeing and trap the warriors within the confines of the village. He would capture them and achieve a quick victory.

Point by point, the plan was not achieved, the underlying theories became false, and Custer and his battalion were annihilated. Reno failed to press the attack, eventually he broke and ran from the field, abandoning his position and troops, in a cowardly rout to safety. This allowed the Indians to devote all their efforts and strengths against Custer's force. When Custer reached Medicine Tail Ford, strong opposition awaited his attempt to ford and he was repulsed incurring light losses. Benteen failed to obey his orders to "come quick" and Custer did not receive his much needed reinforcements. Before Custer could reunite his separated battalions, they each came under attack and were soon surrounded by upwards of 3,000 Sioux and Cheyenne Warriors. Finally, without any hope of aid coming, Custer's plan deteriorated to waiting, watching as his men were killed one by one, until all fell dead!

CHAPTER 7
Manpower Problems of the 7ᵗʰ Cavalry

The 7ᵗʰ Regiment United States Cavalry was organized by an Act of Congress July 28, 1866. Congress had authorized and allowed the Army through the Military Appropriations bills in effect, in 1876, to organize ten regiments of Cavalry. Pursuant to these acts, each regiment of cavalry was authorized to have on its roster[74]:

- 1 Colonel
- 1 Lieutenant Colonel
- 3 Majors
- 1 Regimental Adjutant (an extra Lieutenant)
- 1 Regimental Quartermaster (an extra Lieutenant)
- 12 Captains - allocated 1 per company
- 12 First Lieutenants - allocated 1 per company
- 12 Second Lieutenants - allocated 1 per company
- 1 each of the following: Chaplain, Sergeant Major, Quartermaster Sergeant, Chief Musician, Saddler Sergeant, Chief Trumpeter,

- 12 First Sergeants - allocated 1 per company
- 60 Sergeants - allocated 5 per company
- 48 Corporals - allocated 4 per company
- 24 Trumpeters - allocated 2 per company
- 24 Farriers and Blacksmiths - allocated 2 per company
- 12 Saddlers - allocated 1 per company
- 12 Wagoners - allocated 1 per company In the aggregate:
- 648 Privates - allocated 54 per company

Total Officers Allotted 44 - of which 36 are allocated 3 per company

Total Enlisted Allotted 845 - allocated 70 per company

Aggregate Allotted Men 889 - allocated 73 per company

According to the official muster roll of the 7ᵗʰ Cavalry its manpower level, on

---

[74]*Secretary of War, Official Army Register for January, 1876,* 260b.

June 25, 1876 was 851, consisting of 48 officers and 793 enlisted men, less than that which Congress had authorized. Custer, however, was in command of only 598 men, consisting of 31 officers and 567 enlisted men. The regiment was at 70 % of its allocated strength, with the percentage of deficiency approximately equal among officers (64.5%) and enlisted (71.5%). The most notable depletions were among the senior officers and that 195 enlisted men were on detached service, incarcerated, AWOL, or otherwise missing or excused from duty. Among the missing were the commanding officer Colonel Samuel D. Sturgis (he was on what amounted to permanent detached service, to allow Custer field command of the regiment.) The two most senior majors Joseph G. Tilford (leave of absence) and Lewis Merrill (detached service); four captains (all on detached service) Owen Hale, Charles Ilsley, Michael Sheridan and John Tourtellotte; five first lieutenants (all on detached service) James Bell, Charles Braden, William Craycroft, Henry Jackson, and Henry Nowlan; four second lieutenants (all on detached service) Edwin Eckerson, Ernest Garlington, Charles Larned and Andrew Nave; and the Veterinary Surgeon Carl A. Stein. Of the 48 active officers on the muster roll 31 were present for action on June 25, 1876, with **17 officers missing, on detached service or temporarily assigned elsewhere, consisting of 1 colonel, 2 majors, 4 captains, 5 first lieutenants, 4 second lieutenants and 1 veterinary surgeon.**[75]

The depletion of the Officer Corps did not allow Custer to organize his regiment according to Army Regulations. In 1876, a cavalry regiment was to be divided into 3 battalions, each consisting of four companies (troops) commanded by a major[76]. The colonel and lieutenant colonel of the regiment were to have overall field command but not be hampered with actual troop command. Because of the paucity of field grade officers Custer was forced to divide his regiment into two battalions or wings, each comprised of six companies, only one, the left, commanded by a major, Major Marcus A. Reno. The other, the right, was under the personal command of Custer.

The division of the regiment into wings was done to compensate for a lack of Majors present, to command the requisite three battalions, required by Upton in section 880 of the 1876 United States Army Cavalry Tactics Manual, as discussed in the evolution of the regiment.[77] Upton in section 880 under the evolution of the regiment, requires that the regiment be formed consisting of three battalions, of four troops each, each commanded by a Major.

Assignments, in order of seniority, on June 25, 1876 were a Left Wing commanded by Major Reno with Captain Benteen second in command, with each having command responsibility for a battalion, consisting of three troops, of that wing.

---

[75]Hammer, *Men with Custer*, 390.
[76]Upton, *United States Cavalry Tactics 1876*, 271 and 340.
[77]Ibid., 340.

Major Reno commanding a battalion consisting of M, A, and G Troops of the nine subordinate officers which should have been under his command (3 each captains, first lieutenants, and second lieutenants) he had only five officers, two captains (French and Moylan) and 3 first lieutenants (De Rudio, MacIntosh, and Wallace).

Captain Benteen commanded a battalion consisting of H, D, and K Troops. Missing from this battalion were five officers, a major to command, one captain, one first lieutenant and two second lieutenants.

The Right Wing was under Custer's personal command and formed into two battalions. One was commanded by the Senior Captain present Myles Keogh of I Troop, it consisted of I, B and L.

It was short one troop, Troop B (B Troop assigned to this battalion, was the rear guard with the pack train) and the second battalion was commanded by Captain George Yates of F Troop, it consisted of F, E and C.

Captain Keogh commanded a battalion consisting of I, B, and L Troops. Missing from this battalion were seven officers, a major to command, one captain, two first lieutenants and three second lieutenants. Further, B Troop was detached from the battalion and being used as a rear guard on June 25, 1876.

Captain Yates commanded a battalion consisting of Troops F, E and C. This battalion was short six officers, two captains, three first lieutenants and one second lieutenant. Captain Tom Custer had been

previously detached from his C Troop to serve as his brother's Aide-de-Camp.

Due to the absence of majors to command battalions, Custer placed the right wing of Keogh's and Yates' battalions under his direct field command. This may well have been one of his most significant errors in judgement, on this day. **By assuming field command of a wing, he lost command of the regiment and put himself in a position where he could not oversee and command the actions of all his troops, only the segment of the regiment he personally commanded.**

He should have had Benteen command a wing and have detached himself from actual troop command. He should have detached C Troop, which was the headquarter's escort on June 25, 1876 from Yates's battalion, and placed himself in a position where he could oversee, direct and command the actions of all the troops, in both wings of the regiment and not just have commanded a single wing.

The Army of 1876 was so depleted, that no unit was at its allotted strength, and there was a severe shortage of officers and enlisted throughout, under staffing was not just an isolated problem of the Seventh. The Officer Corps of the 7th on June 25 more resembled the work of a master juggler trying to balance assignments than a regiment of cavalry organized by the United States Army. **The unfamiliarity of officers with the enlisted men under their command and vice versa could well have led to some units fighting poorly and perhaps**

was the cause of the break downs in tactical command that the 7th suffered on June 25, 1876. These changes and reassignments included:

Smith 1st Lt. of A
- assigned to command E

Varnum 2nd Lt. of A
- assigned to command the scouts

Hodgson 2nd Lt. of B
- assigned as Adjutant to Reno

Tom Custer Captain of C
- assigned as Aide-de-Camp to G. A. Custer

De Rudio 1st Lt. of C
- assigned to A

Calhoun 1st Lt. of C
- assigned to command L

Van Reilly 2nd Lt. of E
- assigned to F

Hare 2nd Lt. of K
- assigned as second in command of scouts

Mathey 1st Lt. of M
- assigned to command the Pack Train Guard

Sturgis 2nd Lt. of M
- assigned to E

Crittenden 2nd Lt. of 20th Infantry on loan and assigned to L

Thus, eleven of the thirty officers under Custer's command that day, 37%, were not with their regularly assigned commands. The effects of this further exacerbated the situation by causing Troops E and L to have none of their regularly assigned officers, Troops M, A, K, and F having only one of their regularly assigned officers and Troops M, K, C and B having only one officer in the aggregate with them. Not one of the twelve Troops under Custer's command had a full complement of officers (a captain, a first lieutenant, and a second lieutenant). Eight troops had two officers each and four troops had but one officer. One must wonder how much the unfamiliarity that the officers had towards the enlisted men under their command effected the outcome of the battle. It has been noted and questioned by many others that a lot of the officers didn't die with their commands, the mass reassignment of the officers may have been a contributing factor.

Of the twelve first sergeants, sixty sergeants and forty-eight corporals on the muster rolls, 1 first sergeant, 15 sergeants, and 6 corporals were not present. This only further diluted the amount of leadership present and contributed to the breakdown in the tactical command of the troops. One of the troops that has been accused, through forensics, of breaking down is I Troop. It is said that I Troop bunched, broke and ran and was the victim of a buffalo hunt type slaughter by the Sioux[78]. In all likelihood I Troop was commanded by First Lieutenant James Porter as Captain Myles Keogh had command of the whole battalion (I, and L) and would have had to devote part of his attention to L Troop, as well as his own I Troop. With regard to the non-commissioned officers of I Troop, the

---

[78]Fox Jr., *Archaeology, History, and Custer's Last Battle*, 168-170.

First Sergeant Varden was present, Sergeant Bustard was the only one of the five assigned sergeants present (three others were on detached service and one was with the packs) and three of four corporals were present[79]. There was only one officer and five non-commissioned officers, most of whom were junior officers, present to direct the activities of 36 enlisted soldiers, as opposed to the allotted 3 officers and 10 non-commissioned officers. If this command group fell early in the battle, or was not sufficient in numbers or strength of will, one could easily see why I Troop would bunch, and subsequently break and run.

Next in importance to having a competent Officer Corps to direct a regiment is the ability to effectively relay commands, which was done by means of bugle calls. Of the 2 trumpeters authorized per company, for a total of 24 per regiment, plus 1 Chief Trumpeter making a total of 25 authorized, the muster rolls showed only 22 were assigned of which three were on detached service, and two assigned as orderlies. Only 17 remained present with their troops on June 25, 1876.

The authorized trumpeters were:[80]

Staff - Chief Trumpeter - Henry J. Voss

A - William G. Hardy, David McVeigh
B - **John Connell, James Kelly - Both were on detached service and not present**
C - Thomas J. Bucknell, William K. Kramer
D - Aloys Bohner
E - Thomas McElroy, George A. Moonie
F - Thomas Way
G - **Cassius R. Carter was on detached service and not present, Henry C. Dose assigned as an orderly to Custer and not with his troop,**
H - William Ramell, **Giovanni Martini a/k/a John Martin assigned as an orderly to Custer and not with his troop**
I - John McGucker, John W. Patton
K - George B. Penwell, Julious Helmer
L - Frederick Walsh
M - Charles Fischer, Henry C. Weaver

After making adjustments for those on detached service and those assigned as orderlies there remained only 17 trumpeters with their troops. There were **none with Troops B and G, one each with Troops D, F, H, and L** and two each in Troops A, C, E, I, K and M plus the Chief Trumpeter Henry J. Voss who was assigned to the Headquarters Group. The lack of a trumpeter in Troop B may have influenced Custer's decision in making it the rear guard and guard for the pack train, as this assignment would make it least likely to become involved in combat and require a trumpeter. There has been much discussion regarding the absence of bugle calls being heard during the Timber Fight. It is alleged that a large portion of G

---

[79]Hammer, *Men with Custer*, 393-404.
[80]Ibid., 393-404.

Troop was left behind because they did not hear the order to withdraw. The absence of any trumpeters with G Troop may well explain this enigma. Troop G was the last of three troops in the Timber when the withdrawal commenced. The M and A trumpeters may have relayed the orders as given, but there was no trumpeter assigned to G Troop to do so for that troop. In the midst of all the other commotion G Troop might not hear the bugle calls of the other troops and having no trumpeter of its own to hear, its members would later claim that there were no bugle calls in the Timber preceding the rout.

A curious aspect of the personnel assignments On June 25, 1876 is that of the medical personnel. There were three surgeons assigned to the 7th, Drs. George Lord, James De Wolf and Henry Porter, plus there were three medical stewards Harry A. Abbotts and William M. Shields of E Troop and John J. Callahan of K Troop. One must wonder why Custer took Dr. Lord and medic Callahan with his battalion and gave Drs. De Wolf and Porter and the medics Abbotts and Shields to Reno, while giving Benteen's battalion no medical staff and in fact taking away the medical staff normally in those troops. Records indicate that De Wolf had made Abbotts a hospital attendant on May 17, 1876, Callahan was Dr. Lord's steward, so it is assumed that Shields was the assigned steward for Dr. Porter[81]. This left both Benteen's battalion and the Pack Train without any professional medical assistance. The question arises as to why either De Wolf or Porter was not assigned to

Benteen and either Abbotts or Shields assigned to pack train? That would have been a more logical distribution of the six available medical personnel to the four active battalions of the regiment. The fact that Custer not only failed to assign a surgeon or medic to Benteen's battalion, but that he took the medical steward who was in Benteen's battalion and reassigned him to his own headquarters staff certainly leads one to question whether Custer anticipated that Benteen might not be involved in combat.

Did Custer expect Benteen not to see any action? Is the lack of medical personnel being assigned to Benteen's battalion proof that Custer knowingly sent Benteen on a scout to nowhere? Or, was this simply a prudent act on the part of a concerned commander who knew that his own battalion and Reno's were to see the greatest amount of combat and that they would need all the medical help possible. The previous statement does not seem plausible as Benteen was sent on his scout well before the location and strength of the Indians was known. Conversely, could he have expected that Benteen would see little or no action because of the territory he was assigned to scout and thus not be in need of medical staff? Is it possible that Custer and Benteen were still in the midst of a tiff resulting from an incident the night before and Custer sent Benteen on a scout to nowhere to calm him down and help him regain his composure. If true, Custer would have reason to believe that Benteen would

---

[81]Ibid., 51, 318.

not need medical staff? The notes of an October 19, 1910 interview by Walter Camp of Lieutenant Edward G. Mathey, commander of Pack Train on June 25, 1876, contain the following statement:

"Mathey says that on the night of June 24 Custer asked him to report which company's packs were giving the most trouble. Mathey said that he remarked that he did not like to make comparisons, seeing that all were doing the best they could, but if required to do so he would have to name the packs of Companies G and H. MacIntosh took the criticism good naturedly, but it made Benteen angry."[82]

As Benteen's ability to pout and sulk is a known fact, one can assume he was in a foul mood on June 25, 1876 as a result of this incident. Terry's suggestions to Custer included that "he constantly feel to his left" to avoid the possibility of the Indians escaping to the west. Perhaps Benteen's foul mood coupled with Terry's suggestions, indicated to Custer that it was time to "feel to his left" when he sent Benteen on his sojourn. Hence, Benteen was sent left to an area where it was not likely he would engage the Indians and have plenty of time and dust with which to cool off.

There were 24 Medals of Honor awarded after the battle, ironically not one to an officer. Was this a left handed rebuke and silent criticism of the officers' performances during the battle? Why was not one awarded to Custer posthumously? To do so would

have mandated Reno's court martial, and of this, the Army wanted no part.

Godfrey certainly deserved one for his actions in dismounting his troop and supplying rear guard coverage for the retreat from Weir Point. If he had not acted as he did, the retreat from Weir Point would have turned into a rout resembling Reno's reverse charge from the Timber. Moylan was ordered to cover the retreat, but almost as quickly as he received the order, he saw the Indians coming and immediately mounted his troop and joined the retreat. Moylan, thereby, left the rear exposed and the retreating troops without cover. Godfrey saw this and absent any orders dismounted his troop and covered the retreat and acted as rear guard. Reno immediately sent a message to Godfrey, telling him that he was not supposed to do this and for him to rejoin the retreat. Godfrey maintained his position as rear guard but was denied his justly due medal of honor because a prerequisite to it would have been Moylan's and perhaps Reno's court martial.

Another reassuring site on Reno Hill had to be Reno himself as described by Lieutenant Edgerly at the Inquiry:

"One of the first officers I saw was Major Reno. He was on his horse, he had lost his hat and had a white handkerchief on his head. He was in an excited condition. As we came up he turned and discharged his pistol towards the Indians."[83]

---

[82]Hammer, *Custer in 76*, 78-79.
[83]Nichols, *Reno Court of Inquiry*, 443.

Here was the inspiring leadership that was to be the first sight of the enlisted men and officers reaching the apex of the hill, an out of control Reno, firing his pistol at Indians 900 yards beyond range, to in Edgerly's words demonstrate an act of defiance. After being routed from the valley and cowardly leading the retreat from the valley to hill, discharging his pistol at Indians 900 yards out of range was the best that Reno could come up with to rally his forces. This pathetic moment had to be the low point in the history of the 7th Cavalry.

Emulating his commanding officer, Lieutenant Varnum was similarly attired and out of control. Edgerly continued in his testimony:

"About the same time I saw Lieutenant Varnum. He had lost his hat and had a white handkerchief on his head. He was excited and crying and while telling us about what had occurred he got mad and commenced swearing and called for a gun and commenced firing at the Indians."[84]

Next on the list of brave offices inspiring and rallying the troops under them had to be Moylan. Benteen claimed that Moylan's conduct was less than exemplary following Reno's rout from the valley.

"On 25th June, 1876, when my battalion got to crest of hill where Reno took refuge from his "charge" from bottom, the first thing which attracted my attention was the gallantly-mustached captain of Troop "A"

blubbering like a whipped urchin, tears coursing down his cheeks."[83]

Edgerly reinforced this stating at the Inquiry that after seeing Varnum, next to come into his view was Moylan. *"About this time Captain Moylan came up and said, 'For God's sake, give me some water!' He said he had 25 wounded men dying of thirst."*[86]

Could he embellish on the truth any further, it is very doubtful. Of the 43 men A Troop put into action, 8 were killed, seven in the valley and one George King who died of his wounds on July 2, 1876.[87] Six other men were wounded in the hilltop fight. Thus, the maximum wounded that Moylan could have had under his command at any one time was seven, not the 25 he alluded to. At a time of crisis, following a disastrous fight and rout from the field of battle, it is an officer's duty to maintain control and rally the troops under him, Moylan hardly filled the bill.

Benteen claimed that French weakened[88] and Mathey broke down. Benteen described the Mathey incident as:

"I don't suppose there was ever an officer of the army got such a 'cussing out' as I gave Mathey at the L. Big Horn on the eve of June 25th, and before crowds of enlisted men, officers and "packs."

---

[84]Ibid., 443.
[85]Graham, *The Custer Myth*, 200.
[86]Nichols, *Reno Court of Inquiry*, 443.
[87]Hammer, *Men with Custer*, 393.
[88]Graham, *The Custer Myth*, 195.

Varnum did not return to the hill in control of himself. Benteen's officers did well, as did McDougall. McDougall heard the firing down field, reported it to Reno and wanted to go to the sound of the guns, Reno denied permission.[89]

Of the eight officers, including Reno, who led Custer's vanguard into the valley, two were killed, MacIntosh the result of being abandoned in the valley and Hodgson during the rout. Had the timber position been held probably neither of these officers would have perished. Of the six remaining officers, Reno was drunk and out of control, Moylan and Varnum were out of control and crying, and Benteen contended that French did not perform well. The only two officers who do not bear blemishes are First Lieutenants Wallace and De Rudio. De Rudio who was trapped in the timber has but his own words to attest to his bravery. Thus, the only surviving officer of the charge, skirmish line, timber fight, rout from the valley and ascent to the hilltop, to maintain control of himself and render a semblance of leadership is First Lieutenant George Wallace. The question is not why there were no medals for surviving officers, but in reality the question should truly be why were there no Court Martials?

There is also the allegation from Godfrey and Benteen that Reno wanted to abandon the wounded and leave the field, Benteen describes this incident,

"I expect Godfrey to say in his article that Reno recommended the abandonment of the wounded on the night of 25th, and of *"skipping off" with those who could ride; well, so he did, to me, but I killed that proposition in the bud. The Court of Inquiry on Reno knew there was something kept back by me, but they didn't know how to dig it out by questioning, as I gave them no chance to do so; and Reno's attorney was 'Posted' thereon."*[90]

As the number of the officers who performed poorly appears to out number the ones who performed well, none of the true officer heroes could have been decorated. There were just too many instances where the decoration of one officer would mandate a court-martial for another.

A large misconception regarding this battle is that Custer sent Reno into battle with a very small force, while promising to support him with his much bigger force. In actuality the difference between the two battalions was only forty-nine men, approximately one troop. After the battalion divisions on June 25, troop strength in the various battalions was: Custer 13 officers, 207 enlisted, 6 scouts[91] and 4 civilians,[92] a total 230; Reno 11 officers, 140 enlisted, 25 scouts,[93]

[89]Nichols, *Reno Court of Inquiry*, 529, 531, 536.
[90]Graham, *The Custer Myth*, 192.
[91]Five Crows-Curly, Goes Ahead, Hairy Mocasin, Half Yellow Face, White Man Runs Him, and One Half Blood Two Kettle Sioux,-William "Billy" Cross.
[92]Boston Custer, Autie Reed, Mitch Bouyer, Mark Kellogg.
[93]Eleven Indian Scouts who fought being one Pikuna William Jackson and ten Arikaras-Black Calf, Foolish Bear, Forked Horn, Goose, Little Sioux, One Feather, Red Bear, Strikes the Bear, Strikes Two and Young Hawk. Two Arikara scouts were killed Bobo Tailed Bull and Little Brave.

5 civilians,[94] a total of 181, Benteen 5 officers, 123 enlisted, a total of 128, and McDougall and Mathey 2 officers, 97 enlisted, 1 scout and 13 civilians, a total of 113. In the aggregate 31 officers, 567 enlisted men, 32 scouts, and 22 civilians, for a force of total of 652 [See Exhibit 11 for a complete reconciliation of the entire regiment, troop by troop.] When Reno proceeded down the valley to attack the village he was in command of 181 men, and when Custer turned to the right he was in command of 230 men. These were two essentially equal sized forces, differing only by one large troop, until 12 of the Indian Scouts attached to Reno, refused to attack[95], leaving Reno with 169 men. It wasn't until the Inquiry, in 1879, that Reno's command started to shrink and shrink greatly in number. There have been tomes written crediting Reno with having to attack the village with as little as 114 men, one must wonder to where and now the other 55 to 67 men of his battalion vanished? The percentage of the regiment represented by each battalion was Custer 41.9%, Reno 32.3%, Benteen 19.4%, and the Pack Train 6.5%. When the disparity between Reno's column and Custer's is expressed in troops, five troops to three, it sounds quite large. When it is stated as 230 men versus 181, the disparity does not sound as large, and when it is 42% to 32% it sounds relatively small. The relative strengths of Custer's battalion (41.9%), Reno's battalion (32.3%) and the reserves represented by Benteen's battalion (19.4%) and the Pack Train (6.5%), if they are compared, show three relatively equal strength battalions, per-

haps a futile attempt by Custer to follow Army Regulations in the proper division of a cavalry regiment into three equal strength battalions.

The first step in understanding what occurred at the Battle of the Little Bighorn, is to properly ascertain what the correct battalion assignments were and which troops functioned together as units. To accomplish this task, we must first refer to the discussion of the Formation of the Battalion, on page 271, in Upton's 1876 edition of the United States Army Cavalry Tactics, which reads as follows:

"704. The battalion is usually composed of four companies, but may be composed of a less number, or a greater number not exceeding seven. In this school the battalion is supposed to consist of four companies.

*When the battalion is formed, companies take their places in line, **in an order depending on the rank of their captains;** the first company on the right, the second on the left, the third the right of centre (of centre, if there be an odd number of companies); the remaining odd-number companies take places in order of*

---

[94]Frederic Francis Girard (interpreter), George B. Herendeen (scout), Bloody Knife (guide/interpreter), Isaiah Dorman (interpreter), Charlie Reynolds (guide).

[95]Twelve Indian scouts who refused to fight were Bear Came Out, Bear Running in Timber, Round Wooden Cloud and White Cloud, (four Dakotas); and Bull, Bull in the Water, Bush, Rushing Bull, Soldier, Stab, Strikes the Lodge, and White Eagle, (eight Arikaras).

rank from the right to centre; the remaining even number companies take place in the order of rank from the left to the centre.

In a battalion of six companies, they take places in the following order from right to left: first, fifth, third, sixth, fourth, second.

In a battalion of seven companies, the companies are in the following order from right to left: first, fifth, seventh, third, sixth, fourth, second.

Companies whose captains are absent, take their places in line according to the relative rank of the officers present in command of them. *A company whose captain is absent for a few days only, may retain its place according to the rank of the captain, at the discretion of the commanding officer.*

After the line is formed, no cognizance is taken of the relative order of the companies."

To determine what this means to 7ᵗʰ Cavalry on June 25, 1876, a seniority list must be prepared, based upon the seniority date of the officer in field command of the respective troop:

- I   Myles Keogh   Captain
        July 28, 1866

- F   George Yates   Captain
        June 12, 1867

- D   Thomas Weir   Captain
        July 31, 1867

- M   Thomas French   Captain
        January 1, 1871

- A   Myles Moylan   Captain
        March 1, 1872

- B   Thomas McDougall   Captain
        December 15, 1875

- K   Edward Godfrey   First Lt.
        February 1, 1868

- E   Algernon Smith   First Lt.
        December 5, 1868

- G   Donald McIntosh   First Lt.
        March 22, 1870

- L   James Calhoun   First Lt.
        January 9, 1871

- H   Francis Gibson   First Lt.
        July 11, 1871 *

- C   Henry Harrington   Second Lt.
        June 14, 1872 **

- Captain Frederick Benteen as Senior Captain was assuming the role of a major and was to have an independent command of a battalion. Thus he was no longer considered in field command of his troop, when the wings were formed.

- **At least from the date of the Powder River Scout of June 10, 1876, Captain Tom Custer had been detached from field command of Troop C and was acting as Aide-de-Camp to his brother Lieutenant Colonel George Custer.

Captain Tom Custer did not accompany his troop on the scout and Second Lieutenant Henry Harrington had field command of Troop C from that date forward, through the battle of the Little Bighorn.

This seniority list produces a right wing containing troops I, D, A, K, G, and H, with a left wing consisting of F, M, B, E, L and C. For some inexplicable reason troops I and M were flipped with I being placed in the left wing and M being placed in the right wing, creating a new right wing (the Army orders right based upon seniority and with Keogh, the senior field commanding Captain now in this wing, it becomes the right wing) of I, F, B, E, L, and C and a new left wing of M, D, A, K, G, and H. When the new right wing is ordered according to Upton (*from right to left: first, fifth, third, sixth, fourth, second.*) It would form a line of: I, L, B, C, E, F. When the left wing is ordered in a similar manner, the line produced is: M, G, A, H, K, D.

It should be noted that when troops M and I were flipped between wings, M transferred into the left wing with the position of Senior Troop, though Captain Weir of D Troop had a higher seniority date that of Captain French of M Troop. It is perhaps that Custer felt this arrangement was more suited to the men assigned to command the respective battalions and desired his trusted friend Weir to be with Benteen whom he did not trust. Major Reno assumed command of the right battalion of the left wing, troops M, A, and G. Captain Benteen assumed command of the left battalion of the left wing, troops D, K, and H.

Custer assumed personal command of the right wing which as ordered according to Upton consisted of troops I, L, B, E, C, F. Troop B had been detached from this wing and assigned to guard duty for the pack train. The 7th Cavalry had functioned in wings, most likely from May 17, 1876 when it left Fort Lincoln, but certainly not later than June 10, 1876 when Reno departed on his scout of the Powder River area, taking with him the right wing consisting of troops I, F, B, E, L, and C. The wing was then further broken down into two battalions of I, B, and L and F, E, and C. These battalion assignments were in place, from at least, the June 10, 1876 scout and there is no reason to believe that they would have been altered, on June 25, 1876, merely because one troop was detached temporarily for day duty as guard to the pack train. The foregoing was noted by Walter Mason Camp in an August 24, 1919 letter to Mrs. Elizabeth B. Custer, where he stated:

"Note the companies that were with Maj. Reno on that scout - "B", "C", "E", "F", "I" and "L". With the exception of "B" they were the same companies as those with Gen. Custer at the Little Bighorn; and I have it authentically that, but for circumstance, "B" would have been with the General on that afternoon of June 25,1876. It was the turn of "B" to lead the column on that day, but because of the tardiness of Capt. McDougall in answering the officers' call that morning, he was directed by the General to march in the rear with his company, as he had done the day before (June 24)."[96]

This is further supported by a letter of Augustus L. DeVoto a member of B Troop who wrote Camp on November 15, 1917 stating that

---

[96]Hardorff, *On the Little Bighorn With Walter Camp*, 146-147.

"we started out before daylight, and B Troop was the advance guard, was the morning of the 25ᵗʰ, and the change to rear guard was made when we were about ten miles from the Indian camp, after Officers Call was sounded, and General Custer had his counsel of war."[97]

This clearly shows that the decision to assign B Troop to the rear guard came after the battalion assignments were issued for the day and that in fact B Troop would have been detached from Keogh's battalion not Yates.'

That B Troop was under the command of Custer and would have been considered in any battalion assignments handed out, by Custer, for his wing that day is supported by Reno's statement in his report:

"I was ordered by Lieut. W. W. Cook, adjutant, to assume command of Companies M, A, and G; Captain Benteen, of Companies H, D, and K. Custer retained C, E, F, I, and L, under his immediate command, and Company B, Captain McDougall, in rear of the pack trains."[98]

B Troop was in Custer's wing and would have been considered in any battalion assignments made by Custer, from possibly May 17, 1876 and certainly from June 10, 1876 to June 25, 1876. B Troop was part of the right wing, its battalion assignment in place regardless of whatever temporary duty it might be assigned to and the remaining troops in its battalion would form up short one troop based upon B Troop's temporary assignment.

This wing had been formed at least for the June 10, 1876 scout and had remained intact thereafter. There was neither need nor reason for Custer to alter the battalion assignments within the wing because of the temporary reassignment of one troop and there is no factual evidence to indicate that he did. Thus, it can be concluded that the battalion assignments that existed from the June 10, 1876 scout remained in effect on June 25, 1876 and they were based upon the seniority of the officers commanding the troops on those dates, being: I, B, L and F, E, C.

Accordingly, on June 25, 1876, Myles Keogh was left with the small battalion and in command of only troops I and L. Captain Yates was in command of the larger battalion having three troops F, E, and C. Magnussen noted that:

"The battalions were going to be split away from each other and as Custer would, no doubt be more inclined to accompany or be in close proximity to the larger element, this would mean that he would place the senior captain in command of the separated, but smaller battalion."[99]

This is a point that has escaped historians for years and has led to numerous faulty theories of how the battle evolved, all based upon the erroneous assumption that battalions were formed after Custer took com-

---

[97]Ibid., 139.

[98]Carroll, *General Custer and the Battle of the Little Bighorn: The Federal View*, 102.

[99]Magnussen, *Peter Thompson's Narrative of the Little Bighorn Campaign 1876*, 123.

mand of five troops. This is totally incorrect, the battalion assignments existed from at least June 10, 1876, and Custer would not reorder the assignments merely because B Troop was detached for the day to guard the pack train. Thus, it was Myles Keogh who commanded the smaller battalion and George Yates the larger battalion. It is for this reason the battle played out as it did, and specific troop movements occurred. When Custer led Yates' battalion down Medicine Tail Coulee, he was leading his stronger battalion, not the weaker one. This is a very persuasive fact which refutes the erroneous feint theories. It strongly supports the aggressive theories of a strong move which contemplated an attempt to attack the village.

CHAPTER 8
Charging While Intoxicated

Much has been made of the condition and conduct of Major Marcus B. Reno, second in command, and the effects it may have had on the battle. Aside from biased opinion, and wishful thinking, there is very little to support the position that Reno was not drinking on June 25, 1876 or for that matter on any of the days of the Battle of the Little Big Horn. There are definitive eye witness statements that not only support that he was drinking, but how much he drank and how long it took him to consume the liquor. De Rudio's statement that Reno was drinking at the river is refuted with allegations that De Rudio is a liar. Taylor's statement that he saw Reno take a swig and offer one to Hodgson during the charge, is countered by comments that it would be difficult to do on horseback. Gerard's statement he saw Reno drink, finish and dispose of a whiskey bottle in the timber, is dispelled with another "liar allegation." Thus, Reno supporters, when confronted with eyewitness statements that Reno was drinking, chose to dispel the evidence, by either besmirching the witness as a liar, belittling the statement, or saying such acts were not possible. Such shallow attempts to try and dispel what is in reality irrefutable testimony, are easily seen for what they are. Even the more objective perspectives gravitate to the position that Reno was drinking but might not have been impaired or drunk, in some cases using the ludicrous rationale that he had a high tolerance to liquor and thus could drink large quantities without being impaired.

Let us attempt to time and track the life of a quart bottle of liquor, in the possession of Major Reno on June 25, 1876. The first sighting of a quart liquor bottle occurs at the river just prior to Reno's battalion fording. Walter Camp's notes of his interview of First Lieutenant Charles De Rudio on February 2, 1910 contain the following passage:

"After passing lone tepee, De Rudio stopped somewhere to fill his canteen and did not catch up with the command until it reached the river. Here he found

Reno and Gerard sitting on horses in the river, Reno drinking from a bottle of whiskey. De Rudio was the first man to ford the river, and as his horse surged ahead he splashed water on Reno, who said "What are you trying to do? Drown me before I am killed?"[100]

The bottle is next sighted, approximately twenty minutes later, during the charge down the valley prior to the establishment of the skirmish line. Private William O. Taylor notes,

"The Major and Lieutenant Hodgson were riding side by side a short distance in the rear of my Company. As I looked back Major Reno was just taking a bottle from his lips. He then passed it to Lieutenant Hodgson. It appeared to be a quart flask, and about one half or two thirds full of an amber colored liquid. There was nothing strange about this, and yet the circumstances remained indelibly fixed in my memory. I turned my head to the front as there were other things to claim my attention. What the flask contained, and effects its contents has, is not for me to say, but I have ever since had a very decided belief."[101]

In a December 12, 1909 letter to Walter Camp, Taylor described the same incident in a very similar manner:

"Charrrage, was the way it sounded to me, and it came in such a tone that I turned my head and glanced backward. The Major and Lieut. Hodgson were riding side by side in the rear of my company (A) perhaps 30 or 40 feet away, possibly more but certainly a very short distance. As I looked back Major Reno was just taking a bottle from his lips and passed it to Lieut. Hodgson. In appearance I should say it was a quart flask, about one half or two thirds full."[102]

This same bottle is seen for a third and last time by Frederic F Gerard. He recalled the incident to Walter Camp during his interviews on January 22 and April 3, 1909:

"As Major Reno left the line and passed into the timber, I saw him put a bottle of whiskey to his mouth and drink the whole contents. The men ran into the timber pell mell, and all resistance to the Sioux had ceased"[103]

The life of that one quart bottle of whiskey, in Major Reno's possession was from forty five minutes to one hour, most likely it lasted less than one hour. Reno was at Ford A approximately 3:00 PM, at which time he starts his charge, by 3:30 PM he has deployed to a skirmish line and by 3:45 PM he is leading the Rout to the Hill. The De Rudio incident is at Ford A, Taylor sees him drinking during the charge perhaps 20 minutes later, and

[100]Hammer, Kenneth, *Custer in 76*, 84.
[101]Taylor William O., *With Custer on the Little Big Horn*, 36.
[102]Hammer, Kenneth, *Custer in 76*, 151.
[103]Ibid., 232.

Gerard sees Reno finish the bottle as he leaves the skirmish line for the timber, another 20 or 30 minutes later. This establishes a chain of events involving Reno possessing and consuming the contents of a quart flask of whiskey. It is corroborated by the statements of three different eye witnesses that Reno consumed a quart of whiskey in forty to fifty minutes, just prior to leading the Rout out of the timber.

One must conclude that after consuming such a large quantity of whiskey in so short a period of time, that no matter how accomplished a drinker Reno might have been, there was no possible way that he was in full command of his faculties when he reached the Hill. How was Reno's physical condition described around the time of his arrival on the Hill? Lieutenant Edward S. Godfrey, at the Court of Inquiry, stated,

> *"He had a handkerchief tied round his head and seemed somewhat excited. I think he was making arrangements to go for Lieutenant Hodgson's body or effects"*[104]

Godfrey's visualization of Reno, upon his arrival on the Hill, as described to Arthur Chapman was:

> *"When Captain Godfrey came up with Benteen's command he found Reno with his hat lost and a handkerchief about his head, 'very much excited.' According to the same authority, Reno had thrown away his revolvers after he emptied them."*

It appears Godfrey may have been more open with Chapman and recalled

for his benefit that Reno had thrown his revolvers away after they were emptied.[105] Godfrey was yet more caustic in his diary,

> *"We [Godfrey and Weir] thought that to Col Benteen we must look for the wisdom to deliver us from our situation or defend us as it was evident that Col Reno carried no vigor nor decision, and his personal behavior gave no confidence in him."*[106]

As to Reno's fitness to command, McClernand contributes,

> *"It was said that as Reno emptied his revolvers, he threw them away. A fine example to set for his men!"*[107]

Was the drinking incident limited to June 25, 1876 or was Reno observed drinking on other occasions during the battle?

John Frett testified at the Court of Inquiry regarding Reno's condition on the night of June 25, 1876 that: *"He had a bottle of whiskey in his hand and as he slapped me the whiskey flew over me and he staggered. If any other man was in the condition he was, I should call him drunk."*[108]

Private Patrick Corcoran, who was wounded in the right shoulder on the morning of June 26, 1876, and was in the hospital observed to Walter Camp that Reno was

---

[104]Nichols, Ronald H., *Reno Court of Inquiry*, 483.
[105]Chapman, Arthur, "Custer's Last Battle," Liberty Magazine, 6/26/1926 Issue, 60.
[106]Godfrey, Edward Settle, *The Field Diary of Lt. Edward Settle Godfrey*, 15.
[107]McClernand, *On Time for Disaster*, 73-74.
[108]Nichols, *The Reno Court of Inquiry*, 505.

drinking on the morning of the 26th: *"Reno came around and asked him how he was getting along. At this time he saw Reno have a quart bottle of whiskey and saw him take a big drink out of it in hospital on morning of 26th."*[109]

Liquor was quite plentiful on the campaign, especially among the officers. A typical example of this is an entry that appears in Dr. Holmes Paulding's, of the Montana Column, diary on April 4, 1876. Paulding remarks that he brought "20 botts of whiskey and 4 of Brandy" along for the campaign.[110]

That Reno was drinking on June 25, 1876 is indisputable. That his drinking affected his ability to perform his duties, lead his men and carry out his orders is unquestionable. That Reno was drunk, out of control and unable to command was demonstrated by his actions and lack thereof. Reno's inebriated state was to become the lynch pin of the 7th Cavalry's disaster at the Little Bighorn.

The Rev. Dr. Arthur Edwards was a close friend of Reno's. Edwards claimed that in a moment of deep sorrow Reno informed him that, **"...his strange actions were due to drink, and drink ultimately caused his downfall. His actions at the Battle of the Little Big Horn was cited as one instance of the result of his use of intoxicating liquor."**[111]

---

[109]Hammer, Kenneth, *Custer in 76*, 150.
[110]Koury, *Diaries of the Little Bighorn*, 75.
[111]Graham, *The Custer Myth*, 340.

CHAPTER 9
Village Location

History has been far too critical regarding the "Maguire" map. While he admitted that his after battle report and map were less than precise and that he gained his insights from appearances only, at the Reno Court, Maguire gave "his" map faint praise, saying that it was only a sketch to illustrate the report and did not purport to be any more than that. It is perhaps that Maguire back peddled in defense of his work, as he was aware that the Army had long since revised his efforts and the map before the Court bore little semblance to the one he had prepared.

Other witnesses severely criticized it, particularly the inaccuracies in the Reno field of conflict. Maguire testified that he did not even go over some of the terrain as the ground was so cut up by hooves that most of his lines and trails were only theories. This may well have been the result of Maguire knowing that the map being presented to the Court Of Inquiry was a far cry from any map he had prepared and that an Army coverup or revision of history had begun as early as the fall

of 1876. On September 27, 1876, a Major George Elliot[112] gave written orders to the Bureau of Printing and Engraving, requiring them to make unsolicited and unwarranted changes to the tracings as drawn by Maguire, McClernand and Becker, thereby changing for posterity what the official map of the battlefield would look like.

Maguire did not draw the entire map. Most of the work was performed by Sergeant Charles Becker under the supervision of Second Lieutenant E. J. McClernand of the Second Cavalry. McClernand and Becker started the map and had a good portion completed when Maguire went to General Terry and asked that he be allowed to be in charge of the map preparation as he was the senior engineering officer present. Terry agreed that Maguire should be in charge and ordered that Maguire finish the project. This is why quotes should be placed around "Maguire" and "his" when referring to the map, at best it was a cooperative

---

[112]King, *Massacre*, Illustration 5.

effort with Maguire making the minority contribution.

The major problem, today, with the "Maguire Map" is the multitude of variations that exist and the conflicting and damning testimony and descriptions that accompany them. W. Kent King in his book *Massacre: The Custer Cover-up* did a magnificent job in analyzing and explaining the history of the Map, including ample detail on the changes made by third parties at later dates. King was able to locate and analyze five different variations of the "Map", they are discussed in the apparent order of preparation:

- King Illustration 2 - which he designated as the First Battlefield Map drawn July 2, 1876, to accompany Maguire's preliminary report. This map shows the line of march of Gibbon's forces and the site of their campsite on June 27, 1876.

  In his report to General Humphreys, which this map accompanied, Maguire stated, "The first stand was probably made by Lts. Calhoun and Crittenden on the hill marked D to protect the troops passing along the ravine at its foot. The men and their empty cartridge shells were found in a semi-circle around the crest."[113]

  Maguire continued on in the report, "Along the ravine and up the side hill to the crest marked E was a line of dead men and horses..." "On the crest E were the bodies of Gen'l Custer, Capt. Custer, Lt. Smith, Capt. Yates,

Lt. Cooke, and Lt. Reilly, with a large number of men.

"Leading from the crest to the ravine marked H was a regular line of bodies, there evidently having been a line of skirmishers on this line as the men fell at skirmish intervals. The ravine marked H contained 28 dead bodies."[114]

In his Report of July 10, 1876, Maguire further explained to Humphreys that the "Men taking to the ravine H for shelter must have been surrounded by Indians.[115]

When Maguire testified at the Court of Inquiry in 1879, pens, pencils, and note taking were banned by the Court. The only record of his testimony became that which the court stenographer wrote: "They separated into two bodies to concentrate at the hill E. The lines represent my idea as to the routes they took..." "From D to E bodies were found at intervals. It was my idea that Calhoun had stopped at D. The other companies formed some sort of skirmish line..."[116]

This was a far cry from Maguire's original report which was never presented to the Court as evidence. With all the alterations and deletions made by Major George Elliott, pursuant to written orders he issued on September 27, 1876,[117] being incorporated in the only map presented to the Court, there can be little doubt that

---

[113]King, *Massacre*, 27.
[114]Ibid., 28.
[115]Ibid., 28.
[116]Ibid., 28.
[117]Ibid., Illustration Number 5.

Maguire understood that "for the Good of the Army" the true facts were not to be presented.

- King Illustration 3 - which accompanied Maguire's final report and is dated July 10, 1876. This version adds a notation for Reno's Skirmish Line but omits Gibbon's line of march and the location of Gibbon's June 27, 1876 campsite.

- King Illustration 4 - An engraved version of the map which was scrapped in the fall of 1876, in deference to King Illustration 1. This version introduces alphabetic keys to indicate points on the map where significant events occurred.

- King Illustration 6 - An engraved version prepared in the fall of 1876 which had red "x's" to indicate where the corpses of Custer's dead were found along with a red dotted line indicating Custer's line of March. This map was then revised pursuant to orders of Major George Elliot, dated September 27, 1876: "Omit the title for the present, and leave out altogether the Red Figures. The Red dotted lines, will be black single dotted lines. Make the Indian Camp distinct. The sketch you have just engraved of this Battlefield is to be abandoned."[118] The final result of these alterations became King Illustration 1.

- King Illustration 1 - deemed the Final Battle Map by King, it is the engraved version which was printed in the Report of the Secretary of War for 1877. The King Illustration Number 1 contains the numerals added by the officers during the Court of Inquiry in 1879.

- Subsequent to the printing of King's book in 1989, yet another version of the "Maguire Map" surfaced [See Exhibit 12]. This version was found among documents comprising part of the estate of Edward W. Smith. Smith was a Civil War General, who in 1876 held the regular Army rank of Captain. He was both General Alfred Terry's Aide-de-Camp and brother-in-law. Smith is acknowledged to be the last man outside those in the 7th Cavalry to see Custer alive. This map, which is now in the author's collection and published herein for the first time, is acknowledged by many experts to be the original and first sketch ever drawn of the battlefield and is hand signed by Maguire himself. The map was found pasted into a scrap book alongside a July 6, 1876 article describing the battle.

John Demer of the United States Department of the Interior, in a letter dated December 12, 1989, to the Superintendent (sp), Custer Battlefield National Monument stated:

"The sketch appears similar in method and material to other sketches of the period. What cannot be determined with any certainty is whether it is the

---

[118]Ibid., Illustration Number 5.

earliest or only sketch drawn by Maguire, or when he drew it. Because the newspaper clipping accompanies the sketch it is reasonable to assume the map was drawn soon after the battle. If the park is able to acquire the sketch, we recommend it do so."

Douglas C. McChristian, the Chief Historian for Custer Battlefield National Monument, stated in a letter dated March 20, 1991:

"I think it safe to assume he prepared it 'on the ground' immediately after the battle. We do know that he made other more refined versions of this map and, in fact, it was his final map that was used at the famous Court of Inquiry for Major Marcus A. Reno in 1879...By comparing the one King labels 'First Battlefield Map,' you will readily see that it has a few refinements not shown on your map, thus making yours the more primitive. I have personally examined this map and am comfortable in saying that I believe it is the earliest one known of the Little Big Horn Battlefield."

- This "new" version, most likely is the very first tracing ever drawn and it shows the position of Reno's Skirmish Line, has no alphabetic keys, does have a black dotted line which shows Custer's line of march to his fate, is annotated in red "Custer fell" where his body was found and shows the Indian Village to be over two miles long and approximately one and one half miles wide. It fixes the village as beginning over a mile east of Medicine Tail Coulee and having a western extremity on a line with Last Stand Hill.

There is physical evidence to support this version of "Maguire's Map" and others with similar references that being where the bodies were found. On the Kent King Map designated Illustration Number 6, red x's were drawn to show the position of dead officers and enlisted men. The most advanced of the red x's, in the area where Reno fought in the valley, are less than a mile and a half from Medicine Tail Coulee. Hardorff in his book *Custer Battle Casualties* indicates that the bodies of John E. Armstrong, John J. McGinnis and two unknowns were found within a three quarters of a mile of Medicine Tail Coulee. Miles O'Hara, George E. Smith, Bloody Knife, Henry Klotzbucher, and George Lorentz were all found less than one and a half miles from Medicine Tail Coulee.

If Reno stopped 500 to 1000 yards from the village, a range of from .3 to .6 of a mile, then the village had to begin east of Medicine Tail Coulee. Knowing where it is alleged Reno stopped, and where the bodies were found provides physical evidence to corroborate the starting point of the village as drawn by Becker, McClernand and Maguire. It begins east of Medicine Tail Coulee and extends to a point just west of Last Stand Hill.

The skirmish line had to be less than 1000 yards from the village, as there are both Indian and Army statements that Army misses and shots went through tepees close to the beginning perimeter of the village. The range of a Springfield is 1000 yards +/-, therefore the skirmish line had to be less than the maximum range of the Springfield for shots to reach the village.

This is supported by the Maps drawn by:

• Capt Henry Freeman 7th Infantry, with the Montana Column, prepared after the battle.[119]

• Russell White Bear, prepared in 1926.[120] [See Exhibit 14]

• Captain Frederick Benteen, a map which accompanied a July 4, 1876 letter to his wife.[121]

• Walter Mason Camp's map which was prepared after his substantial discussions with both numerous Army and Indian combatants, had similar beginnings and endings.[122]

• Lieutenant Philo Clark, the Army's expert in sign language, prepared a map [See Exhibit 13] based upon his interviews of the Sioux who had surrendered in early 1877 and were being held at Fort Robinson. This map also shows the village began approximately one mile east of Medicine Tail Coulee and extended west to a point slightly past Last Stand Hill.[123]

• Godfrey's map starts with an Uncpapa circle north of Garryowen Loop and ends with a Cheyenne circle past Last Stand Hill[124]

• Sitting Bull's Map starts with the Uncpapas even with Reno's entrenched position and ends with the Cheyenne circle well past Last Stand Hill.[125]

Clearly the early maps drawn by Maguire, McClernand and Becker were accurate representations of the Battlefield. It is not until these renderings are doctored on the order of Major George Elliot on September 27, 1876 that they lose their value and appropriate place in history. It is thus most conceivable that the village ran from a location parallel to Weir Pt approximately one mile east of Medicine Tail Coulee, to a point one mile west of Medicine Tail Coulee and approximately parallel Last Stand Hill.

E. J McClernand's report, in the Report of the Chief of Engineers for the Fiscal Year Ending June 30, 1877, states:[126]

"Making an early start, we go but a short way when two tepees are seen through the timber, and crossing a narrow sandstone point we see just in front of us where a very large village was yesterday. The fate of Custer is

---

[119]Freeman, *The Freeman Journal*, 26.
[120]Original Map in Author's Collection.
[121]Graham, *The Reno Court of Inquiry*, 306-307.
[122]Hardorff, *Camp, Custer and The Little Bighorn*, 92.
[123]Original Map in Author's Collection.
[124]Godfrey, *Custer's Last Battle*, 23.
[125]Graham, *The Custer Myth*, 64.
[126]Carroll, *General Custer and the Battle of the Little Big Horn: The Federal View*, 59.

now more puzzling than ever. We are not left much longer in suspense. Lieutenant Bradley sends in word he has counted one hundred ninety six dead cavalrymen lying on the hills to the left."

Gibbon states:[127]

"The next morning the march was resumed, and after proceeding about 3 miles we came in sight of a large deserted Indian camp, in which two tepees were still standing..."

Gibbon continues later on,

"After marching 8 3/4 miles we encamp on the Little Big Horn, near Colonel Reno's position, which is on a high steep bluff."

Gibbon's column travels approximately three miles and reaches the northern perimeter of a village. This spot is two miles northwest of Medicine Tail Coulee. One of the first things encountered, in the Northwest fringe of this abandoned village, is two tepees with dead Indians inside. One with ten bodies and one with five or eight bodies. This is the northwesternmost extremity of the village. It is where the Indians exited as they abandoned the valley, as evidenced by the tepees with the deceased Indians inside.

The sandstone point and timber are northwest of Last Stand Hill, if the village had ended at Medicine Tail Coulee the sandstone point would be near there. It is nearly two miles northwest of Medicine Tail Coulee, thereby establishing this point as the western extremity of the village.

It is approximately four miles from the Little Bighorn river to Medicine Tail Coulee, Reno stopped between .3 and .6 miles before the village, after charging 2 plus miles. We also know that the 8 ¾ miles Gibbon's column marched stretches from his prior camp to the river and includes the length of the village. Thus, if the two extremities are added 5 plus miles are accounted for. Gibbon's march to the village was 3 miles, Reno's charge was 2 plus miles and Reno stopped approximately ½ of a mile before the village for a total of 5 ½ non village miles. If the 5 ½ non-village miles are subtracted from Gibbon's total march distance of 8 ¾ miles, the remainder is 3 ¼ miles which is the approximate length of the village. The village would have a starting point approximately 2 ½ miles from the river, at or near one mile east of Medicine Tail Coulee, approximately at Shoulder Blade Creek and extending approximately ¾ mile west past Last Stand Hill, approximately to Squaw Creek.

Far too many statements and reports from the members of Gibbon's column, along with the other maps previously mentioned support the location of the village as shown on the Maguire, McClernand, Becker maps for it to be slandered as it has in the past.

The Indians tell us there was a village running from near the Shoulder Blade Creek which is very near to Garryowen Loop, a point approximately one mile east of Medicine Tail Ford, to approximately one mile west

---

[127]Ibid., 99.

of Medicine Tail Ford, or Squaw Creek.

Two Moons in a interview with Richard Throssel during the summer of 1909 stated: "Sitting Bull and his band were camped right at Big Shoulder's place."[128] As the beginning of the village is positioned below Medicine Tail Coulee, Custer could see a large portion of the village from the bluffs and Weir Pt, and this is why he sent Martin back with the note "Big Village." This village position is supported by the following quotes:

Respects Nothing in his interview with Ricker November 9, 1906 put the village between, Box Elder and Chasing Creek, Shoulder Blade Creek and Squaw Creek being the modern names respectively. This puts the village between Garry Owen Loop on the south and just below Last Stand Hill on the north.[129]

Moses Flying Hawk in an interview with Ricker on March 8, 1907 described the village as four circles with an extreme length of one and one half miles. The distance from Garry Owen Loop to Medicine Tail Coulee is about 3/4 of a mile. If it started at Garryowen Loop then it ended near Last Stand Hill.[130]

Standing Bear in an interview on March 12, 1907 with Ricker shows a village from Garryowen Loop to near Calhoun Hill.[131]

In 1910 He Dog told Walter Camp there were 1800 lodges in the village - this could not be contained in a small village area.[132/133]

George Bird Grinell's map shows the village running from Garryowen Loop to past Deep Ravine.[134]

White Bull said the Cheyennes had 200 tepees 3000 people.[135]

Russell White Bear, a Crow, based upon his research has the village running from Garryowen Loop to well past Last Stand Hill.

- Two Moons states the camp ran from below Big Shoulder's allotment to past Medicine Tail Coulee.[136/137]

- Mrs. Spotted Horn Bull in a map printed in 1883 starts with a Blackfeet circle near where McIntosh died and ends with a Minneconjous circle on a line even with the monument.[138]

There seems to be as much, if not more, Native American support for a larger village than there is for a smaller village. This is augmented by the statements of the Army men who were present immediately after the battle. The Army had odometers affixed to wagon wheels which measured distances accurately to within hundredths of a mile over all types of terrain. This strongly suggests the village was of a very large size and

---

[128]Hardorff, *Lakota Recollections of the Custer Fight*, 134.
[129]Ibid., 26.
[130]Ibid., 49-50.
[131]Ibid., 58.
[132]Hammer, *Custer in 76*, 206.
[133]Graham, *The Custer Myth*, 57 and the Original Map in the Author's Collection.
[134]Hardorff, *Cheyenne Memories of the Custer Fight*, 22.
[135]Ibid., 81.
[136]Hardorff, *Lakota Recollections*, 134.
[137]Ibid., 79.
[138]Graham, *The Custer Myth*, 83.

was located from near Garryowen Loop to just past Last Stand Hill.

If Reno, starting at Ford A, trotted for one mile and galloped/charged for another mile to where he stopped and deployed, approximately, one half mile from the village perimeter, this would place the village start 2 ½ miles from the river.

On many maps, there is the notation "abandoned lodges", just south of the Garryowen Loop. These lodges were abandoned because the village was moved slightly for sanitary reasons the day before Custer attacked. Perhaps some of the foggier memories confused the first location with the second, and the interpreters and interviewers, with their own agendas, included these lodges in the village, making it even larger than it was.

Based upon Army records, there were between 1500 to 1800 lodges and 400 wickyups in the village. Lieutenant Luther Hare testified at the Court Of Inquiry that:

"I was with the battalion that burned the tepee poles after the fight. I counted 40 lodges at a place where I stood, and estimated the area of that, and from that I estimated the whole of the village. I estimate that there were 1500 lodges and 500 wickyups, making a fighting force of 4000 men and that is a very low estimate."[139]

The Russell White Bear Map contains the following annotation:

"The entire Indian encampment contained about 2000 tepees. There were about 17000 Indians. Indians - men & boys - participating

in the Custer battle, numbered about 6000"[140]

Lieutenant W. Philo Clark, 2nd U.S. Cavalry in the report which accompanied his map described the village as having:

"1200 standing lodges, 400 wickyups and 3500 fighting men."[141]

The composite village created from the Maguire, Clark and White Bear Maps and the Hare testimony would contain:

"Approximately 1600 lodges, approximately 450 wickyups, and approximately 4500 Indian combatants of various ages."

Such a complex would have required a vast amount of land, of from three to five square miles for sanitary purposes, general living needs and the pasturing of the pony herds required to transport such a mass of humanity.

Clearly the early Maguire maps were drawn correctly, the Indians were in a large village that was approximately 2 ½ miles long and 1 ¼ miles wide, situated between Shoulder Blade Creek, approximately 1 mile south of Medicine Tail Coulee and Spotted Tail Creek [Squaw Creek] approximately ½ mile north of Last Stand Hill.

The foregoing strongly suggests that the boundaries of the Indian village were, on the south and east, a line running from Garryowen Loop to Shoulder Blade Creek and on the north and west, a line running from

[139]Nichols, *Reno Court of Inquiry*, 297.
[140]From original map in author's collection, see Exhibit 14 to this text.
[141]See Addendum to this text.

Squaw Creek to Last Stand Hill, stopping at the river by Ford C, a distance of more than two and one half miles, with the width determined by the land between the Little Big Horn River and the western bluffs, ranging from one to one and one half miles. The total land between these four boundaries is approximately four square miles. The northern and southern extremities are shown on a modern map prepared by the Custer Battlefield Preservation Committee, circa 2001. [See Exhibit 15].

The first Maguire Map, as shown in Exhibit 12, was prepared with the perspective of going east to west and north on top. The Custer Battlefield and north appear to the right of, and above, the river. The Indian Village conversely appears to the left of, and below, the river. This is the classic view most people are used to seeing in maps of the battlefield and would represent the view Custer had as he approached his doom, going southeast to northwest.

The W. Philo Clark map shown in Exhibit 13, was prepared with the reverse perspective of going west to east and north on the bottom. The Indian village appears on the right of and above the river. The Custer Battle field and north are on the left and below the river. This map represents the view Colonel Gibbon and his men had as they approached the valley going northwest to southeast.

When the W. Philo Clark map is flipped over to create the same perspective as the Maguire map, and the two are compared, they show that the two maps are virtually identical in

concept, positioning of geographical landmarks, marking of Custer's Route and the movements of his troops during the battle. Both maps position the village in virtually identical areas, that being the land mass in the valley between Shoulder Blade Creek and Squaw Creek.

If these two maps are compared with the map made in 1926, by Russell White Bear, Exhibit 14, prepared from a composite of the Indian oral histories of the battle and discussions with Indian survivors of the battle, all three maps clearly show that Custer descended Medicine Tail Coulee to near the river, got very close to but did not cross the river, turned to the right, then pulled back retreating up along the bluffs to Last Stand Hill. All three maps show a retreat from the river north to Last Stand Hill. The McGuire and Russell White Bear maps show a single line of retreat from the river across the bluffs to Last Stand Hill.

The Clark map shows two lines of retreat from the river, the eastern one is up Medicine Tail Coulee [This depicts the F Troop]. The second comes from Ford "C" and forks. The eastern fork goes from the river to Last Stand Hill [This represents the retreat of C Troop]. The western fork commences about one half mile from the river and runs for less than one quarter mile [This represents the entrapment of E Troop in Deep Ravine].

The three maps appear virtually identical for the area bounded by Reno's Timber, on the south and east and Squaw Creek and Ford C, on the north and west, which is quite remarkable as the Maguire map had to be enlarged to have its original scale of one mile to the inch conform to the apparent scale of the Clark and Russell White Bear maps of one mile to two inches. There is no scale indicated by Clark or Russell White Bear on their maps. The major variations occur east of Shoulder Blade Creek and it appears that Clark may have lost interest in the true course of the river beyond that point. An interesting difference between the two maps is that Maguire has Reno's Skirmish Line approximately one quarter mile south or below Shoulder Blade Creek while Clark has it positioned one quarter mile north or above the Creek and Russell White Bear has it positioned exactly at Shoulder Blade Creek.

Maguire prepared his map after walking the battlefield, going over Custer's route and being there two days after the battle. Clark prepared his map after interviewing and debriefing the Sioux Indians who had surrendered and were being held at Fort Robinson the year following the battle, and then walking the battlefield with three Indians, one of which may have been Iron Cedar, a Sioux, another captured Sioux and one of Reno's scouts.[142] Russell White Bear prepared his map based upon the oral histories of the Crow, Sioux and Cheyenne Nations and discussions with Indian survivors fifty years after the battle. It can be said that the Maguire map was prepared from the Custer or Army perspective and the Clark and Russell White Bear maps

were prepared from the Indian perspective. The Maguire and Clark maps were prepared within a year of each other and both of these were prepared within a year of the battle, while the Russell White Bear map was prepared fifty years after the battle. All three contain nearly identical representations of Custer's line of march and the flow of the battle. Maguire prepared his map by reviewing the forensics on the field days after the battle. Clark prepared his after interviewing many of the combatants, walking the field with Indians who fought in the battle, before any attempt was made to clean up the battlefield and with the forensics still in place except for effects of the burials and nature. Russell White Bear prepared his based upon the oral histories of the tribe involved and the discussions held with many of the Indian Survivors fifty years after the battle.

As all three of these maps were prepared from entirely different perspectives and are mutually corroborating, they therefore must accurately depict the topography of the battle, including, Custer's line of march, the flow of the battle and the position and size of the village. The village as shown on all three of these maps runs from Shoulder Blade Creek to Squaw Creek, a distance of 3 miles and ranged from 1 to 1½ miles wide, for an aggregate area of approximately four plus square miles. These maps, both individually and in concert,

---

[142]Graham, *The Custer Myth*, 136.

accurately and properly define the geographic boundaries of this extremely large Indian village. The composite created from these three maps must be far more accurate than any modern day map prepared based upon archeological interpolations. It should settle once and for all the questions of whether Maguire's maps were accurate, what the geographic size of the village was, and where the geographic location of the village was.

Maguire did his job correctly by supervising the production of accurate maps. These renderings were concealed from the public, distorted and changed versions were presented to the public based upon the orders of Major George Elliot and perhaps other higher ranking officers in the War Department. The Indian village definitely was more than 3 miles long and ranged from 1 to 1½ miles wide, approximately 4 plus square miles in total area. As per the Philo Clark Report, the village was 3 ½ miles long and 2 miles wide. (See page 231 herein.) Its southeastern extremity was between Shoulder Blade Creek and Garryowen Loop, while its northwestern extremity was between Squaw Creek and Ford C.

CHAPTER 10
Village Head Count

To obtain a relatively accurate estimate of the head count and warrior density of the village, several sources must be examined. Primary sources are the estimates of the Indians who lived in the village and the Army personnel who were on site and saw the village and its remains. Secondary sources are acknowledged experts and any corroborating facts that may exist.

As the Indian sources should be the best for determining the composition of their own village, their estimates are presented first. However, when considering the Indian estimates one must understand that the Plains Indians' vocabularies (means/ways of communication) and methods of counting and quantifying items differed from the standard English methods being employed by the Frontier Military at this time.

In his annual report for the year ending June 30, 1877,[143] Lt. Maguire described the sophistication of the Rees vocabulary, counting and communicative abilities: "Their language contains about 750 words.

Their composition is crude, their most definite rule of grammatical construction being that for distinguishing the genders. Masculine is changed to feminine by prefixing an S. They can count up to 1000, but beyond that they must resort to sticks. Their term for twenty signifies a man, from the fact that a man has ten fingers and ten toes."

This was the case for most Plains Indians, so one can then easily see how accuracy would be lost to the translation process. When going from the Native American Tongue to an interpreter or sign language expert, to the flowery Victorian prose of the day or early twentieth century English, misstatements became the rule not the exception. It is also likely that interpreters added their own words for Indian words they could not understand or translate properly or did not want to use. So even though Indian sources are primary and should be the best available, they can not be

---

[143]Carroll, *General Custer and the Battle of the Little Big Horn: The Federal View*, 36.

accepted at face value and must be augmented by further verification or support.

The Cheyenne estimates are:

- Big Beaver in a 1928 interview at the Custer Battlefield[144] stated: *"As the Cheyenne camp was the one on the north or lower end of the great Indian camp, this made them the nearest to the [Custer] battleground. He says all the Indians from this end of the camp went north along the river, then to the right or east, and came up towards Custer from the north side."*

- George Bird Grinell points out that there were at least 200 lodges in the Cheyenne circle. Two Moons had 50 lodges - there were several Cheyenne bands and six villages of Sioux each as large as or larger than the Cheyenne camp which would have meant at least 1400 lodges. Grinell adds the Cheyennes told him there were 3-4 fighting men per lodge, thus 4500 to 6,000 warriors in the whole camp.[145]

- Tall Bull - July 10, 1910 to Walter Camp as interpreted by Thaddeus Red Water[146] - *"The Cheyenne village was at north end of camp and there was a population of 3,000, with Chiefs Two Moons, White Bull, Lame White Man who was killed as the Head Chiefs."*

- Tall Bull in a July 22, 1910 interview with Walter Mason Camp claimed there were 3,000 people in the Cheyenne circle. This footnote appeared *"On June 20 , 1876 Capt Pollock telegraphed the Dept Commander from Ft Laramie that "Jordan under date of June 19 says Little Wolf, chief of Northern Cheyennes, left Agency Thursday [June 15] with 1,000 of his people, including 200 warriors for the north."*[147]

- Two Moons in an 1882 interview with the Harness Gazette[148] stated: *"It is estimated that there were 1000 lodges in the Indian camp along the bottom of the Little Bighorn River. This means that there were from 4000 to 6000 Indians, probably half of whom were able-bodied fighting men."*

- Two Moons, in his 1901 interview with J. M Thralls[149] stated that his band had 50 lodges.

- White Bull - July 22, 1910 to Walter Camp as interpreted by Thaddeus Red Water,[150] *"The Cheyennes had about 200 tepees and about 3,000 people."*

- Wooden Leg stated to Dr. Marquis[151] that *"The Uncpapa circle*

---

[144]Hardorff, *Cheyenne Memories of the Custer Fight*, 148.
[145]Stewart, *Custer's Luck*, 311.
[146]Hardorff, *Cheyenne Memories of the Custer Fight*, 75.
[147]Ibid., 212.
[148]Ibid., 118.
[149]Ibid., 108.
[150]Ibid., 81.
[151]Marquis, *Wooden Leg a Warrior Who Fought Custer*, 177.

was the largest followed by the Ogallalas then the Minneconjous, the Sans Arcs and the Brules, with the Cheyennes having the smallest circle." He claimed the Cheyennes had 300 lodges and 1600 people, the Blackfeet about the same, the Sans Arc more, and the Minneconjous and Ogallalas still more, with the Uncpapas having the largest circle and it was twice the size of the Cheyenne's.[152] This would equate to a village consisting of:

—Cheyenne and Blackfeet circles each having 300 lodges and 1600 people,

—a 400 lodge, 2120 person Sans Arc circle,

—a 500 lodge, 2650 person circle for both the Minneconjous and Ogallalas, and

—a 600 lodge, 3180 person circle for the Uncpapas, or

—a combined village of 2,600 lodges and 13,800 people.

- Young Two Moons, the son of Beaver Claws who was an older half brother to Two Moons, was interviewed at the Custer Battlefield in 1929[153] and stated that *"The Cheyennes had 200 lodges and three warriors to a lodge. There were 6 Arapahoes with the Cheyenne, they did not have tepees. The Two Moon family had 40 ponies. The moving camp was ½ mile wide, and it took one horse to carry a tepee and eighteen poles. Eighteen buffalo skins is eighteen poles."*

The Sioux estimates are:
- Crazy Horse estimated the village had 1800 lodges and 400 wickyups, with each lodge having 3-4 warriors, with a low estimate of 7000 people.[154]

- Flying By, a Minneconjous and the son of Lamedeer in a May 21,1907 interview stated, *"Our village the winter before was on the Tongue River. Lamedeer had between 600 and 800 tepees... Was in village two or three days before battle."*[155]

- He Dog, an Ogallala, in a July 13, 1910 interview with Camp said, *"Moved to the Little Big Horn third day after Crook fight."* He also stated, *"Ogallalas were not on Little Big Horn June 25 but back from river northwest of Uncpapa...Brules not on Little Big Horn in village June 25 but over by Ogallalas."* This conforms exactly with the placement of the circles on the Philo Clark map.[156] More Uncpapas than any other tribe. Minneconjous next. Hunk and Blackfeet together had 600 or 700 lodges. Thinks 1800 lodges in whole village about right.[157]

---

[152]Graham, *The Custer Myth*, 106.
[153]Ibid., 158.
[154]Graham, *The Custer Myth*, 63.
[155]Ibid., 209.
[156]Exhibit 13.
[157]Hammer, *Custer in '76*, 206.

- He Dog also gives a good description of the geography of the village by stating the Ogallalas were not on the river but northwest of Uncpapas. This situates them on the bluff side of the valley floor, leading to the conclusion the village was more likely in a square layout, similar to that shown in Maguire's map.

The Army estimates are:
- De Rudio put the number of warriors between 3,000 and 4,000.[158]

- Gibbon estimated 2500 warriors.

- Hare estimated that there had been 1500 lodges in the camp and 400 wickyups which at a low estimate would mean a fighting force of about 4,000 warriors.[159]

- Herendeen estimated the village at 1800 lodges and 3500 warriors.[160]

- Moylan said the village was three miles long, had 1800 lodges.[161]

Expert Opinions are:
- Fred Dustin estimated the village to be between 10,000 to 12,000 of whom 3,000 to 3,500 were warriors, with 2,500 actually fighting.[162]

- W. A. Graham, estimated 4,000 warriors.[163]

- Edgar Stewart concludes, "The probability is that there were not more than four thousand warriors and possibly not that many."[164]

- Stanley Vestal put the "top estimate of the effective manpower of the Western Sioux when all together at three thousand."[165]

Corroborating Facts include:
- The June 8, 1876 telegram, Exhibit 6, reports commanding officer at Fort Laramie informing Sheridan in Chicago, that a scout Hand had observed Sitting Bull and Crazy Horse's village on the Powder river consisting of 1273 lodges.

- The Battle of the Rosebud had from 1000 to 1200 Sioux warriors participating. It is most likely that these Indians represented approximately half the available warriors, as the village would not be left unguarded and without sufficient warrior strength to protect it. Approximately 1000 to 1200 of the less virile warriors were likely to have been left behind.

   At that time of the Rosebud, the village size would have approximated 7500 people. There were new bands, groups and individuals continually arriving in numbers. There were many summer roamers leaving the reservations and joining the gathering. The average growth rate of the

[158]Ibid., 321.
[159]Nichols, *The Reno Court of Inquiry*, 297.
[160]Ibid., 262.
[161]Ibid., 234.
[162]Dustin, *The Custer Tragedy*, 106.
[163]Graham, *The Reno Court of Inquiry*, 30.
[164]Ibid., 312.
[165]Stewart, *Custer's Luck*, 310.

village appears to have been up to 500 people per day with 200 being warriors. Thus the village would have grown to approximately 10,000 people, with a warrior density of 3,500, by June 25, 1876.

- The population of the village can be estimated by looking at the populations of Indian Bands as they surrendered, following the battles after the battle of the Little Big Horn, through the end of the Great Sioux Wars.

- Yellow Hand's band, after his defeat at War Bonnet Creek in July 1876, contained 200 lodges, 400 warriors and 1000 Cheyennes in total.

- American Horse's band after the battle of Slim Buttes in September 1876 had 37 lodges. 100 warriors and 200 Sioux in total.

- Bands under the leadership of Sitting Bull, Gall, No Neck, Red Shirt, Bull Eagle, Small Bear, Pretty Bear after their defeat at Spring Creek and Cedar Creek in October 1876, consisted of 600 lodges, 600 warriors and 2000 Uncpapas, Minneconjous, Sans Arc Sioux in total.

- Dull Knife in November 1876 surrendered 200 lodges, 400 warriors, 1000 people in total.

- Crazy Horse in January 1877 surrendered 600 lodges, 800 warriors for a total of 3500 Ogallalas and Cheyennes.

- Lame Deer in May 1877 surrendered 51 lodges, 100 warriors and 300 Sioux in total.

The aggregate of all these bands was 1688 lodges, having 2400 warriors and 8000 Sioux and Cheyenne in total. A fair assumption would be that this composite represents a comparable number of lodges to those that were on the Little Big Horn on June 25, 1876. Due to depletion resulting from death, runaways and those that returned to the reservations the head count has been approximately reduced by forty percent and the warrior count by sixty percent, from those that were present at the Little Big Horn.

All of the foregoing suggests that the combined village on the Little Big Horn on June 25, 1876 consisted of approximately 1800 lodges and 400 wickyups, containing 5800 warriors and 13,000 people present. A probable subdivision by bands would be:

	Lodges	Warriors	People
• All other	100	300	700
• Brules	100	300	700
• Blackfeet	200	600	1400
• Cheyennes	200	600	1400
• Sans Arc	250	750	1750
• Minneconjous	250	750	1750
• Ogallalas	300	900	2100
• Uncpapas	400	1200	2800
• 400 - Wickyups	0	400	400
• TOTAL VILLAGE	1800	5800	13000

Indian custom did not require adolescents and the aged to engage in combat. Additionally, fathers, who had sons who could and did fight, were not themselves required to fight. It is reasonable to assume that these exempt categories of males comprised 40% to 60% of the total warrior strength. Thus the net deduced fighting strength of the Indians gathered ranged from 2,320, 40% of 5,800, to 3,480, 60% of 5,800, with the median approximating 2,900.

The trail left by the migration of the Indians was extremely wide and deep, showing the impression of thousands of human feet and many thousands of hooves. Such markings could only have been left by one of the largest gatherings of Plains Indians ever and were strongly indicative of a huge gathering, far greater than the cavalry force pursuing it. The village when Custer clearly visualized it, extended for over three miles and was one and one half mile wide. It was common practice for military men to estimate that an Indian village contained 2,000 to 3,000 inhabitants per square mile of camp, with 60% of the village being males and fighting warriors being half of the total males. A camp such as this, with four and one half square miles of occupied land, would generate an estimate of 9,000 to 13,500 inhabitants, of which from 5,400 to 8,100 would be estimated as males, and from 3,240 to 4,860 of which would be estimated as fighting warriors. A median estimate would be 4,050.

The pony herd when it was pointed out to Custer, by his scouts, was estimated to be 30,000 ponies. It was fairly common for Indians to have from three to five ponies for each tribe member above the age of puberty gathered. A herd of 30,000 ponies would indicate an approximate gathering of from 6,000 to 10,000 inhabitants. As the primary purpose of the gathering was military in nature, it is reasonable to assume that the warrior population of the group was in the range of 40% to 50% of the adults present. The warrior strength thus could range from a low of 2,400, 40% of 6,000, to a high of 5,000, 50% of 10,000, with a median estimate of 3,700.

The estimate of total fighting warriors produced by the analysis of the village population by band was 2,900, the estimate of fighting warriors based on land occupied by the village was 4,050 and the estimate based upon the size of the pony herd was 3,700. The average of the three calculations is 3,550. It is thus fair to assume that the 7th Cavalry faced an approximate total of 3,500 fighting warriors on June 25, 1876.

The village at the Little Big Horn has been described through history as the largest gathering of the Plains Tribes, ever. The winter village at Washita contained approximately 6,000 people camped in a long thin line, 12 miles long, against the river bank.[166]

General Hazan estimated the number of Indians in the Washita Valley at 8100.[167] "At the Medicine Lodge Council of October, 1867, Thomas Murphy Supt. of Indian

---

[166]Connell, *Son of the Morning Star*, 195.
[167]Quaife, *My Life On The Plains*, 353.

Affairs, reported that 852 lodges would be in attendance, averaging 6 Indians per lodge, or a total of 'over' 5,000 souls. Reporter Henry M. Stanley recorded that 756 lodges were in actual attendance."[168] If the foregoing average of 6.5 Indians per lodge is extended to the 1500 to 1800 lodges plus 400 wickyups [estimated one warrior each] found at the Little Big Horn site, it would suggest that the village Custer found contained between 10,150 and 12,100 souls. If a warrior density ranging from 20% to 40% is assumed, augmented by the 400 wickyups which contained only warriors, then the number of warriors Custer faced ranged from 2430 to 5252, with a median count of 3841. The interpolations from the Washita Valley population strongly support the calculations above for the Little Big Horn Village. It is thus quite fair to assume that Custer and the Seventh Cavalry faced approximately 3,500 Lakota and Cheyenne warriors on June 25, 1876.

Washita was a gathering of the less populous southern plains tribes for winter lodging. During the winter a large amount of space is required as the village is not often moved due to the weather conditions. The Little Big Horn was a gathering of the more populous northern tribes, immediately following a Sun Dance, in defiance of a government ultimatum and during a very warm early summer. It easily could have had twice the people of Washita in the space it occupied.

The common description of this village was the largest gathering, ever, in the history of the Plains Indians. This in and of itself evokes the image of a great mass of humanity. They were not few in number, living in an ordered community, on a small plot of land, in high rise condominium tepees, as current revisionist thinking would have one believe. They occupied a large land area of four plus square miles, the pony herd was estimated at between 20,000 and 30,000 head, when they traveled they cut a swath in the ground a half mile wide. We know that there were six to seven people for a normal lodge, this gathering was at the upper end of the range. The warrior density was high, probably 40% of that gathering. The above composite village so closely conforms to all the correct criteria that describe the gathering, that it must be as close to an accurate representation of the tribes, Indians and warriors who were present at the Little Big Horn on June 25, 1876, as one can achieve today.

[168]Ibid., 354.

CHAPTER 11
Was the Village Surprised?

When discussing this aspect of the battle one is likely to fall victim to semantics. Two different debaters having the same facts will reach two different conclusions. To answer this part of the Custer enigma one must define the difference between "tactical surprise" and "emotional surprise." "Emotional surprise" is when people are caught completely off guard by the occurrence of an event which they had no inkling would take place. "Tactical surprise" occurs when a person is caught off guard by the occurrence of an event which they felt could take place, but they were unsure of when or where it might happen.

Further differentiation between "emotional surprise" and "tactical surprise" evolves from the application of the words aware, prepared, and surprised versus the words unaware, unprepared, and not surprised. The presence of awareness, in and of itself, eliminates the possibility of "emotional surprise." One simply can not be aware that an event will occur and then be "emotionally surprised" by it. If a person is aware that an event is

possible to occur, but does not know when or where, then that person can still be a victim of "tactical surprise."

The Indians were aware that soldiers were in the area. The Army column contained approximately 600 soldiers and 55 civilians, with well over 650 horses and 200 pack mules. It most likely stretched in length for over one mile. It had to raise a dust cloud of immense proportion, and despite all attempts at being quiet, it must have made a severe amount of noise. It is therefore impossible to make the statement that the Indians were unaware of the presence of the soldiers in the vicinity of the village. The Army column had been sighted by bands heading towards the village and seen by lookouts and scouts. Thus, it cannot be said that the village was "emotionally surprised" by the attack.

The Indians had previously received an edict from the United States government to return to the reservation or be deemed hostile and suffer the consequences. As they had not returned to the reservation, they knew that soldiers would be heading towards their village, to force the issue. This is why they rode out from the village and met Crook's column on neutral ground, they did not want their village attacked. The Indians were aware of the Army's presence in the vicinity of their village and knew its intentions would be aggressive. This condition, also, eliminates the possibility that the Indians were "emotionally surprised" by Reno's attack.

Were the Indians prepared, were they ready to respond to an attack? The answer quite simply is no. They were not ready to meet the onslaught, their defenses were not up and ready. They were caught off guard by the event and its timing. They ignored alarms and warnings that soldiers were coming. They were neither prepared for Reno's attack nor were they in position to repel it. The Indians were unprepared for Reno's attack, thereby creating one of the essential elements for being "tactically surprised."

Did the attack surprise them and catch them off guard? Yes. They had received an ultimatum from the United States Government which they defied. They knew they were declared hostile and as such, subject to attack. This was the modus operandi of the Government through the army. Were they caught off guard by the attack? Yes, because they felt the village was so large that no enemy would dare to attack it. Thus, the Indians did not feel they were going to be attacked by Reno's force, though they knew they were subject to attack by the Army. The vast majority of the village was surprised and caught off guard by the timing and location of the attack. This provides the final element necessary for being "tactically surprised."

The Indians were aware that an attack was imminent. They were surprised when the village was attacked. They were caught off guard by the date, location and time of Reno's attack, and they were unprepared to defend themselves. In fact, they were the victims of "tactical surprise" but not "emotional surprise" when Reno attacked the village.

- Crow King stated: "We were in camp and not thinking there was any danger of a battle, although we had heard that the long-haired chief had been sent after us. Some of our runners went back on our trail, for what purpose I do not know. One came back and reported that an army of white soldiers was coming, and he had no more than reported when another runner came in with the same story, and also told us that the command had divided, and that one party was going around to attack us on the opposite side.[169]

- Eagle Elk said, "Just at that time, an Unkpapa woman called me and said, 'Attackers are approaching fast, they say.' While I was with the others, a second call from the same woman repeated the same thing, 'I am going home.' There is something to that [warning]. Someone said, 'Don't go. They are not going to kill us all at once.' We

---

[169]Graham, *The Custer Myth*, 76-77.

started together across the camp circle. Just then we heard shooting towards the river. Red Feather and I ran and got to our home. Just at this moment my brother had driven the ponies in from the water. As we were running to our tepee, I came across a pony that I knew belonged to a relative, so I caught the pony and rode him. I got my own horse and gun."[170]

• Foolish Elk, in 1908, told Walter Mason Camp:
"There was not much concern about the soldiers, as the Indians thought they had enough men to whip any force that would come against them, seeing that the Indians were all together for once - all the different tribes."[171]

• Gall's narrative states;
"We saw the soldiers early in the morning crossing the divide. When Reno and Custer separated, we watched them until they came down into the valley. A war cry was raised that the white man soldiers were coming, and orders were given for the village to move immediately. Reno swept down so rapidly on the upper end that the Indians were forced to fight. Sitting Bull and I were at the point where Reno attacked. Sitting Bull was big medicine. The women and children were hastily moved downstream where the Cheyennes were camped. The Sioux attacked Reno and the Cheyennes, Custer, and then all became mixed up."[172]

• He Dog in 1919 told General Hugh L. Scott that:
"The alarm was given first that soldiers were coming below, by women who had been on the north side of the river (Greasy Grass), digging turnips. They could see the dust and were certain they were soldiers. There was great confusion everywhere, and most of the women and children stampeded to the bluff."[173]

• Hollow Horned Bear told Sewell Weston, in 1909, that:
"He, in the company with about 20 Two Kettle Indians, was out looking for these horses. While at Heart Creek, a branch of the Yellowstone, he first saw soldiers. The soldiers were headed westward. He states that he was informed that this was Custer's outfit. This bunch followed the soldiers for two days and then cut across to the Greasy Grass and joined Sitting Bull."[174]

• Hump's version of the initial attack was:
"The sun was at the meridian when the fight began. That was the first we knew that the white warriors were coming. They attacked the Uncpapas first.

---

[170]Hardorff, *Lakota Recollections of the Custer Fight*, 100-101.
[171]Hammer, *Custer in 76*, 198.
[172]Graham, *The Custer Myth*, 88.
[173]Hardorff, *Lakota Recollections of the Custer Fight*, 74.
[174]Ibid., 178.

They were at the upper end of our camp. The Minneconjous, Sans-Arcs and Cheyennes were near the center of the camp, but nearer the end of the camp farthest from where the attack was made. The charge was from the upper end of the camp. The Indians gave way slowly, retreating until they got their horses and got mounted. Just as soon as they got sufficient force—for our warriors were rushing to help them as fast as they could—they drove the white warriors back and they retreated. These were Reno's men."[175]

- Iron Hawk told Ricker in 1907 that:
  "Two young men were going back on the Indian trail toward the east looking for ponies, and they discovered the troops coming. One of these boys was killed. The other returned to the camp and gave the alarm, and the camp was thrown in the utmost confusion."[176]

- Respects Nothing and his wife, White Cow Robe both told Eli S. Ricker in 1906 that:
  "Custer's advance was discovered in this way. Some Oglalas had started for the Red Cloud Agency. One of the number was slow in getting started and was behind. The others had gone forward, and he was following; he saw the dust rising from Custer's column, and also saw the soldiers; he

went back and notified the Indians. This was on the morning the battle began."

"Reno crossed at the mouth of Trail Creek [the Lakota name for Reno Creek]. When the Indian returned and gave warning of the approach of Custer there was a good deal of excitement and a rush was made for the ponies, and before the people could get out, the village was attacked.

"Reno crossed and came down the bottom of the river to the mouth of the Box Elder [Lakota name for Shoulder Blade Creek] and began firing from a clump of woods at that point. The Indians left their lodges standing. The women fled down the river, toward the mouth of Chasing Creek [the Lakota name for Squaw Creek]"[177]

- Red Horse, in an 1881 sign language interview with Dr. Charles E. McChesney, said:
  "One hot day around noon Sioux scout mounted horse to look for soldiers at Red Cloud tepees. When Sioux scout had ridden short distance from tepee, he saw cloud of dust rising. He turned back and said, 'I think many buffalo are moving near.' I, Red Horse, and four women were short distance away digging wild turnips. Suddenly,

[175]Graham, *The Custer Myth*, 78.
[176]Ibid., 63-64.
[177]Hardorff, *Lakota Recollections of the Custer Fight*, 25-26.

one woman pointed to cloud of dust rising. I saw white man soldiers moving where Sioux had many tepees. Women and I ran back to camp. When I, Red Horse, arrived, Sioux scout told me to hurry to council tepee. But we Sioux could not talk. We saw white men soldiers moving on trail."[178]

- Runs the Enemy is quoted as saying:
  "*About ten o'clock a band of Sioux, who had been visiting the camp and had gone home, came rushing back with the tidings that the soldiers were so near, and we were not very much depressed because of the report for two reasons: the soldiers had gone back to Wyoming, and **we did not think they were near enough to attack us; and from the history of all our tribe, back for generations, it had never been known that soldiers or Indians had attacked a Sioux camp in daytime; they had always waited for night to come.**"*[179]

- Standing Bear told Ricker in 1907 that: "*An Oglala Indian went out on opposite side of the L. Big Horn to look for horses and came back saying that there were white soldiers coming, and then they sent out a scout. The Indians saw Custer about noon when he made a charge on them. The first fighting of all the fighting was down on the river bottom and began about noon.*

He did not fight against Reno. Reno's bullets came right into the camp. Standing Bear was in or just back of the camp when Reno attacked it."[180]

- Mrs. Spotted Horn Bull said, "*The man who led those troops must have been drunk or crazy. He had the camp at his mercy, and could have killed us all or driven us away naked on the prairie. I don't believe there was a shot fired when his men commenced their retreat. But when they began to run away they ran very fast, and dropped their guns and ammunition. Our braves were not surprised by this time, and killed a good many when they crossed the plain to the river, while they were fording the river and on the hill beyond. I saw boys pull men from their horses and kill them on the ground.*"[181]

- Turtle Rib, in a 1908 Walter Camp interview stated:
  "*He (Turtle Rib) was asleep when the soldiers were first reported in the valley but got in before the fighting stopped and killed one of the Rees.*"[182]

---

[178]McGaw, *Chief Red Horse Tells About Custer*, Pages un-numbred.
[179]Dixon, *The Vanishing Race*, 171.
[180]Hardorff, *Lakota Recollections of the Custer Fight*, 58-59.
[181]Ibid., 85.
[182]Hammer, *Custer in 76*, 201.

- White Bull, in 1910, told Walter Camp that:

  "Did not learn of approach of soldiers until Reno attacked. Did not get into Custer fight until it was nearly over."[183]

- Wooden Leg's narrative as retold by Thomas B. Marquis:

  "In my sleep I dreamed of a great crowd of people who were making lots of noise. Something in the noise startled me. I found myself wide awake, sitting up and listening. My brother was too awakened, and we both jumped to our feet. A great commotion was going on among the camps. We heard shooting. We hurried out from the trees so we might see as well as hear. The shooting was somewhere at the upper part of the camp circles. It looked as if all of the Indians there were running away toward the hills to the westward or down toward our end of the village. Women were screaming and men were letting out war cries. Through it all we could hear old men calling: 'Soldiers are here! Young men, go out and fight them.' We ran to our camp and to our home lodge. Everybody was excited. Women were hurriedly making up little packs for flight. Some were going northward or across the river without any packs."[184]

Statements like those of Crow King, Foolish Elk and Runs the Enemy further propound the argument for an immense village containing an extremely large number of people and warriors. Only a huge, highly populous village would inspire the confidence that the village was totally safe from attack and had sufficient warriors to defeat any foe which might dare to attack it.

- Crow King: *"We were in camp and not thinking there was any danger of a battle."*[185]

- Foolish Elk: *"There was not much concern about the soldiers, as the Indians thought they had enough men to whip any force that would come against them, seeing that the Indians were all together for once - all the different tribes."*[186]

- Runs the Enemy: *"We did not think they were near enough to attack us; and from the history of all our tribe, back for generations, it had never been known that soldiers or Indians had attacked a Sioux camp in daytime; they had always waited for night to come."*[187]

This overconfidence permeated the village, it was compounded by the feeling of safety in numbers, stemming from the immense land mass occupied by the village and the huge number of people contained within its boundaries. The village, collectively, became an overconfident sleeping giant, ready to

---

[183]Hammer, *Custer in 76*, 211.

[184]Marquis, *Wooden Leg A Warrior Who Fought Custer*, 217.

[185]Graham, *The Custer Myth*, 76.

[186]Hammer, *Custer in 76*, 198.

[187]Dixon, *The Vanishing Race*, 171.

be defeated by an attack utilizing "tactical surprise." When Reno advanced down the valley, he had the advantage of "tactical surprise," no opposition in his path and the opportunity to ride through the village, driving the Indians before him:

- Crow King - *"If Reno had held out until Custer came and then fought as Custer did, they would have whipped the Indians."*[188]

- He Dog - *"The alarm was given first that soldiers were coming below...There was great confusion everywhere, and most of the women and children stampeded to the bluff."*[189]

- Hump - *"The charge was from the upper end of the camp. The Indians gave way slowly, retreating until they got their horses and got mounted."*[190]

- The Iron Hawk - *"The camp was thrown in the utmost confusion."*[191]

- Kill Eagle - *"Before retiring across the creek the soldiers [Colonel Reno] got into our camp and set fire to some of the lodges."*[192]

- Low Dog said, *"If Reno and his warriors had fought as Custer and his warriors fought, the battle might have been against us. No white man or Indian ever fought as bravely as Custer and his men."*[193]

- Mrs. Spotted Horn Bull - *"The man who led those troops must have been drunk or crazy. He had the camp at his mercy, and could have killed us all or driven us away naked on the prairie."*[194]

- Standing Bear - *"Reno's bullets came right into the camp"*[195]

- Two Moon - *"That morning [June 25, 1876] I remember well. We were going to have a dance, but it did not come off. All were preparing for all the dancers to gather, when another chief came and told our haranguer to call off the dance. I started to get my horses to drive them to the river for water, and as I went back onto the hills, I looked up the valley and saw a great dust coming. Puzzled over its meaning, I went on and took my horses to the river, then back to the hills from where I saw the fight commence. I realized the soldiers were here, and instead of a dance it was to be a fight."*[196]

Reno's cowardice which was induced by his timidity, and exacerbated by alcohol caused his defeat and the subsequent rout of his battalion. His drunken stupor made him see Indians

[188]Graham, *The Custer Myth*, 77.
[189]Hardorff, *Lakota Recollections*, 74.
[190]Graham, *The Custer Myth*, 78.
[191]Hardorff, *Lakota Recollections*, 64.
[192]Graham, *The Custer Myth*, 53.
[193]Ibid., 75.
[194]Ibid., 84.
[195]Hardorff, *Lakota Recollections*, 58.
[196]Ibid., 134-135.

where there were none. His timidity made him stop his charge before he engaged the enemy. His forming a skirmish line gave the enemy time to prepare a defense and organize a counterattack. His cowardice caused him to be confronted by an overwhelming force and led to his abandoning the field of battle with a disorganized rout. He abandoned part of his command in the timber. He showed no regard for the safety of any human being save himself. It was solely due to his actions that his battalion suffered the high loss of life and number of wounded that it did. It was his abandoning the field that instilled bravery in the Indians and allowed them to prepare a defense for Custer's attack at Medicine Tail Ford. It was Reno's timidity, drunken state, and cowardice that inspired the Indians to fight and effectively caused the demise of Custer and his battalion.

Crow King, Foolish Elk, Gall, Hollow Horned Bear, Iron Hawk, Respects Nothing, Runs the Enemy, Standing Bear and White Cow Robe all state that the Indians were aware that soldiers were in the area. They neither believed that the soldiers would attack, nor did they do anything to prepare for an attack. Many of the village were in their tepees sleeping, like Turtle Rib and Wooden Leg, and did not learn of the attack until they were awoken by it. Eagle Elk, He Dog, Hump, Two Moons and White Bull learned of the attack when it happened; even though Hollow Horned Bear, Iron Hawk, Red Horse, and Standing Bear all say reports were made and alarms given that soldiers were coming.

The Indians were aware that soldiers were in the area, so they could not be the victim of "emotional surprise" when Reno's attack came. Though they were aware that soldiers were in the area, they regaled in over confidence that the soldiers would not attack a village so large, that no Sioux village had ever been attacked during daylight and that they had enough warriors to whip any enemy who dared attack the village.

Hence, they made no preparations to defend the village and did not heed the warnings of their scouts and others who sounded alarms that there were soldiers coming to attack the village. They were caught flat footed and totally unprepared for Reno's attack, as Mrs. Spotted Horn Bull stated, "He [Reno] had the camp at his mercy, and could have killed us all or driven us away naked on the prairie." For Reno's attack the Indian village was clearly a victim of "tactical surprise."

They were not surprised by Custer's attack at Medicine Tail Ford. They were prepared for the attack, as warriors were hidden and waiting for Custer to attack. They were ready for and able to repel Custer's attack. In this instance, they were not the victims of "tactical or emotional surprise" but the perpetrators of a "tactical surprise" upon Custer.

CHAPTER 12

Did Custer Order a Feint or Die Early?

Custer was victimized by misinformation, that he errantly failed to confirm when Cooke relayed Girard's erroneous assumption that the Indians were running.[197] This caused Custer to aggressively deviate from his plan of supporting Reno from behind and make a bold move in an attempt to outflank the "running Indians" by turning to the right and heading up the bluffs. Custer and his men were seen on the bluffs by Reno's men in the valley. De Rudio testified at the Court of Inquiry that:

"The only observation I made was while I was in the woods. General Custer, Lieutenant Cooke and another man I could not recognize came to the highest point of the bluff and waved their hats and made motions like they were cheering, and pretty soon disappeared. I judge by that, that probably his column was behind the bluff."[198]

"I supposed General Custer's command was coming down some of those coulees and was watching for it, but did not see it, and as pretty soon after that the fire began on the other side of the village, I argued that General Custer went to the rear of the village to attack it that way."[199]

One can only assume that the opposite was true and Custer saw, from the bluffs, Reno's men in action in the valley. As Custer proceeded along the bluffs he saw for the first time the village. It appeared to be a sleeping or deserted village. The illusion occurred as the warriors had left the area heading towards the Reno fight. The women, children and other non combatants had already vacated this part of the village, in response to the alarm, and were heading towards Squaw Creek. John Martin described Custer's reaction to what he visualized: "After General Custer saw the village with no Indians in it I suppose he was glad and he pulled off his hat and gave a cheer and said, 'Courage boys, we will get them and as soon as we get

---

[197]See Chapter 7.
[198]Nichols, *The Reno Court of Inquiry*, 337.
[199]Ibid., 338.

through we will go back to our station."[200] On his way from Custer to Benteen, when trumpeter John Martin reached the bluffs again, Martin could see Reno's troops engaged.[201]

John Martin, the trumpeter who carried Custer's last order back to Benteen, the sole eyewitness who lived, that was with Custer when he ascended Weir Point. He testified at the Inquiry, and was interviewed twice, later in life. He saw essentially what Custer did, but, when his statements did not fit a desired conclusion, his testimony was impugned.

Gray's time estimates appear accurate up until 4 PM. Gray's chronologies generate the following time frames:

Reno's battalion[202]

3.18 deploys to the skirmish line

3.18 Custer is seen on bluffs

3.30 De Rudio claims to see Custer on the bluffs

3.33 Reno retreats to timber

3.53 Reno departs the timber

Custer's battalion[203]

3.13 passes Reno hill and sees Reno charge

3.15 if you believe Knipe was a messenger it is now that he is sent back

3.18 Custer passes sharpshooters ridge and sees Reno deploy to skirmish line

3.24 Custer stops and ascends Weir Point

3.34 Custer returns from Weir

Point and sends Martin back with order

3.35 Custer continues down Cedar Coulee, then down Medicine Tail Coulee

Custer arrives at the junction of Cedar Coulee and Medicine Tail Coulee approximately 4.05 PM. It is during his decent down Cedar Coulee to Medicine Tail Coulee that his view of the village is obscured by the bluffs. If we assume that the above Gray time frames are essentially correct, and assume that Custer is on top of Weir Point, no later than 3.30 PM, allowing for the round trip up and down Weir Point, then we can conclude that Custer would have had to have seen Reno on the skirmish line holding his own against the Indians, with minor casualties, and no visible problems. The only negative Custer could observe was that Reno has abandoned the charge, in favor of the skirmish line. Reno, though, was holding his own and occupying the Indians, thereby diverting their attention from Custer.

This was his probable view from Weir Point:

To the west and south of Weir Point was essentially an empty village. Martin claimed they saw no bucks, just squaws and children. The warriors had already left to confront Reno, but Custer did not know this. Martin states that Custer's

---

[200]Nichols, *Reno Court of Inquiry*, 389.
[201]Ibid., 390.
[202]Gray, *Custer's Last Campaign*, 290.
[203]Ibid., 338.

reaction after this, when he returned to the command was to pull off his hat, give a cheer and say, "Courage boys, we will get them and as soon as we get through we will go back to our station." At the Reno Inquiry, Martin says the timber and skirmish line could not be seen because they were obscured by a hill, and that they could only see children, dogs and ponies, but no Indians at all.

Custer saw dust and movement going south and east, this was the warriors going to meet Reno.

To the north and west he saw a dust cloud, too. This was generated by the non combatants heading towards Squaw Creek.

When he looked to the east of the village towards Medicine Tail Ford, he saw a third dust cloud created by the early non-combatants who fled the village first and went in that direction, to seek safety.

The only way Custer could interpret this multitude of dust clouds, in multiple directions, was that the village was fleeing and scattering. When he returned to his command per Martin he said to them, *"Courage, boys, we will get them, and as soon as we get through, we will go back to our station."*

Martin's comments have been picked apart for a myriad of reasons, none of them good ones. Martin was a decent person, he served his country well, achieved the rank of sergeant and bore no prejudice towards any of the participants. The only challenge

that could have some validity was fluency in English. If there was a language problem in the 1876-1879 period, it could not have been severe. There surely was no communication problem when Graham interviewed him. His statements sounded convincing, he appeared to have no ax to grind, demonstrated no prejudice and sounded lucid and coherent.

Martin had to speak English fairly well by the date of the battle, as he had already achieved the rank of corporal. By the Inquiry, he had to be quite fluent, which his testimony certainly bore out. He arrived in the US in 1873, and joined the Army in June 1874. By June 1876 he has about 2 ½ years in the United States, of which two were in the Army. He was capable of describing what he saw, at least in simple words. By January, 1879, the date of the Inquiry, after four plus years in the Army, he must have been fluent. Either his testimony supported a theory of fluency, or the theory that the scribe embellished on his testimony. Here is one germane paragraph of testimony from the Inquiry, to lend support:[204]

> Q - *Tell how fast General Custer's column then went, and tell all you know about what direction and how far from the river, and whether you could see anything on the other side of the river.*

> A - *General Custer left that watering place and went 300 yards in a straight line. Then after he turned to the right a little more*

[204]Ibid., 388.

and traveled that way four or five hundred yards. Then there was a kind of big bend on the hill. He turned these hills and went on top of the ridge. All at once we looked on the bottom and saw the Indian village at the same time. We could see only children and dogs and ponies around the village. No Indians at all. General Custer appeared to be glad to see the village in that shape and supposed the Indians were asleep in their tepees.

Unless this is more scribe than Martin, the man is fluent in English and does not have either a comprehension or communication problem by 1879.

Then the adjutant called me. I was right at the rear of the general. He said "Orderly, I want you to take this dispatch to Captain Benteen and go as fast as you can." He also told me if I had time and there was no danger in coming back to do so, but if there was danger or there were any Indians in the way not to come back but to remain with my company.[205]

Martin was a dutiful and obedient soldier who followed orders to the letter, as given. He did not deviate from orders, as they were given. A person with this type of loyalty and dedication simply would not distort facts as he saw them or those where he participated in their evolution. Martin testified at the Court of Inquiry that, "The adjutant told me to follow the same trail we came down,"[206] when describing how he was told to find Captain Benteen and the routing he followed. He responded to the Question, "Tell us what you saw going back," with "After I started from General Custer to go back I traveled 5[00] or 600 yards, perhaps 3/4 of a mile. I got on the same ridge where General Custer saw the village for the first time. On going back over that ridge I looked down into the bottom, and I saw Major Reno's battalion was engaged..."[207] This statement sheds light on several points:

- Martin would not deviate from an order, as given, even if a shortcut to obedience presented itself. He was ordered to follow the trail back to Captain Benteen, and follow the trail he did, even if it included a trip up to the top of Weir Point. He could have availed himself of a shorter routing, by not going up and down Weir Point, but he followed the order he was given, exactly. He was telling the truth.

- He tells us that he was sent to Benteen from a point, from one-third to three-quarters of a mile past Weir Point. This indicated the column kept moving while Custer ascended Weir Point and that Custer did not send Martin back with the order to Benteen until after he returned to the Head-quarters Group and consulted with his aides.

---

[205]Ibid., 390.
[206]Ibid., 390.
[207]Ibid., 390.

- That when Custer sent Martin back, Custer was already in the blind spot where his view of the village was obscured and he was relying on his observations of a few minutes past.

- Martin, on his trip to Benteen, visualized Reno's battalion engaged in the Valley. This reinforced the fact that Custer had no knowledge that Reno was in trouble. It suggests that when Custer observed the Valley, Reno was either charging, first deploying to a skirmish line, or deployed on the skirmish line and holding his own.

- That, yet and still, on Martin's return, Reno was engaged and holding his own. He was not in desperate need of assistance and Custer did not need or have to take immediate action, to take pressure off of Reno's forces. This totally negates the need for a feint or any other similar action.

- It shows that Custer was now aware that there would be at least one "hot fight," hence the urgent need for the reserve ammunition and men.

- It shows that Custer could have thought, that he still had an anvil upon which he could drive the Indians, by utilizing a flank attack, with his battalions acting as a hammer or multiple hammers.

- He believed the Indians opposing Reno were a rear guard action.

- That there would be a need for more men, if he were to have any chance at containment. The concept of the fleeing village, instills in Custer the need to divide his forces, still further, in the hopes of capturing as many of the bands as possible and blocking as many escape routes as possible.

- He feels that he was up against a running or fleeing enemy who would not stand and fight. Accordingly, he felt there was neither risk involved in further dividing his forces nor in attacking the Indians with smaller units. He would not be aware of a need to keep his battalion together, as a contiguous unit.

- He had no time to wait for Benteen to come up. He must take action now, while leaving orders for Benteen, with Keogh, to give Benteen further directions when he does arrive. However, if Custer was to have any chance at containment and victory he must act swiftly.

- He intended to position his forces to be capable of blocking all escape routes to the east, north and south while allowing him to attack going east to west and south to north. This would give him the ability to drive the escaping villagers into the direction from which he believes Terry and Gibbon would eventually be coming.

- There was sufficient reason to believe that based upon his observations,

- Custer could only have been in a positive mood,
- inspired to aggressive action,
- unaware of Reno's actions and ensuing problems,
- unaware of the size of the overwhelming enemy forces arrayed against him,
- of the belief the village was unprepared for an attack,
- that the Indians were scattering and running,
- and that he had to move and act quickly and decisively to achieve victory.

Martin was there, he was the last person to see Custer alive, he saw exactly what Custer saw up to but not beyond Weir Point. His statements are the best evidence we have today of what Custer saw, what his mood was and how he could have been thinking. Martin offers fact that strongly contradicts the guesses and postulations of the revisionist writers and theorists. These groups have long belittled him, to down grade the value of his statements. Martin's facts prove Custer acted prudently based on how the facts were presenting themselves to Custer. From Weir Point, Custer saw Reno on the skirmish line in good order, he saw an empty village, he saw major dust clouds in the village going in three different directions towards Reno, Squaw Creek, and Medicine Tail Ford; thereby giving him the impression the Indians were fleeing and scattering in multiple directions. The empty village gave him the impression the Indians were sleeping and unprepared for an attack.

John Martin died in 1922, shortly before his death he granted an interview to a friend of E. A. Brininstool, who in turn reproduced the interview in his book, *"Troopers with Custer."*[208]

"The general (Custer) seemed to be in a big hurry. After we had gone about a mile or two (after the separation of the regiment) we came to a big hill that overlooked the valley, and we rode around the base of it and halted. Then the general took me with him and we rode to the top of the hill where we could see the village in the valley on the other side of the river.

We didn't see anything of Reno's column when we were on the hill. I am sure the general didn't see them at all, because he looked around with his glasses, and all he said was: 'We have got them this time.'

Then the general and I rode back to where the troops were, and he talked with the adjutant, telling him what we had seen. We rode on pretty fast, until we came to a big ravine that led in the direction of the river, and the general pointed down there and then called me. This was about a mile down the river from where he went up on the hill, and we had been going at a trot and gallop all the way. It must have been three miles from where we left Reno's trail.

The general said to me:

---

[208]E. A. Brininstool, *Troopers with Custer*, 189.

'Orderly, I want you to take a message to Col. Benteen. Ride as fast as you can and tell him to hurry. Tell him it's a big village, and I want him to be quick and to bring the ammunition packs.'

He didn't stop at all when he was telling me this, and I just said to him: 'Yes, sir;' and checked my horse, when the adjutant said: 'Wait, orderly, I'll give you a message,' and he stopped and wrote it in a big hurry in a little book and then tore out the leaf and gave it to me."

For the approximately 20 to 30 minutes it took him to descend Cedar Coulee, until he reached Medicine Tail Coulee, Custer's view was completely obstructed by the hills of anything on the west side of the river. Custer had no way of seeing Reno's rout or the warriors turning from Reno and heading north to meet the new threat, him.

This indicates that Custer saw nothing to indicate impending danger, that he saw a big sleeping village and needed more men and ammunition to achieve the victory that he anticipated. The visualization dispels fear, gives no awareness of enemy size and it suggests that the village may be in the process of scattering and void of Indians as not many are visible. Thus, Custer tells Martin, "...if I had time and there was no danger in coming back to do so, but if there was danger or there were any Indians in the way, to stay with my company."[209] It was when Custer descended Medicine Tail Coulee and attempted to ford and

attack, he first determined the inaccuracy of his observations.

Maguire on his maps indicated that as Custer marched down Cedar Coulee he moved with his troops five abreast, going from left to right E, F, L, C, I. This is an incorrect formation the basis of which is not discernible. If it were a single battalion, the troops would have been aligned, from left to right, F, C, E, L, I. This would be the required formation, based upon the United States Army's Cavalry Tactics Manual for 1876, under the School of the Battalion.[210] Upton requires that battalions form in order of seniority of their captains, or commanding officers if the captain is not present. Upton describes proper formation as "the first company on the right, the second company on the left, the third company in the center, the remaining odd numbered companies take their place in order of rank from the right to center and the remaining even numbered companies take their place in order of rank from left to center." Custer's troops traversed Cedar Coulee in two wings, the right wing consisting of the I and L, the battalion depleted by the loss of B Troop to guard the pack train, and a left wing of F, E, and C. This was borne out by members of Reno's battalion seeing the gray horse troop on the edge of the bluffs. According to Upton they would have been aligned left to right E, C, and F.

Custer's formation down Cedar Coulee gave indication that he intended

---

[209]Ibid., 390.
[210]Upton, *United States Army Cavalry Tactics 1876.*

from that point forward to operate with two wings, each of which would operate independently. Custer's mind set was highly aggressive at this time, as indicated above, and confirmed by John Martin when he related how he described Custer's whereabouts to Captain Benteen:

"Captain Benteen asked me where General Custer was. I said I supposed that by that time he had made a charge through the village and that was all I said."[211]

Boston Custer's arrival was significant as it brought more critical incorrect information to Custer. Since he had started from the pack train, Boston had passed Benteen, met briefly with and spoken to Trumpeter Martin, and then continued on to Custer. When he joined his brothers he informed them of his sightings. Surely Boston would have informed Custer of Benteen's relative proximity, and that Martin was safely en route to Benteen. Boston would probably say that by the time he was informing Custer of his sightings, Martin had already delivered Custer's order to Benteen and Benteen should be complying with it. This new erroneous information could only stir Custer into a more aggressive mood, if such was conceivably possible. Custer now felt that Benteen would be arriving very shortly with his 125 men, the 25,000 extra rounds of ammunition from the pack train and a substantial number of the 84 extra men who were handling the pack mules carrying the ammunition. Their arrival would give Custer the resources he felt necessary to take on a large village containing

the estimated 1500 warriors the Army anticipated engaging.

When Custer heard Boston's report he had every reason to expect and assume that Benteen would be making his appearance very shortly. Boston had informed his brother that he had passed both Martin and Benteen and that Benteen should now be in compliance with the orders delivered by Martin and coming forward to reinforce Custer. Custer ordered Keogh with I and L troops to cross Medicine Tail Coulee and wait on the bluffs on the opposite side. Custer, by so doing, had established a rally point for Benteen to come to and a strong defensive position to cover his advance. Custer left further orders with Keogh, for both Keogh and Benteen. Based upon Custer's highly aggressive mood, the orders left for Benteen likely would have been to follow Custer's trail into the village. The further orders left for Keogh probably would have been to proceed northwest, find a ford and finally outflank the village and attack from there. Custer then proceeded with a highly aggressive act and attempted to capture the non-combatants with the resources then available to him, Yates' battalion. He was in the belief that reinforcements were coming very soon and in minutes he would be attacking the village with nearly 400 men. He moved forward with his stronger battalion of F, E and C with an aggressive move to the ford.

There is sufficient Indian testimony that the village was virtually

---

[211]Nichols, *Reno Court of Inquiry*, 390.

unprepared, and a cavalry charge at the moment of Reno's attack could have been devastating if it were brought to a conclusion. Many Indians have stated that if Reno kept going he would have ridden right through the village.

- Low Dog said, *"If Reno and his warriors had fought as Custer and his warriors fought, the battle might have been against us."*[212]

- Crow King said, *"If Reno had held out until Custer came and then fought as Custer did, that they would have whipped the Indians."*[213]

- Mrs. Spotted Horn Bull said, *"The man who led those troops must have been drunk or crazy. He had the camp at his mercy and could have killed us all or driven us away naked on the prairie. I don't believe there was a shot fired when his men commenced their retreat. But when they began to run away they ran very fast, and dropped their guns and ammunition. Our braves were not surprised by this time, and killed a good many when they crossed the plain to the river, while they were fording the river and on the hill beyond. I saw boys pull men from their horses and kill them on the ground."*[214]

- Kill Eagle said, *"Before retiring across the creek the soldiers [Colonel Reno] got into our camp and set fire to some of the lodges. On retreating across the creek to take position on the hill, they left their dead behind them."*[215]

The penetration of the village by some of Reno's command would lend credence to Gall's contention that his family was killed by soldiers in their tepees. Based upon the statements of Peter Thompson, Red Horse, Sitting Bull and Gall one can fairly accurately conclude that at some point some of Reno's troops entered the Uncpapa village and burned tepees.

Custer had visualized Reno moving to the attack against what appeared to be a basically unprepared village. Custer had seen Reno charge, he had seen what appeared to be a surprised village, and he had received horribly incorrect and misleading information from Girard through Cooke that "the Indians are running" and his brother Boston regarding Benteen's imminent arrival. He had seen across the river non-combatants heading towards sanctuary at Squaw Creek. He was aggressively moving towards what he believed would be a quick and easy victory, based upon the facts as he knew them and the information that he had received up to that time.

With Custer's aggressive mind set and an apparently surprised and unprepared village before him, with no knowledge of Reno's rout and ensuing debacle, there was neither reason nor factual support that Custer ever intended to or did in fact order a feint at Medicine Tail Coulee. If the action at the river was a feint, then one or more of the following statements would be true, but were not.

---

[212]Graham, *The Custer Myth*, 75.
[213]Ibid., 77.
[214]Ibid., 85.
[215]Ibid., 53.

1- The ridges on either side of Medicine Tail Coulee afforded visibility of Reno Hill and Custer could have seen the comings and goings there when he got to this position and decided on a feint to relieve the pressure upstream.

2- Martin left him approximately 3:35 PM and passed Boston Custer some minutes later, Boston could have become aware of the Reno disaster by making a side trip to Weir Point and he visualized the rout. He would then report this information to Custer.

3- Curley was on Weir Point with Bouyer approximately 3:55 PM and they reported to Custer about 10 minutes later informing him of Reno's rout.

4- He had sent the last order to Benteen "to come quick", he had visualized the village and realized he needed reinforcements to take it on and had decided to wait for Benteen to come up with the packs. The feint bought him time and allowed him to wait for reinforcements.

5- He used the feint to buy time while he continued to the Northwest looking for a place to ford further up river. This was to allow him to finally outflank the village and attack it on the end opposite to the one Reno attacked.

A feint is an excellent maneuver to employ in any of the above circumstances, another name for it is a diversion. The enemy does not know its a feint, so they are forced to commit assets to thwart it, while there can be an attack elsewhere without having to face all the opposition.

While a feint may sound good in theory it does not fit Custer's personality and mood of the moment which required bold and aggressive action. Therefore the move to the ford was an aggressive act, in conformity with Custer's personality and mood at the time and his intent to achieve a quick victory, not a feint.

The premise that Custer was either killed or wounded at the ford is also bogus because all of the following would have occurred immediately thereafter. These events did not occur and there are no sustaining facts to show that Custer was in any way impaired when his forces retreated from Medicine Tail Ford:

- Keogh would have assumed command.

- Cooke as Adjutant would have moved to Keogh's side as it was his duty to be with the commanding officer. Had Custer been incapacitated at the Ford with a severe and likely fatal wound, the Adjutant, Cooke, would have attached himself to Keogh, the next in rank. Cooke's body would have then, presumably, been found with Keogh's.

- Keogh would have ordered a retreat towards Reno. Custer's incapacity or death would merely have given Keogh temporary command of the battalion. Keogh would then be under a duty to return to Reno who would then have been in command of the entire regiment.

- If there was a retreat, the bodies would have fallen in a Northeast to East pattern as opposed to the Northwest to West pattern actually found. The retreat would have been a retracing of the advance, back up Medicine Tail Coulee and then back down Cedar Coulee.

- The fact that the body pattern heads North to Northwest, strongly suggests it was the result of an aggressive not defensive movement.

- An aggressive northwest move means Custer was well and still in command and he had not been killed or incapacitated early in the battle. If he had been killed or incapacitated, then there would have been a defensive move, a retreat, towards help, heading northeast.

- Custer's aggressive move continuing on from the ford is what got him into deeper trouble and caused him to be eventually surrounded and annihilated.

CHAPTER 13
Army Views of Custer's Attempts to Ford

Custer made two aggressive and costly attempts to cross the river at Medicine Tail Ford and Ford C, what would entice him to do so? Surely he was unaware of Reno's circumstances, and he was not taking heavy casualties to his own battalion to merely take the pressure off of, or to support Reno. No, there was a very valuable prize on the village side of the river that he wanted to capture, and it was worth major sacrifice. The prize was the non-combatants, women and children. Squaw Creek is between Ford B and Ford C, and it derived its name from being the place where the women and children first sought shelter when Reno attacked. Custer could see Squaw Creek from both Weir Point and the bluffs of Medicine Tail Coulee. Both positions should have given him excellent views of the non-combatants, women and children heading towards Squaw Creek. He quickly decided that if he crossed the river and captured the non-combatants the village would surrender and he would achieve victory. This created a risk reward scenario in his mind which made it appear worthwhile to make an all out effort to ford the river and attempt to capture the non-combatants. Unfortunately, his attempt was met by heavy resistance, and he was repelled.

Statements of Army personnel describing Custer's attempt to cross the river:

Benteen's first description of the action at the ford comes in a letter to his wife dated July 4, 1876:[216]

"Whether the Indians allowed Custer's column to cross at all, is a mooted question, but I am of the opinion that nearly - if not all of the five companies got into the village — but were driven out immediately — flying in great disorder and crossing by two instead of the one ford by which they entered. 'E' going by the left and 'F, I , and L' by the same one they crossed. What became of 'C' Co no one knows - they must have charged there below the village,

---

[216]Graham, *The Custer Myth*, 298.

gotten away - or have been killed in the bluffs on the village side of stream - as very few of 'C" Co. horses are found. Jack Sturgis and Porter's clothes were found in the Village. After the Indians had driven them across, it was a regular buffalo hunt for them and not a man escaped."

Walter Mason Camp in an April 22, 1910 letter to General Charles A. Woodruff wrote:

"Curley does say that Custer remained a short time on the flat, near the river and just south of Greasy Grass Hill, before starting for Custer Ridge. I could not, however, get from him much of an idea as to the length of time Custer and his command stopped here. (You know how difficult it is to get an Indian to estimate time according to our standards.) He is rather hazy as to what was done while Custer was on this flat, except that he says that shots were exchanged by both sides across the river at this point, the soldiers firing into the village and the Sioux firing at the soldiers in return. From all that Curley told me about the shooting at this point, I do not think that he (Curley) got as near the river as did the soldiers. I just surmise this from the fact that he is so indefinite about matters. About what happened on the retreat up to Custer Ridge and the fighting on the ridge, he is more explicit. I want to tell you that I think considerable fighting was done by

soldiers right on top of Greasy Grass Hill, but whether all of Custer's men were up there or not, I am not clear. I rather think that only part of them were there."[217]

Lieutenant W. Philo Clark in his report dated September 14, 1877, describes Custer's attempt to cross, based on the information supplied by captured Ogallalas and Cheyennes as:

"...General Custer's column, which came down and made an attempt to crofs [sp] at the mouth of the little stream at "K" finding it impossible turned up the ridge, then turned again as the trails leading down to the ford "D" were reached. The Indians had massed in the ravines and timber and opened such a terrific fire from all sides that the troops gave way. The Indians rushed in and made it a hand to hand conflict. The troops attempted to rally once or twice but literally overwhelmed with numbers and in few moments not one was left alive to tell the story..."[218]

Curly stated:

"I came down with Custer as far as the creek; then he gave me a message to take to Reno. I did not know the import of the message. I brought the answer back from Reno to Custer. While I was delivering the last message, Reno

---

[217]Hardorff, *Camp, Custer and the Little Bighorn*, 116-117, Footnote 3-a transcript of the original letter in the possession of the Little Big Horn National Monument.
[218]Addendum.

was fighting his battle, but it was not very fierce, and when I go to Custer with the message he was fighting at the mouth of the creek."[219]

Richard Anderson Roberts was Captain George Yates' brother-in-law and for a time served as Custer's secretary. As such he was privy to comings and goings within the Army and had access to later classified documents. In 1890, he wrote a tome which contained a version of Curly's story:[220]

"The only survivor of the massacre was the Crow Indian scout Curly and from him we have a partial description of General Custer's movements and charge, as given to General Alfred H. Terry the notes of which I was permitted to see on the Far West.

Custer had to go farther down the river, and farther away from Reno than he wished, on account of the steep bank along the north side; but at last he found a ford and dashed for it. The Indians met him and poured in a heavy fire from across the narrow river; Custer dismounted to fight on foot, but could not get his skirmishers over the stream. Meantime hundreds of Indians on foot and on ponies poured over the river which was only about three feet deep, and filled the ravine on each side of Custer's men.

Custer then fell back to some high

ground behind him and seized the ravines in his immediate vicinity. The Indians completely surrounded Custer and poured in a terrible fire on all sides. They charged Custer on foot in vast numbers, but were again and again driven back."

Goes Ahead stated:
"Custer also opened fire just beyond the Medicine Creek where he had crossed. Soon after Reno opened fire Custer began his fire."[221]

"He led his men to where he was repulsed and driven to where the Custer Monument now stands."[222]

General Fred D. Grant, son of President Grant, visited the battlefield in 1878. His conclusion, based upon what he felt was clear evidence of fighting, regarding the action at Medicine Tail Coulee, as related to Walter Mason Camp in later years was:

" Custer had come down Medicine Tail Coulee and turned to the right , out upon the flat next to the river, as though to cross into the village. Presumably the first firing from the village side was from the fringe of timber or brush along that side of the stream, while the troops occupied this flat. This fire may have been so

---

[219]Dixon, *The Vanishing Race*, 163.
[220]Roberts, *Custer's Last Battle Reminiscences of General Custer*, 41-42.
[221]Ibid., 168.
[222]Coffeen, *The Custer Battle Book*, 52.

strong as to cause the men to hesitate, and, at all events, they had moved to *Greasy Grass Hill,* [*Calhoun Ridge*] *as a more commanding position"*[223]

"Leaving this hill and passing a slight depression, they reached higher ground where the group of bodies, including those of Sergeants Finley and Finckle, was afterwards found. Here again they saw unoccupied higher ground still to the north, beyond a slight depression, and they had gone to it, the evidence of dead bodies marking the trail to where the Calhoun and Crittenden markers now are. **It then impressed him that men whose bodies lay along the route had probably been killed by fire from the rear or left flank"**[224]

Maguire stated in his report[225]
"In the mean time, Custer had gone down stream and attempted to make a crossing at the point B, but was met by an overpowering force and the troops retreated to the hills in rear in order to procure a more defensible position. From the position of the dead bodies on the field I conclude that they retreated on the two lines marked on the sketch to concentrate at E..."

"The column which retreated along the line B H E must have been dismounted, and, fighting along the whole distance, a portion of its men taking to the ravine H for shelter, must have been surrounded by the Indians."

Mc Clernand's report contained:[226]
"The trails I saw, and the dispositions indicated by the positions of the dead men and horses, incline me to the belief that he went further down this coulee with the intention of crossing but was deterred therefrom by the Indians as they commenced to arrive in great numbers after having temporarily disposed of Reno."

Mc Clernand in a 1910 interview with Walter Mason Camp asserted that:[227]
"He saw a double column of fours down MTC and turned across into dry coulee and up this to forks and then to Finley [on Calhoun Ridge]. No doubt about this being a cavalry trail, so regular."

Reno states in his report[228]
"That he did charge, but his march had taken so long, although his trail shows he moved rapidly, that they were ready for him; that Companies C and I and perhaps part of E, crossed to the village, or attempted it at the charge, and were met by a staggering fire, and that they fell back to secure a position from which to defend themselves, but were followed too

---

[223]Hardorff, *Markers. Artifacts and Indian Testimony,* 27-28.
[224]Hardorff, *Camp, Custer and the Little Bighorn,* 115.
[225]Carroll, *Custer and the Battle of the Little Big Horn: The Federal View,* 29.
[226]McClernand, *On Time For Disaster,* 91.
[227]Hardorff, *Markers, Artifacts and Indian Testimony,* 27.
[228]Ibid., 34.

closely by the Indians to permit him to form any kind of line."

n.b.: Reno is confusing the dark bay horses of F Troop with those of I Troop when making this statement. The horses as well as the soldiers were stripped of all equipment and could only be identified by color. Stanislas Roy, in a March 4, 1909, letter to Walter Camp, stated: "All the bodies were nude and equipments and clothing carried away by the Indians. Dead horses the same, all stripped."[229]

Sheridan commented:[230]

"The point where Custer reached the river, on the opposite side of which was the village, was broken into choppy ravines and the Indians crossing from Reno got between the two commands and as Custer could not return he fell back over the broken ground.

Peter Thompson has these comments regarding the action at the Fords:[231]

"...we were further astonished by seeing General Custer dash out of the fording place and ride rapidly up to the Crow and commence to talk to him."[232]

"Custer was mounted on his sorrel horse and it being a very hot day he was in his shirt sleeves; his buckskin pants tucked into his boots; his buckskin shirt fastened to the rear of his saddle; and a broad brimmed cream colored hat on his head, the brim

of which was turned up on the right side and fastened by a small hook and eye to its crown. This gave him the opportunity to sight his rifle while riding. His rifle lay horizontally in front of him; when riding he leaned slightly forward. This was the appearance of Custer on the day that he entered his last battle and just one half hour before the fight commenced between him and the Sioux."[233]

When he was passing us he slightly checked his horse and waved his right hand twice for us to follow him. He pointed downstream, put spurs to his horse and disappeared at the ford, never uttering a word. That

---

[229]Hardorff, *On The Little Bighorn With Walter Camp*, 41.

[230]Carroll, *General Custer and the Battle of the Little Big Horn: The Federal View*, 76.

[231]When reading Peter Thompson's Narrative one should be forewarned that even the wildest lie is based upon some truth and even what appears to be absolute truth can be based on slight falsehoods. Parts of his tale appear incredulous, others seem to be highly accurate but could have been gleaned elsewhere and at different times, while others may be pure fact. The reader is cautioned to exert care when reading these excerpts and relying upon them as absolute, but Thompson was a survivor of the battle and perhaps the last man to see Custer alive who survived. Accordingly his tale cannot be either dismissed in total or completely ignored.

[232]Magnussen, *Peter Thompson's Narrative of the Little Bighorn Campaign 1876*, 144. [This part sounds incredulous.]

[233]Ibid., 145-146 [This is one of the most accurate descriptions of Custer on the day of the battle available. It could however have been from earlier recollections.]

was the last time I ever saw
Custer alive. He must have gone
thence directly to his
command."[234]

"I could see Custer's command
drawn up in battle line, two men
deep in a half circle facing the
Indians who were crossing the
river both above and below
them."[235]

"The Indians while fighting
remained mounted, the cavalry
dismounted. The horses were held
back behind and inside of the
circle of skirmishers. The odds
were against the soldiers for they
were greatly outnumbered, and
fought at a great disadvantage."[236]

"The Indians were riding around
in a circle and when those who
were nearest to the cavalry had
fired their guns (riding at full
speed) they would reload in
turning the circle. The well
formed ranks of the cavalry did
fearful execution, for every time
the soldiers fired I could see
ponies and riders tumbling in the
dust."[237]

"During the fight between Custer
and the Sioux, scores of Indians
had stationed themselves on the
bluffs overlooking the village as
far as we could see, so that any
movement on our part would have
led to discovery."[238]

"Looking in the direction of the
battle, I saw that the cavalry were
being driven towards the foot of a
small hill; their number greatly

reduced. The firing was growing
less every minute, but the Indians
still kept up their seemingly
tireless circling, making a great
cloud of dust."[239]

Terry stated in his report[240]
"Then it comes down the bank of
the river, but at once diverges
from it as if he had unsuccessfully
attempted to cross."

White Man-Runs-Him stated:
"We went with Custer down a dry
gulch to near the river. Near the
mouth of the gulch some
dismounted and fired into the
village. There were a good many
Sioux around firing at us. Mitch
Boyer said that Custer had told
us to go back to the pack-train
and we went."[241]

When these statements are
interpolated correctly, combined with
Indian accounts of the battle and
augmented by Army post battle
forensic examinations of the battlefield
a reasonable description of the action
at the ford and subsequent fighting
can be derived. Such an interpolation
is put forward in Chapter 15.

---

[234]Ibid., 146. [This excerpt is a bit hard to
  believe.]
[235]Ibid., 160. [This could be accurate of E Troop's
  formation on the river bank.]
[236]Ibid., 161. [This could be accurate.]
[237]Ibid., 163 [This could be accurate.]
[238]Ibid., 164. [This could be accurate.]
[239]Ibid., 165. [This could be accurate.]
[240]*Report of the Secretary of War, Volume 1-1876
  to 1877*, 463.
[241]Coffeen, *The Custer Battle Book*, 46.

CHAPTER 14
The Indians Tell How Custer Repulsed

As the Indians moved back from the Reno Valley fight to the Ford B area they were on the left of the column descending Medicine Tail Coulee. If they continued past Medicine Tail Coulee, that portion of the Indians covering the mouth of the coulee was on the front of the descending column. There is very strong reason to believe that the force Custer sent down Medicine Tail Coulee was in a double column of 4 as these are the tracks that were noted by McClernand.[242] As the coulee was not wide enough for Custer to form a line and charge, he utilized the tactic of double columns of four. This would allow him to achieve the maximum impact of a cavalry charge as dictated by the limitations of the terrain. This formation also confirms that the force coming down Medicine Tail Coulee was participating in a highly aggressive act, a cavalry charge, and not a feint, as a single column of four galloping would be more than adequate for a feint. This group included E troop as the gray horses were seen descending Medicine Tail Coulee and ascending Deep Ravine.

The battle was fluid and the same Indians that were on the left flank, eventually moved forward a few hundred yards and were then on the front of the column. The Indians talked of advancing to the Ford on both sides of the river. The Indians on the N or E side of the river, the bluffs side, were on the descending columns left flank while those returning from the valley fight, across the plain towards the Ford, through the village, became the group that was on the front. The descending column when it reached the flat, turned right around the base of the lower part of Calhoun Ridge and continued towards Ford C. The same two groups of Indians previously mentioned were then on the right and rear of the column.

This created an "illusion" of the column being surrounded as two Indians in the same spot, at different times, could both accurately say one was on the 'left' of the soldiers and the

---

[242]Hardorff, *Markers, Artifacts, and Indian Testimony*, 27.

other say he was on the 'right' of the soldiers. The determining factor was the moment in time each was referring to and whether the column was descending Medicine Tail Coulee or continuing on to Ford C or ascending Deep Ravine.

There is a consistent theme within most of these statements, that the group that charged had grey and sorrel horses and the group that remained on the bluffs had black horses. Keogh's I and L troops had black horses while E and C had grey and sorrel horses respectively. F Troop had bay horses, and if it were driven back up Medicine Tail Coulee, then all the black horses would have been in one area, creating an illusion of all the black horses retreating by the way they came. There is support for the E troopers being dismounted as their horses were frightened away in the Deep Ravine area by the Indians. They were then trapped there and met their demise **while attempting to retreat towards Last Stand Hill, not from it.** It appears that the Sioux just weren't there when Custer was descending Medicine Tail Coulee and advancing towards Ford C, while the Cheyenne were there. It thus appears that the Custer fight was predominantly with the Cheyennes and the Reno fight was exclusively with the Sioux.

Indian statements describing the flow of the action at Medicine Tail Ford and Ford C:

Sioux Chief American Horse, in 1895, described Medicine Tail Coulee,

"While they were doing this, they heard shooting and calling down

the river-a man calling out that the troops were attacking the lower end of the village. Then they all rushed down below and saw Custer coming down the hill and almost at the river. I was one of the first to meet the troops and the Indians and the soldiers reached the flat about same time. When Custer saw them coming, he was down on the river bottom at the river's bank. The troops fought in line of battle and there they fought for some little time. Then the troops gave way and were driven up the hill. The troops fought on horseback all the way up the hill. They were on their horses as long as the horses lasted, but by this time the Indians had got all around them and they were completely surrounded."[243]

Brave Wolf, in 1895, said

"The soldiers (Custer's) were right down close to the stream, but none were on this side. Just as I got there, the soldiers began to retreat up the narrow gulch. They were drawn up in line of battle, shooting well and fighting hard, but there were so many people around them that they could not help being killed. They still held their line of battle and kept fighting and falling from their horses - fighting and falling all the way up, nearly to where the monument now stands. I think all their horses had been killed

---

[243]Hardorff, *Cheyenne Memories of the Custer Fight,* 29.

before they got quite to the top of the hill. None got there on horseback and only a few on foot."[244]

John Stands in Timber 1956:
"Custer came toward the village from the ridges to the east. The Custer men tried to cross the river at a ford west of the present railroad tracks, on what is now the Willy Bends place. Cheyennes hidden in the brush on the south side of the ford drove the soldiers back and killed a couple of them in the brush by the river. Then the Custer men retreated to the flats below where the superintendent's house is now located. They waited there for about half an hour, while Indians assembled in the vicinity and fired on the soldiers from the ridges north of the flats. (Six empty 45/70 cases were found there subsequent to this interview, in a place where the cartridges could not have been fired at targets anywhere but on the flats mentioned). The horses of the Gray Horse Soldiers were frightened away by the Indians coming up the big ravine on the Battlefield."[245]

Nicholas Ruleau, in 1906:
"The Indians forced the troopers back to where the first stand was made on Calhoun Hill and the ridge running therefrom towards the river. At this place the soldiers stood in line and made a very good fight. The soldiers delivered volley after volley into the dense ranks of the Indians

without any perceptible effect on account of their great numbers."[246]

Red Horse describes the action in this way,
"I saw white man soldiers moving where Sioux had many tepees. Women and I ran back to camp. When I, Red Horse, arrived, Sioux scout told me to hurry to council tepee. But we Sioux could not talk. We saw White Man Soldiers moving on trail. Straightway we ran out of council tepee in all directions. Then we Sioux mounted horses and took guns to fight White Man Soldiers. Women and children mounted horses to flee. White Man Soldiers forded Greasy Grass Creek farther up than Sioux had crossed and fought Sitting Bull's tribe. Suddenly White Man Soldiers charged among us set fire to many tepees. Sioux charge White Man Soldiers and drove them into confusion across Greasy Grass Creek. Creek was so rapid that many white man soldiers drowned. White Man Soldiers stopped on hill. Sioux surrounded them. **Sioux scout rode up and said, 'Different White man soldiers may make women and children prisoners.' Like whirlwind word spread and Sioux heard. We Sioux left White Man Soldiers on Hill and hurried to save women and**

---

[244]Ibid., 35-36.
[245]Ibid., 169-171.
[246]Hardorff, *Lakota Recollecctions of the Custer Fight*, 43.

children. *Sioux feared White Man Soldiers on Hill would charge Sioux in rear. When White Man Soldiers on Hill did not charge, Sioux thought they had no cartridges. On level ground by creek I, Red Horse, saw different White Man Soldiers moving on trail. In front of soldiers, White Man Soldier Chief was riding horse with feet like snow. White Man Soldier Chief had long hair, big brimmed hat, and deerskin clothes. White Man Soldier chief had divided soldiers. One band was charging many tepees. I, Red Horse, Sioux Chief, spoke: 'Sioux warriors, watch White Man Soldiers on Hill. Do not let them join different White Man Soldiers.' Immediately all brave Sioux ran short distance, separated, surrounded soldiers, and charged to save women and children. Brave different White Man Soldiers fought hand to hand and stopped five charges. Different White Man Soldiers shot guns not many times. We Sioux charged in the midst of white man soldiers. They scattered in confusion."*[247]

Soldier Wolf, in 1898,
 "By this time, Custer had gotten down to the mouth of the dry creek and was on the level flat of the bottom. They began firing and for quite a time fought in the bottom, neither party giving back. There they killed quite a good many horses, and the ground was covered with horses of the

Cheyennes, the Sioux and the white men, and two soldiers were killed and left there. **But soon the Indians overpowered the soldiers and they began to give way, retreating slowly, face to the front. They fell back up the hill until they had come nearly to where the monument now is.** *Then they turned and rushed over the top of the hill. From this point on, everything was mixed up, for there was a grand charge and nothing clear could be seen for the dust and the people, until all the troops had been killed."* [248]

Tall Bull 1910 to Camp,
 "After returning from Reno, women going over east to get on high ground to overlook Reno fight discovered Custer coming. Custer got onto flat near ford B and within easy gunshot of village and Indians drove him back."[249]

Two Moons to Harness Gazette 1901:
 "One bunch of soldiers had black horses, another had gray horses and one had red (sorrel) horses. The black horse men dismounted down there (pointing along the ridge toward the place where Keogh and his men made their last stand). We killed lots of them and pretty soon they were all gone. The gray horse men fell back along the ridge (Evidently

[247]Red Horse, *Chief Red Horse Tells about Custer* - Edited by Jesse Brewer McGaw, 42.
[248]Ibid., 43-44.
[249]Hardorff, *Cheyenne Memories of the Custer Fight*, 75.

this was the group with Custer, who fell near the end of the ridge.) Pretty soon they were all gone, too. The red horse men were the last to be killed."[250]

Two Moons to Throssel 1907, in the version maintained in the notes of Walter Mason Camp:

"Custer and his men rode up nearly to the river on their horses and were being fired upon by the Sioux posted on the west bank. Here Custer stopped momentarily and supposing that he would cross, the Sioux began to appear on his right and rear. He says that here some soldiers were killed and were afterward dragged into the village, dismembered and burned at the big dance that night. Two Moons retracted the part about killing soldiers at the dance, Little Knife (Sioux) admitted that a soldier with stripes was killed at the dance).[251]

Custer now turned and charged down the river at Indians who were opposing him and his (Two Moons') warriors had by this time arrived in [a] large force with their horses. **He therefore forded and followed in Custer's rear the soldiers fighting on foot, into wings, with horses led between them.** *As Custer passed onto the high ground, the Cheyennes split and passed into ravines surrounding the soldiers.*

Two Moons in 1909 said, **"They (Custer's command) dismounted and slowly moved back up the ridge with their horses on the inside and the soldiers around them.** *We circled around and around. We had them surrounded, and first the Sioux and the Cheyennes would charge them. In our first big charge, when all swept in together—, nearly one whole band was killed. (From the location and the grouping of the markers on the field, it appears [to Throssel] that this was Company I, under Captain Keogh.) I rode back through my men telling them to fight hard and shoot good and prepare for the next big charge."*[252]

White Bull 1895 to Grinnell,
"Custer rode down to the river bank and formed a line of battle and prepared to charge. But then he stopped and fell back up the hill; but he met Indians coming from above and all sides and again formed a line. It was here that they were all killed."[253]

A very significant theme flows through all the Indian Statements which has great bearing on how we have historically, incorrectly, viewed the flow of the battle. The statements say that the soldiers were

---

[250]The gray and red horses' colors were unique to E and C troops respectively, F had bays which could be called black, it appears that Two Moons was referring to the ridge where F and I troops were positioned.

[251]Hardorff, *Cheyenne Memories of the Custer Fight*, 126.

[252]Hardorff, *Lakota Recollections of the Custer Fight*, 137.

[253]Hardorff, *Cheyenne Memories of the Custer Fight*, 39.

dismounted, with their backs to Last Stand Hill and walked up the hill backwards shooting at the Indians. When Army personnel reviewed the field a few days after the battle, they would have seen footprints that appeared to be heading towards the river. This gave the impression of E Troop rushing, on foot, from Last Stand Hill to Deep Ravine and being trapped there. The opposite is in fact correct, E Troop was trapped in Deep Ravine and it attempted to get from Deep Ravine to Last Stand Hill by a walking retreat marching backwards. C Troop dismounted and retreating backwards from the lower part of Calhoun Ridge, combined with the mounted Headquarters Group and marched backwards across the bluffs towards Last Stand Hill. F Troop, mounted, first retreated back up Medicine Tail Coulee and then across the bluffs, firing at the Indians as they went. When these footprints were viewed a few days later, they all gave the impression of soldiers rushing towards river when the reverse was true, that it was a backwards retreat from the river, of dismounted soldiers. Walter Camp was aware of this and he wrote, in a September 28, 1910 letter, to Daniel Knipe:

> *"The battle was fought as we have understood it heretofore. Custer and his five companies retreated back from the direction of the river and the fighting started where Sergeant Finley was killed."*[254]

---

[254]Hardorff, *On The Little Bighorn With Walter Camp*, 110.

CHAPTER 15
The Fiasco at Medicine Tail Ford

On the Kent King version of the Maguire Map, (King illustration 6 - see page 69 herein,) with the location of the bodies shown with red "x's" there is a thin line of eight bodies forming a line running from southwest of where Calhoun's body was found to southwest of where Keogh's body was found and it appears along the edge of a ridge.

The line of bodies correlate well with a scenario of the men of C Troop being dismounted and forming an east-west line to cover the abortive attempt to ford the river.

There are many documents, in Kent King's book *Massacre*, which conclusively prove that the published Maguire Maps were altered by the Army, however, the early unpublished versions are correct.

Maguire has been overly criticized for his poor renderings in the maps we have seen. If one reads the Kent King book and looks at the maps we were not allowed to see and reads Maguire's pre-coverup report we get an entirely different view of the battle. Maguire in his report dated July 10, 1876 gives what is probably the most detailed and perhaps accurate descriptions of Custer's battle and his movements:

*"In the mean time, Custer had gone down stream and attempted to make a crossing at the point B, but was met by an overpowering force, and the troops retreated to the hills in rear in order to procure a more defensible position. From the position of the dead bodies on the field, I concluded that they retreated on the two lines marked on the sketch to concentrate at E, which was the highest point of the ground. At the hill D a stand was undoubtedly made by the company under command of Lieutenant Calhoun to protect the men passing up to E. Lieutenant Calhoun and Crittenden were killed on this hill. Captain Keogh was killed about half way up the slope to E. The column which retreated along the line B H E must have been dismounted, and, fighting along the whole distance, **a portion of its men, taking to the ravine H for shelter, must have been surrounded by the Indians.***

There were twenty-eight bodies found in this ravine. From H to E stretched a line of dead men with skirmish intervals. The crest E was literally covered with dead officers and men. Here we found General Custer and his brother Captain Custer, Captain Yates, Lieutenant Smith, Lieutenant Cook and Lieutenant Riley. The Indians must have been present in overwhelming numbers, for this part of the fight did, from all accounts, last over two or three hours."

Two and half years later when Maguire is brought to testify at the Court of Inquiry, he is shown the doctored version of his map and his description of the battle becomes:[255]

"Question - Were there any evidences of fighting at or near the point "B"? If so, state what evidences and how near the first was.

Answer - There were empty shells lying all around and the marks of ponies or horses having been ridden all around; the whole field was covered with tracks. Every now and then we would find an empty shell and as we advanced up further we found dead bodies in a circle around the crest of a little hill and quite a number of empty shells. There were dead bodies stretched from "D" to "E" and in the ravine "H" there were 28 dead bodies found.

Question - How near to the point "B" was it that you found empty shells and evidences of fighting?

Answer - Upon a little rise, on the slope, as if persons had lain there to take advantage of whatever protection there was in the formation of the ground. There were government shells and Winchester shells and one peculiar brass shell was found that nobody knew anything about but which was supposed to belong to General Custer's pistol."

Hence for all time Maguire becomes the village idiot and his work is deemed incompetent. His map is hence described as flawed, his testimony as babble. He was the Chief Engineering Officer and he could not describe the field in a professional manner, of course, the map he was shown bore no resemblance to the one he had drawn and had been altered pursuant to orders issued by Major George Elliot, in September 1876.

Had proper legal techniques been utilized by Recorder Lee, the following Questions would have been asked and the Answers received might have been:

Question - Lt. Maguire is this your report dated July 10, 1876 [a few months before the coverup started] and is this the unaltered sketch that accompanied it?

Answer - Yes

Question - Do you believe the report and sketch accurately describe the battle as you determined it from the forensics on the field two days later?

———————————————

[255]Nichols, *Reno Court of Inquiry*, 9.

Answer - yes.

It is requested that the report and sketch become part of the official record.

If the original Maguire sketch, the Philo Clark map derived from debriefing captured from Ogallalas, the Russell White Bear map, and all the pre-coverup maps and sketches prepared by the combatants are examined together, they all clearly show that Custer came down Medicine Tail Coulee, attempted to cross, met heavy resistance, continued on the river bed to Ford C and then retreated up the hills to his destiny.

As F Troop was trapped in the coulee when Gall attacked and Custer was further down river with the other two troops, Gall would have thought Custer didn't make the river. But Custer did make it to the river, and this is well documented within the Cheyenne versions. Many Indian versions talk of a retreat from the river and the slaughter of the last troop in the retreat, the grey horse troop.

Custer attempted to get to the river with three troops. He got close to and perhaps into the river, but almost immediately was repulsed. I and L troops were left to wait for Benteen and to cover the advance. They eventually wound up covering what became a disorganized retreat to Last Stand Hill by the other three troops.

- F was dismounted and returned by the route it came up Medicine Tail Coulee.

- E troop became dismounted and their horses were frightened away as they retreated up Deep Coulee. They were dismounted and facing the river as they marched backwards up the bluffs and became trapped in Deep Ravine, where they were slaughtered.

- C was dismounted and positioned on the lower part of Calhoun Ridge. A number of their horses, too, were frightened off. Heavy losses were sustained and the remaining troopers retreated, dismounted towards Last Stand Hill. At least six sorrels made it to Last Stand Hill to provide the breastworks for the top of the knoll. No gray horses were found at or near Last Stand Hill.

Based upon Reno's Report, Benteen's Letter, Philo Clark's and Maguire's Maps and strong corroborating Indian testimony, especially Cheyenne, that Custer attempted to or succeeded in fording at two places and that some portion of his troops may have entered the perimeter of the village is without question. The Indian corroboration is augmented by the Philo Clark Map as it is derived from Indian testimony.

Did they enter the village proper? This depends on how close the tepees were to the river and where they crossed. The Maps show Ford C is above the Cheyenne circle so it would appear that they did cross but did not enter the village there. Ford B used to be known as Minneconjous Ford and was right at the Minneconjous Circle, it is most likely if Custer's troops entered the village it was here. This is a topic which becomes a victim of semantics. Too often "crossing the river" is given the same meaning as "entering the village," and it is quite doubtful it translated very well into sign language during the interviews with the Indians. It is doubtful that the tepees were up to the water's edge, so that the minute a soldier crossed the river he was in the village. The tepees had to be some distance from the water, so soldiers may have crossed the river without entering the village proper.

Neither Reno nor Benteen time framed their descriptions of the fight. This appears to be a fallacy of most of the other descriptions as well. It causes most people to think that all events occurred simultaneously. Put the statements together in a logical time sequence and they make wonderful sense. Also consider that when Benteen was giving his description, he was standing in the village looking at Last Stand Hill. Reno said that C and I Troops (Reno believed the dead bay horses next to the sorrels came from I Troop, when in fact they came from F Troop) entered the village. Benteen said that F, I and L Troops all entered and left the village by the right ford. As he was facing Last Stand Hill from the village, Medicine Tail Coulee was the right ford.

Utilizing the Philo Clark report and the statements of Knipe, Martin and Peter Thompson a composite scenario can be created beginning when Martin looked back and saw Custer descending Medicine Tail Coulee and specifically identified the Gray Horse troop as being in the center of the column. Keogh had led

out with I troop followed by L beginning his crossing of the coulee, to establish a rally point on the bluffs on the opposite side. Custer then followed leading C, then E and F, with Yates guarding the rear.

All of the foregoing when interpolated properly suggests that the action at Medicine Tail Coulee and subsequent Last Stand occurred as follows:

- Custer traveled with two wings along the bluffs from Reno Hill, through Cedar Coulee. He had a right wing of L and I, with I on the far right and L on the left of I. His left wing was E, C, and F. E traveled along the edge of the bluffs and being seen by Reno's troops in the valley, C was in the center and F on the far right of this wing. [See Exhibit 17]

  Magnussen states that, "Therefore the order of advance along the bluffs would have been Company F, Company C, and Company E."[256]

- I troop, with Keogh commanding, followed by L, moved across Medicine Tail Coulee to the opposite bluffs. L Troop formed a dismounted skirmish line and I Troop was held in reserve in a depression. They were positioned to cover the advance and waited for Benteen to come, holding further orders for him.

- Five men, one sergeant and four

[256]Magnussen, *The Thompson Narrative of the Little Bighorn 1876*, 119.

enlisted, from F Troop, were 100 yds. in front of headquarters and lead out. This could explain the dead troopers and horses from F Troop found in the village.

Peter Thompson notes, *"When the companies came in sight of the village, they gave the regular charging yell and urged their horses into a gallop. At this time a detail of five men from Company F was sent ahead to reconnoiter and from this point I was gradually left behind."*

"Private William Brown of F Troop and his horse were found dead in the village. Brown's body lay 250 yards from the river his horse farther."[257]

Walter Camp noted, *"Rooney says he [William Brown] was found in the village opposite to where Custer charged down the river."*[258]

• The Headquarters Group followed, with as many as twenty men, depending on whether the Crows were still with the column. As Custer intended for no one other than himself to lead this charge.

• C Troop, the headquarters guard, followed Custer when he led out. Augustus L. DeVoto wrote in a November 15, 1917 letter to Walter Camp,[259] *"When we were about ten miles from the Indian camp, after officers call was sounded, and General Custer had his counsel of war, C Troop*

was made advance guard."

• E Troop the next in the line.

• F Troop acts as rear guard, Yates commanding. [See Exhibit 18]

• The Custer led advance down Medicine Tail Coulee was, in order of march, troops C, E and F. This is what John Martin saw descending Medicine Tail Coulee and what he described to the Reno Court of Inquiry:[260]

Q - State if you know where the Gray Horse Company was on that march.

A - In the center of the column.

• Approximately three quarters of the way down Medicine Tail Coulee, Custer observed an essentially empty village except for a large dust cloud created by the non combs who were seeking shelter in the Squaw Creek area north and west of his position, directly across the river, per the Clark Report.

• Boston Custer arrived and informed Custer he had passed Benteen and Martin and by now Martin should be delivering his orders to Benteen and within minutes he could expect Benteen to arrive.

• The Coulee's terrain did not afford

---

[257]Hardorff, *The Custer Battle Casualties*, 109.
[258]Ibid., 109.
[259]Hardorff, *On The Little Bighorn With Walter Camp*, 139.
[260]Nichols, *The Reno Court of Inquiry*, 389.

him a good area to launch an attack, he could not form a line and charge so he ordered his battalion into double column of fours, to give his attack as much force as the terrain permitted.

Edward J. McClernand asserted to Walter Camp in 1910 that: *"He saw a double column of fours down MTC and turned across into dry coulee [Deep Coulee] and up this to forks and then to Finley [on Calhoun Ridge]. No doubt this being a cavalry trail, so regular."*[261]

- Custer ran into opposition from the Wolf Tooth band, about 75 strong, on the right side of the river, in the trees on the east bank. He deployed the Headquarters Group mounted and one platoon of C troop dismounted onto the lower part of Calhoun Ridge. Custer positioned C Troop platoon so as to return fire to the Wolf Tooth Band and to supply covering fire for the continuing advance.

- Custer remaining mounted established a Headquarters position behind C Troop's dismounted skirmish line.

- Yates' battalion of F and E continued down Medicine Tail Coulee intending to cross the river at Ford B and attack the village.

- They met stiff resistance from the Uncpapas coming north from the Reno fight, led by Gall, Rain-in-the-Face and Crow King, and they were quickly repelled with limited losses.

- Second Lieutenant Sturgis was shot when he reached midstream. His body was recovered by the Sioux, and it was carried into the village. This explains why Sturgis' body was never identified nor recovered though his underwear and other belongings were found in the village. This also explains the Indian version of Custer being shot at the river.

- Gall attacked and split Custer's force, driving F Troop back up Medicine Tail Coulee and sending E Troop towards Ford C.

- F Troop was forced to retreat back up Medicine Tail Coulee, it then proceeded across the bluffs between the positions occupied by L and C Troops. I and L troops remained in the positions where Custer sent them and the bodies of their dead were found. This could have created the illusion that conforms to the opinion Benteen formed that F, I and L retreated by the route they came.

- E Troop continued along the river bed to Ford C, again it attempted to cross and again it was repulsed. E Troop commenced a dismounted retreat. Their backs were to Last Stand Hill, and they were firing at the Indians pursuing them from the river. [See Exhibit 19]

- The Indians, primarily the Cheyennes, came across the river,

---

[261]Hardorff, *Markers, Artifacts and Indian Testimony*, 27.

attacked E Troop and caused most of E Troop's gray horses to stampede.

- The dismounted E Troop retreated towards Deep Ravine and took cover there, while Two Moons and the Cheyennes followed and attacked them.

- E Troop now took the brunt of the battle. It had lost most of its horses and the dismounted survivors were trapped in Deep Ravine, under heavy attack by the Cheyennes.

    Augustus L. DeVoto formerly of B Troop wrote, in a July 24, 1917 letter to Walter Camp that, *"I helped bury Custer's dead. Those that I helped bury were in a dry ravine, and could have been easily identified. There were members of E Company among them."*[262]

- Custer now had the dismounted C Troop commence a retreat across the bluffs, on foot, facing the river and firing all the way, heading towards Last Stand Hill. They had and continued to incur losses on the way.

    Daniel Knipe in a July 20, 1908 letter to Walter Camp stated: *"I saw Sergeant Bob, Finley, [and] Finckle; they were lying along the line of march as the company was retreating for the last stand."*[263]

- Custer's horse was killed approximately 150 feet from the knoll. Its body was found in a running position facing the knoll, by Lieu-

tenant Edward McClernand.[264] The loss of his horse may have also helped inspire Custer to choose Last Stand Hill as a rally point.

- Custer reached Last Stand Hill with part of C Troop and reunited with F Troop. Custer then established a headquarters position and field hospital on Last Stand Hill.

- Custer next ordered F troop to move independently, to the area where the cemetery now is and beyond, looking for yet another place to ford, as he was still of an aggressive mind set and anticipating the imminent arrival of Benteen and the reserves.

- On nearing the river, near Ford D, F Troop encountered a large group of Sioux, the Crazy Horse band coming from the village side of the river, and returned to Last Stand Hill, where it again reunited with Custer.

- Yates informed Custer that a large party of Sioux were coming from the river, and it appeared that the position was becoming surrounded. Custer deployed F Troop in a dismounted line, on the southwest side of the knoll, to face the threat coming from the west.

- The remnants of C Troop attempted to fill the gap in the lines between Last Stand Hill and

---

[262] Hardorff, *On The Little Bighorn With Walter Camp*, 131.
[263] Ibid., 8.
[264] McClernand, *On Time For Disaster*, 93.

Keogh's position, by establishing a line facing east on the top of the knoll.

- He now had, as a left flank, L troop deployed as line running east to west, with I as a reserve.

- His right flank consisted of what remained of E troop trapped in Deep Ravine. F Troop as dismounted skirmishers facing west, and C Troop facing east, trying to fill the gap between I and F's positions. [See Exhibit 20]

- The Oglalas' attack under Crazy Horse separated the Keogh battalion from Custer's remaining force. The Uncpapas, Minneconjous and Sans Arc, under Gall, Crow King and Rain-In-The-Face attacked, overwhelming L Troop in a single rush and then slaughtered I Troop, buffalo hunt style. Concurrently, the Cheyennes under Two Moons engulfed and slaughtered the members of E Troop trapped in Deep Ravine.

- The few survivors of I and L attempted to retreat to the apparent safety of Last Stand Hill, but its refuge proved to be momentary. As this was taking place, the last remaining members of E Troop, trapped in Deep Ravine, were killed. [See Exhibit 21]

- Custer was now in command of approximately 80 men, approximately 35 from F Troop, 20 from C Troop, 10 from I and L troops, 5 from E Troop and the 10 members of the Headquarters group. They were completely surrounded by from 2500 to 3000 Sioux and Cheyenne.

- Defenses were established, as best as possible, with the limited resources available. The remnants of C formed a semi-circle on the top of the knoll facing east to thwart the Sioux threat coming from that direction. F Troop, the only troop still relatively intact, had formed a line facing northwest to defend against the Sioux threat from that direction. The remaining men had formed a loose line against the Cheyenne threat coming from the river. The backside of the hill and the north and northeast were undefended.

- The Indians attacked with a grand rush from all sides, with Crazy Horse leading the attack from the Northwest, Two Moons coming from the South, and Gall, Rain-in-the-Face and Crow King coming from the South and East. All but a very few were immediately killed,

- The few survivors left tried to escape by running towards the river, the only area where they might be able to hide. The Indians hunted them down until all were killed. [See Exhibit 22]

Battle scholars have previously presented portrayals of the flow of fighting, but they have erred by presenting the flow, in a slow motion, freeze frame, step by step methodology. This is not what occurred, many events occurred simultaneously or concurrently. The Indians were not unit fighters, they were individual fighters who occasionally banded into a unit for a charge or single act. They then disbanded as a unit and waited until another leader asked them to form a new band and perform a new act. Further, when the Indians told their versions of battle, they only told it from their individual perspectives. They spoke of where they were and what they saw and did. If they arrived after an event occurred, in their minds, it did not occur. They did not judge time in a western sense. Most told time by the movement of the sun around a lodge pole, i.e., a sundial.

Custer's right flank was under attack by the Lakota warriors returning from the Reno fight and Minneconjous and Sans Arc warriors whose circles abutted Ford B. As Custer vacated the Ford B area, they crossed the river and followed him. The Lakota advance divided Custer's battalion causing F Troop to retreat on foot up to the Calhoun Ridge area. There they received support from I and L troops, mounted and proceeded towards Custer's position on Last Stand Hill. L Troop then came under full attack from the Lakota warriors and fell. I Troop bunched, broke, attempted to run and were killed buffalo hunt style.

Custer's left flank was under attack by the Cheyennes under Two Moon's leadership. The Cheyennes crossed the river and followed them up Deep Coulee and then to Deep Ravine, causing E Troop to lose most if not all its horses. They surrounded the Trapped E Troop soldiers in Deep

Ravine and quickly killed them. They then followed Custer's Headquarters Group and the remaining members of C up the bluffs to the Last Stand Hill vicinity.

The attacks on the right and left flanks were not in step motion, they were simultaneous or concurrent, as the Lakota decimated part of C, and then L and I; the Cheyenne were slaughtering the men of E Troop trapped in Deep Ravine. These events were concurrent, and there was not a momentary lull in the fighting, until Custer formed his last stand defenses while the Lakota and Cheyenne regrouped from decimating two thirds of his command. At this point, after the initial carnage, the question arises - how many men was Custer left with for the final fighting? It appears that perhaps 10 members of the Headquarters Group reached the last stand area, the only loss being Kellogg by Ford C. As many as 20 men from C Troop could have made it safely, up to 35 men from F Troop and 5 members of E Troop and perhaps 10 survivors from the I and L position. Yates, Van Reilly, Smith and perhaps Harrington were the surviving officers with Custer in addition to those in the Headquarters Group, being Custer, Cooke, Lord, and Tom Custer. The remaining members of the Headquarters Group were 4 enlisted, Sharrow, Voss, Hughes and Callahan and 3 civilians, Boston Custer, Autie Reed and Mitch Bouyer. Custer had up to 72 enlisted men, 7 or 8 officers and 3 civilians, for a total force of 82 or 83.

Custer formed a bi-level defense, on the top of the knoll he positioned the remaining men of C Troop and the Headquarters Group. This is actually where Custer fell, not the 100 or so feet down the slope where the marker exists. The markers on Last Stand Hill as well as the rest of the battlefield are an artist's rendition of where the dead fell and not actually where the bodies were found. The top of the knoll was a circular area roughly 30 to 40 feet in diameter. This is where Custer's body was found, in close proximity to where the monument now stands. *"On top of Custer Hill - a nearly level knoll, some thirty feet in diameter and only a few feet higher than the adjacent ridge - lay the bodies of four officers, six enlisted, and six horses, the latter bloated to the extreme. The horses, all sorrels of Company C, were killed along the perimeter of the knoll, the convex of the circle being towards the east."*[265] This was the defensive position Custer established to repel the Lakota advance coming across Battle Ridge after eliminating I and L Troops.

Below the crest of the knoll a second defense was established that faced west and presumably was to thwart the Sioux advance from the river. The men here were predominantly from F Troop. *"Some thirty-two soldiers and thirty-three horses were found on the southwestern slope, just below the crest."*[266]

From these two positions Custer was able to maintain his defenses thwarting two sides of what was soon about to become a triangular shaped death vise. The Ogallala circle was on the far western extreme of the village, this forced them to cross the river by a northern ford, loop around the area where the cemetery presently is and descend on the Last Stand Hill from the rear. When Crazy Horse finally got his magic ready for battle, most of the damage had been done by the Two Moons led Cheyennes and the Gall and Crow King led Lakota. These two groups had thwarted Custer's attempt to cross the river and decimated two thirds of the soldiers and trapped the remainder on Last Stand Hill. The trapped soldiers and the two attacking groups were trading shots when Crazy Horse and Ogallalas descended on the rear of Last Stand Hill coming from the west and the north. The Ogallalas closed the triangular vise and sealed Custer's fate. He simply did not have enough men to defend against the three sides of the triangular vise. In one grand rush from all three sides his forces were overwhelmed and annihilated.

The consensus of the statements draws a clear picture of what happened at Medicine Tail Coulee. Custer came down the coulee at a charge, he attempted a crossing at Ford B and was repelled. He continued along the river bank and attempted to cross at Ford C, severe losses of horses forced E Troop to dismount and retreat on foot getting trapped in Deep Ravine, Custer with part of C Troop made it up the ridges to Last Stand Hill.

Custer was in an offensive mode until he reached Last Stand Hill. It was then the unfortunate realization came to him that Benteen and help were not coming. Right up until the

---

[265]Hardorff, *The Custer Battle Casualties*, 33.
[266]Ibid., 33.

virtual end, the fight by Custer was an aggressive, offensive effort. Custer left Ford B aggressively looking for a point further up to ford which offered less resistance and would give him an opportunity to outflank the defenders at Ford B. There were some 50 to 75, and possibly more Sioux , east of the river, that had been firing upon Custer's companies.

Reno deployed a skirmish line without ever firing a shot at a great distance from the village. His timid actions inspired the Indians and enticed them to come out and attack. His turning tail and running convinced the Indians the soldiers were vulnerable and inspired them to even bolder action against Custer.

At Ford C, Custer suffered losses and lost the offensive momentum and element of surprise that he thought he had. He did not know that Reno's charge failed. He had seen a basically empty village and a target, that if he could capture it, would enable him to win the battle. He failed in his attack on the village. He then formed a defensive position to wait for the reinforcements he had ordered to come. Little did he know that now more than half his command, seven-twelfths to be precise, had come under the command of the biggest coward in the United States Army never to face a Court Martial. He did not know that his second in command would wantonly disobey orders, fail and refuse to engage the enemy when his way was clear and refuse to come forward, even when there was scant resistance in his path. It was Reno's duty as an officer to report to his commander and inform

him of the failure of his mission as soon as practical thereafter. Or, as stated by General Miles, *"No commanding officer can win victories with seven-twelfths of his command remaining out of the engagement when within sound of his rifle-shots."*[267]

As Benteen came under Reno's command when the two battalions merged, the order to Benteen became Reno's responsibility to carry out, though Reno had the right to not comply if he had good reason. Reno would be subject to court martial if his reasons for failing to obey the order proved inadequate. This was aptly summed up by General of the Army Nelson A. Miles in his autobiography: *"Under rules governing all military forces-, whenever two commands come together the senior officer is responsible for the whole. And the senior officer should give the necessary orders. Major Reno was the responsible commander at that point."*[268]

The entire battle did not exceed one and a quarter hours, as Custer had neither the men nor ammunition to survive longer. It began at 3:45 PM when Martin saw Custer descend Medicine Tail Coulee. Custer reached the river by 4 PM, was repelled by 4:20 PM, and the "Last Stand" was over before Weir departed to find Custer at 5 PM.

It will not be until after the collapse of the I and L battalion that Custer will realize that he has been hung out to dry, abandoned by Reno,

---

[267]Miles, *Personal Reflections of Nelson A. Miles*, 290.
[268]Ibid., 209.

and that the only form of Custer's Luck
he will experience that day will be bad!

George Armstrong Custer

Copy Telegram.

Headquarters Military Division of the Missouri,

Chicago, Illinois, _____ July 9 _____ 1876.

Mrs George A. Custer

Fort Lincoln, via Bismarck, D. T.

I take this opportunity to convey to you and to the ladies of the 7th Cavalry who have been so deeply bereaved by the terrible loss you have sustained, my sincere sympathy and condolence. And while conscious that nothing I can say will assuage your great sorrow, I can at least share in the grief you all feel. My acquaintance with General Custer and the officers who fell with him was most intimately both officially and personally, and in a long service with them they sustained the high character now so justly appreciated by the Army and the country, for their gallantry and devotion to duty.

Official

L. v. B⸺ (Signed) P. H. Sheridan

Assistant Adjutant General   Lieut. General. (Over)

Copy condolence telegram sent to Mrs. Annie Yates by General Sheridan. The original telegram was sent to Mrs. Elizabeth Custer with original copy telegrams being sent to the widows of each of the officers killed with Custer.

Mrs. Elizabeth B. Custer, from the original cabinet card by Gilbert of Philadelphia, Pennsylvania, circa 1880s.

Thomas Ward Custer, from an original carte-de-viste, by W. McClellan, Monroe, Michigan, 1867.

Sleigh Ride, Winter 1875, from the original oversized albumen print by O. S. Goff. Seated in the sleigh from left to right: William Winer Cooke, Tom Custer, Nellie Wadsworth.

Lt. Henry M. Harrington, West Point.

1st *Lt. James Calhoun, from a partially hand tinted presentation cabinet card, attributed to O. S. Goff, taken at Fort Lincoln in 1875, inscribed on the reverse "Lieut. James Calhoun, 7th Cavalry, U.S.A. To Annie G. Yates, from her devoted friend, Maggie E. Calhoun."*

Lt. William Winer Cooke, from an original carte-de-viste believed to be unpublished, photographer unknown, taken between January 26, 1864 and June 24, 1865. Signed on the reverse "W. W. Cooke, Lt. 24 N.Y. Cav."

Sleigh Ride, winter 1875, from the original unpublished oversized albumen print by O. S. Goff. Seated in the sleigh from left to right: "Maggie Custer Calhoun, Tom Custer, Libbie Custer, Boston Custer, George Custer. The sleigh bore the name "Frolic."

2nd *Lt. Charles Roe of New York, West Point Album photograph.*

2ⁿᵈ Lt. Charles A. Varnum from West Point.

2ⁿᵈ Lt. Charles A. Varnum, from an original oversized albumen print attributed to O. S. Goff, circa 1874. Inscribed on the reverse: "For John P. Varnum, Lowell Mass." John P. Varnum was his father.

Below, Capt. Algernon E. Smith, from the original unpublished carte-de-viste by W. C. North, Utica, N.Y., taken between October 12, 1864 and May 15, 1865. Inscribed on the reverse: "Yours Truly, A. E. Smith, Aid de Camp, 2d Div, 10ᵗʰ U.C., Capt. 117ᵗʰ N.Y. Vols."

Below, Boston Custer, period carte-de-viste photographer unknown.

Comanche and Sergeant Gustav Korn, taken May 1888 by Coules & McBride of Deadwood, Dakota Territory. Comanche was 24 years old at the time of the photograph.

Seventh Cavalry Officers on a picnic at the Hat River, near Fort Lincoln, By O. S. Goff July, 1875. From left to right, 1ˢᵗ Lt. James Calhoun, Leonard Swett, Capt. Steven Baker 6ᵗʰ U.S. Infantry, Boston Custer, 2ⁿᵈ Lt. W. S. Edgerly, Miss Emily Watson, Capt. Myles Keogh, Mrs. Margaret Custer Calhoun, Mrs. Elizabeth Custer, Dr. Holmes Paulding, Lt. Col. George Custer, Mrs. Nettie Smith, Dr. George Lord, Capt. Thomas Weir, 1ˢᵗ Lt. W. W. Cooke, 2ⁿᵈ Lt. Richard Thompson 6th U.S. Infantry, Miss Nellie Wadsworth, 1ˢᵗ Lt. Thomas Custer, 1ˢᵗ Lt. Algernon Smith.

Original montage of the "Custer Men," from the original carte-de-viste by Wing's Photographic of Monroe, Michigan, B. D. Jackson, Operator. Undated. (Top to bottom, L to R) Lt. Calhoun, Capt. Custer, Gen. Custer, Autie Reed, and Boston Custer.

A parlor scene at the Custer Home in Fort Lincoln, from the original oversized albumen print by O. S. Goff, July, 1875. From left to right: Boston Custer, Mrs. Margaret Custer Calhoun, 2nd Lt. Winfield S. Edgerly, Mrs. Elizabeth Custer, Mr. Leonard Swett, 2nd Lt. Richard Thompson, Miss Nellie Wadsworth, 1st Lt. Thomas Custer, Lt. Col. George Custer, Miss Emma Wadsworth and Miss Emily Watson.

2nd Lt. Edward S. Godfrey, from an original unpublished carte-de-viste, by Jay Noble, Leavenworth, Kansas, 1867.

Capt. Myles Keogh, from an original cabinet card by D. F. Barry, circa 1875.

Brig. Gen. Alfred H. Terry, from an original carte-de-viste by Mathew Brady.

A unique tintype approximately 1¼ inches in diameter, in a screw close gutta-pecha case, photographer unknown. Believed to have been carried on the person of Mrs. Yates. Photograph acquired from the estate of Mrs. Annie Yates, widow of Capt. George Yates.

Original unpublished carte-de-viste by J. W. Turner, Meridian, Mississippi, November 7, 1871, of Capt. George Yates in full field dress standing next to a 7th Cavalry horse. Photograph acquired from the estate of Mrs. Annie Yates, widow of Capt. George Yates.

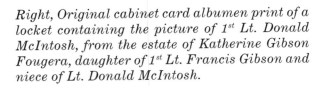

1ˢᵗ Lt. Charles De Rudio, from a believed unpublished original carte-de-viste, by O. S. Goff, circa 1875. Inscribed on the reverse "Yours ever truly, Charles C. DeRudio, 1ˢᵗ Lt. 7ᵗʰ Cavalry."

1ˢᵗ Lt. Edward Maguire, from his West Point Album photograph.

Right, Original cabinet card albumen print of a locket containing the picture of 1ˢᵗ Lt. Donald McIntosh, from the estate of Katherine Gibson Fougera, daughter of 1ˢᵗ Lt. Francis Gibson and niece of Lt. Donald McIntosh.

Bloody Knife, from a believed unpublished carte-de-viste attributed to W. H. Illingsworth, approximately 1872, formerly in the James O. Aplan Library Collection.

Curly, from an oversized albumen print by D. F. Barry. This is Curly as a young man and believed to have been taken within a few years of the Battle of the Little Bighorn.

Uncpapa Chief Gall, from the original cabinet card albumen print by D. F. Barry. Circa 1880s.

Uncpapa Chief Rain-in-the-Face, once arrested by Tom Custer and sometimes credited with killing George Custer, from the original card albumen print by D. F. Barry.

Cheyenne Chief Two Moons, from the original photogravure, by Rodney Wanamaker, 1913.

Five Sioux Chiefs from the original stereo view by F. J. Haynes, reading left to right: "Rain-in-the-Face, Gall, Low Dog, Running Antelope, Spotted Eagle."

Sitting Bull and his favorite wife, from the cabinet card sized stereo view by Bailey, Dixon & Mead, circa 1882.

Chief Spotted Tail, from the oversized albumen print by D. F. Barry.

Sioux Chief Standing Soldier, from the 10 by 13 studio albumen print, by Heyn of Omaha, Nebraska, copyright 1900.

Sioux Chief White Bull, from the original cabinet card albumen print by Kern Brothers, New York, New York.

Uncpapa Chief Rain-in-the-Face, from the original cabinet card albumen print by Huffman's of Miles City, Montana Territory.

The British Bulldogs, holding either five rounds of 32 or 38 caliber ammunition and weighing 11 ounces. The one on the left is an 1878 Webley made model, and the one on the right is a Belguim made model circa 1880s.

An 1867 Webley, R.I.C. used by the Royal Irish Constabulary and became known as the R.I.C. model, was 9.25 inches long, with 4.5 inch barrel, double action, held six rounds of 45 caliber ammunition.

An 1875 "Frontier Bulldog." A Belgium made modification of the R.I.C., it was 9.5 inches long, with a 4.5 inch barrel, double action, held 6 rounds of Winchester 44 caliber ammunition.

CHAPTER 16
There Weren't Any Survivors?

"MASSACRED
GEN. CUSTER AND 261 MEN THE VICTIMS
NO OFFICER OR MAN OF 5 COMPANIES LEFT TO TELL THE TALE"

So read the headlines of the Bismarck *Tribune's Extra* published July 6, 1876, giving the country its first distorted version of "Custer's Last Stand." Over the ensuing 125 plus years have come an onslaught of articles, books and movies all echoing the same inaccurate theme "not a man left to tell the tale." Quotes like, "They found Custer and all of the two hundred and sixty four men who had died on the ridge and on the slopes of the ridge. There was not a single survivor," "Comanche was the only survivor of Custer's Last Stand," and "Only Comanche knew the real story of Custer's Last Stand. But Comanche never said a word."[269] The cited tome and the quotes are not singled out for any particular reason other than to show examples of the distorted facts the public has been handed since the Bismarck *Tribune* initiated this theme.

Even a rudimentary study of Custer and the Battle immediately generates questions which attack the obvious inaccuracies. The first question that is asked is, what happened to the other 300 plus men in the regiment who were not under Custer's direct command that day? It usually receives a curt response of "they were trapped and survived." The second question that is raised is, "But, Custer did not have that many men with him, who are the other dead?" The answer to this is that 39 of the dead were from Reno's command. Much like an individual who becomes infected with an incurable disease, after asking these two questions, an individual is then infected with the "Custer Bug." The Custer Bug creates an incurable thirst for knowledge about Custer, the Battle and the long enduring challenge of how "NO OFFICER OR MAN OF 5 COMPANIES LEFT TO TELL THE TALE" and why.

---

[269]Reynolds, *Custer's Last Stand*, 183-185.

As many have previously written, if all the self proclaimed sole survivors of Custer's Last Stand were in fact with Custer, his force would have outnumbered the Indians by five to one, or more. That being stated, we must still deal with the reality that the numbers published do not conform to the Regiment's Records and Muster Rolls. Bradley initially counted 194 bodies on the Custer Battlefield, and he so reported to Colonel Gibbon.[270] In his July 25, 1876 letter to the Helena *Herald*, Bradley stated there were 206 bodies.[271] General Charles F. Roe stated that when Benteen came back from Custer's battlefield on June 27, a roster of officers of Custer's five companies had been made out and the names called off one by one, and Benteen claimed to have identified the bodies of all but Harrington and Dr. Lord. Later the list of unidentified officers was increased by Porter and Sturgis, possibly because the next day the bodies were badly decomposed and could not be identified any more.[272] The Monument is inscribed with 212 names, one of which is Nathan Short's, whose remains were found miles from the field. The remains of Lts. Porter, Harrington, and perhaps Sturgis were never found or identified, yet their names appear on the Monument. The battlefield was littered with the mutilated, rotting corpses of Custer's command, which were in an advanced stage of decomposition.

It is without a doubt that less bodies were found and buried than the 212 names inscribed on the Monument, and for over 125 years the public has been led to believe that this is the true and complete accounting for the dead, that Custer commanded 212 men, they all perished, and there were no survivors. The word survivors requires definition. When does one become a survivor, how long must one live after the battle to be deemed a survivor, and how far must one travel while escaping the field to be classified a survivor? In the narrowest of terms, one would have had to have been on Battle Ridge while Custer was fighting the Indians and had lived to tell about it. There is one who might even meet this stringent definition, and that is Curly. Certainly Nathan Short was a survivor, his name is on the monument, but his remains were found miles from the field. Knipe claims to have been a messenger, and Martin actually was a messenger, so they should qualify as survivors. Peter Thompson and Joe Watson claimed their horses gave out, and they walked to Reno's position. Gustav Korn's horse bolted, ran wild and he somehow wound up with Reno's troops. Custer released the four other Crows in addition to Curly, so Goes Ahead, Hairy Moccasin, Half Yellow Face and White Man Runs Him can qualify as survivors. Now, two more questions arise:

• How many men were actually under Custer's command when he turned to the right?

[270]Secretary of War, *Report of the Secretary of War Volume I 1876*, 473.
[271]Bradley, *The March of the Montana Column*, 173.
[272]Hardorff, *The Custer Battle Casualties*, 105.

• How many of these men survived the battle?

Survived will be defined as being with Custer when his battalion turned to the right and either winding up on Reno Hill the evening of June 25, 1876 or having their remains found somewhere other than on the battlefield.

After allowing for the return of Mitchell and McIlhargey, the messengers sent by Reno to Custer whose bodies were found with their fellow members of I Troop, the return of Cooke and Keogh, transfers into the battalion of orderly trumpeters Henry Dose of G Troop and John Martin of H Troop, Robert H. Hughes, Custer's Battle Flag Bearer, and John J. Callahan, a Medical Steward, both from K Troop, and deducting a transfer out, Edward Davern of F Troop, John Martin back to H and counting Custer, there were 230 men in the battalion. There are only 210 known dead [13 Officers, 193 Enlisted and 4 Civilians], leaving 20 men not killed in the battle, 6 Scouts and 14 Enlisted, these are the actual survivors from Custer's battalion.[273] All the enlisted men shown below and listed as survivors had no reason for being with Reno's force on the hilltop, other than the weak excuses noted. There is no record of them being assigned to pack train detail or having any legitimate reason for being there. Peter Thompson and John McGuire claimed that John Fitzgerald and John Brennan of C Troop were deserters. It is quite probable that Morris Farrar was a deserter, too. There is no way to

determine what caused Nathan Short's remains to be where they were found, other than to assume he was either a deserter or an escapee/survivor of the battle who subsequently died of wounds suffered in the battle. William Reese, Bernard Lyons, John Sweeney and Philip McHugh had no valid reason for not dying with their respective troops and instead surviving on the hilltop.

It is noted in Peter Thompson's narrative that fourteen men from Company C, nine from Company E, fifteen from Company F, ten from Company I and thirteen from Company L, were found on Reno Hill, far more than was supposed to be tending each company's respective packs.[274]

Thus the total of those killed in Custer's battalion is 210 men, consisting of 13 Officers, 193 Enlisted and 4 Civilians. The total that survived was 20, 14 enlisted men and 6 civilian scouts.

---

[273]Carroll, *They Rode with Custer*, 5.
[274]Magnussen, *Thompson's Narrative of the Little Bighorn Campaign 1876*, 113.

CIVILIANS-INDIAN SCOUTS - 6

WILLIAM "BILLY" CROSS	MAY OR MAY NOT HAVE GONE WITH CUSTER
CURLY	CROW SCOUT RELEASED BY CUSTER
GOES AHEAD	CROW SCOUT RELEASED BY CUSTER
HAIRY MOCASIN	CROW SCOUT RELEASED BY CUSTER
HALF YELLOW FACE	CROW SCOUT RELEASED BY CUSTER
WHITE MAN RUNS HIM	CROW SCOUT RELEASED BY CUSTER

ENLISTED MEN - 14

C-DANIEL KNIPE	CLAIMED TO BE A MESSENGER
C-JOHN FITZGERALD	DESERTER PER PETER THOMPSON & JOHN MAGUIRE
C-JOHN BRENNAN	DESERTER PER PETER THOMPSON & JOHN MAGUIRE
C-MORRIS FARRAR	STRAGGLER WHO APPEARED ON RENO HILL
C-PETER THOMPSON	CLAIMED HORSE QUIT - APPEARED ON RENO HILL
C-JAMES WATSON	CLAIMED HORSE QUIT - APPEARED ON RENO HILL
C-NATHAN SHORT	MESSENGER, DESERTER, SURVIVOR?
E-WILLIAM SHIELDS	ON RENO HILL - MAY HAVE BEEN MEDIC FOR PORTER
E-WILLIAM REESE	APPEARED ON RENO HILL
F-BERNARD LYONS	APPEARED ON RENO HILL
F-JOHN SWEENY	APPEARED ON RENO HILL
H-JOHN MARTIN	ORDERLY, RETURNED WITH A MESSAGE
I-GUSTAV KORN	HORSE BOLTED RAN WILD, FOUGHT ON HILLTOP
L-PHILIP McHUGH	APPEARED ON RENO HILL

THE OFFICERS, CIVILIANS AND HEADQUARTERS ENLISTED KILLED

OFFICERS - 13		HEADQUARTERS ENLISTED - 5	CIVILIANS - 4
CUSTER, G	PORTER, J	SHARROW, W	CUSTER, B
KEOGH, M	HARRINGTON, H	VOSS, H	REED, A
YATES, G	STURGIS, J	DOSE, H	BOUYER, M
CUSTER, T	VAN REILLY, W	HUGHES, R	KELLOGG, M
COOKE, W	CRITTENDEN, J	CALLAHAN, J	
SMITH, A	LORD, G		
CALHOUN, J			

ENLISTED MEN KILLED BY TROOP - TOTAL 188

C - 35 KIA	E - 37 KIA	F - 36 KIA	I - 36 KIA	L - 44 KIA
1S BOBO	1S HOHMEYER	1S KENNY	1S VARDEN	1S BUTLER
S FINCKLE	S JAMES	S GROESBECK	S BUSTARD	S CASHAN
S FINLEY	S OGDEN	S NURSEY	C MORRIS	S WARREN
C FOLEY	C BROWN	S WILKINSON	C STAPLES	C GILBERT
C FRENCH	C EAGAN	C BRIODY	C WILD	C HARRISON
C RYAN	C MASON	C COLEMAN	MCGUCKER	C SEILER
BUCKNELL	C MEYER	C TEEMAN	PATTON	WALSH
KRAMER	MCELROY	WAY	BAILEY	HEATH
KING	MOONIE	BRANDON	BARRY	SIEMON
HOWELL	BAKER	MANNING	BROADHURST	PERKINS
ALLAN	BARTH	ATCHESON	CONNORS	ADAMS
BRIGHTFIELD	BOYLE	BRADY	DOWNING	ANDREWS
CRIDDLE	BROGAN	BROWN B	DRISCOLL	ASSADALY
EISEMAN	CONNOR	BROWN W	GILLETTE	BABCOCK
ENGLE	DARRIS	BRUCE	GROSS	CHEEVER
FARRAND	DAVIS	BURNHAM	HETESIMER	CRISFIELD
GRIFFIN	FARRELL	CARNEY	HOLOCOMB	CROWLEY
HATHERSALL	FORBES	CATHER	HORN	DYE
LEWIS	HEIM	DOHMAN	KELLY	GALVAN
MEIER	HENDERSON J	DONNELLY	LEHMAN	GRAHAM
MEYER	HENDERSON S	GARDNER	LEHMANN	HAMILTON
PHILLIPS	HUBER	HAMMON	LLOYD	HARRINGTON
RAUTER	KNECHTKLEIN	KELLY	MCILHARGEY	HAUGGI
RIX	LIDDIARD	KLEIN	MITCHELL	HUGHES
RUSSELL	O'CONNOR	KNAUTH	NOSHANG	KAVANAGH
SHADE	REES	LEROCK	O'BRYAN	LOBERING
SHEA	ROOD	LIEMANN	PARKER	MAHONEY
ST JOHN	SCHELE	LOSSEE	PITTER	MAXWELL
STUART	SMALLWOOD	MADSEN	POST	MCCARTHY
STUNGEWITZ	SMITH A	MILTON	QUINN	MCGUE
THADUS	SMITH J1	MONROE	REED	MILLER
VAN ALLEN	SMITH J2	OMLING	ROSSBURY	O'CONNELL
WARNER	STAFFORD	RUDDEN	SYMMS	PARDEE
WRIGHT	STELLA	SAUNDERS	TROY	REIBOLD
WYMAN	TORREY	SICFOUS	VAN BRAMER	ROBERTS
	VAN SANT	WARREN	WHALEY	ROGERS
	WALKER			SCHMIDT
				SCOTT
				SIEMONSON
				SNOW
				TARBOX
				TESSIER
				VETTER

1S= FIRST SERGEANT
S=SERGEANT
C=CORPORAL
NO KEY=PRIVATE

SURVIVOR BILLY CROSS?

There appears to be no known statement, in any known account, or in Walter Camp's unpublished notes, that Cross was assigned to, was supposed to go with Custer, or actually had gone with Custer. Cross was with the Ree Scouts, which is documented in Camp's notes. Although there is little documentation that he crossed the Little Bighorn. Cross's job, in part, was to interpret for the Arikara scouts who were on the expedition and were all involved in the valley fight.

William "Billy" Cross a Native American Scout may have been with Custer. As per Walter Camp's notes, as Weir started towards Custer on June 25, the troop met Billy Cross coming in the opposite direction from that in which the troop was moving (that is Cross was coming south along the bluff), with a handkerchief tied around his head. Billy Cross was named in a New York Herald story of August 1, 1876 as being suspected of betraying Custer. It inferred that he possibly went to the "hostile" camp the night before the battle, and that he left the battle as did most of the Arikara Scouts. This allegation was never substantiated.

The passage about Cross coming from the north refers to the fact that the "Ree" group, having come back to the battlefield from the pack train where they took the captured ponies, was now wandering about looking for something to do. They seem, by their accounts, to have gone down towards Weir point in advance of the Weir "advance," and stated that they saw some of Custer being defeated. They then came back towards Reno Hill from that direction, which was north. Herendeen, who was coming up from the timber after Weir went by, recalled seeing Cross and the "Rees" as they passed Weir and then came down past him towards the river to water their horses, as was documented in the "Ree" accounts. Suggesting that Billy Cross was supposed to have gone with Custer, lagged behind Custer, or left Custer, appears to have no basis in fact.

THE FIVE CROW SCOUTS

Four of the five Crow Scouts, Goes Ahead, Hairy Moccasin, Half Yellow Face and White Man Runs Him, were released early, before the actual fighting began. It is believed Custer released them from their duties some time after his ascent to Weir Point and before he reached Medicine Tail Ford. Curly adds a twist in this version of his story that he carried messages back and forth between Custer and Reno. While there is no other corroboration for this claim, there may be circumstantial support for it. It is incredulous to believe that Custer did not try to communicate with Reno, though he made several attempts to communicate with Benteen.

Curly stated:

"Custer split up his command at this point, and told Reno to follow the creek down, which is now called Reno Creek. Then we crossed over the ridge. I came down with Custer as far as the creek; then he gave me a message to take to Reno. I did not know the

import of the message. I brought the answer back from Reno to Custer. While I was delivering the last message, Reno was fighting his battle, but it was not very fierce, and when I got to Custer with message he was fighting at the mouth of the creek. Then Custer told me to go save my life. I made a circle around, and I found my ammunition was getting low. I found a dead Sioux. I took his ammunition and gun and horse, and got out. I stayed near where the dead Sioux was until the fight was pretty fierce. I went up on a high butte to the east of the battlefield where I could see the fight. When I got on the high hill I looked back and saw that Custer was the last man to stand."

Goes Ahead:[275]

"...Custer crossed the ridge, going over to the Medicine Tail Creek which runs into the Little Horn. There on the creek General Custer dismounted and said prayers to the Heavenly Father. Then he rose and shook hands with me, and said: 'My scout if we win the battle you will be one of the noted men of the Crow Nation.' In a moment or two he turned around again and said to me: 'I have forgotten to tell you, you are not to fight in this battle, but to go back and save your life.'"

Hairy Moccasin

"We four scouts turned and charged north to where Custer was headed for. Three of us stopped to fire into the village. We saw no more of Curley after that. I don't know where he went. When we met Custer he asked, 'How is it?' I said, 'Reno's men are fighting hard.' We went with the command down into a dry gulch where we could not see the village. Custer told Mitch Boyer to tell us to go back to the pack-train which we did."

White Man Runs Him:[276]

"Finally they wiped out Reno, and he retreated to the hills. Custer and all of us got off our horses here. At that time the enemy was surrounding us. They were banging away at us. We had a heavy skirmish. Custer then came up and said, 'You have done your duty. You have led me to the enemy's camp. And now the thing for you to do is to obey my orders and get away'...Custer when he told me to go said, 'You go; I am now going with my boys.'"

SURVIVOR SERGEANT DANIEL A. KNIPE - C TROOP

Reno communicated with Custer twice via Mitchell and McIlhargey. Custer communicated three times with Benteen through Voss, Sharrow and Martin. Benteen responded twice to Custer with Voss and Sharrow. There is no known communication from Custer back to Reno after Keogh and Cooke departed from Reno's battalion. It is possible that Custer sent two messengers back to Reno with responses to the Mitchell and

[275]Ibid., 166-167.
[276]Dixon, *The Vanishing Race*, 156.

McIlhargey messages, one with Nathan Short, who may have decided to take a circuitous routing, and possibly with Knipe. It is possible that when Kanipe saw the mess Reno was in, in the valley, he just continued on. Unfortunately for Knipe, he ran into Benteen instead. He then came up with a story about looking for the packs, which Benteen bought into and in turn sent him to McDougall. It appears Knipe never made it back to the packs and just went with the flow to the hill. As the hill was in a highly agitated state of flux, when Knipe arrived it appears that no one paid particular notice to his being there and no one bothered to verify his story. It is entirely unlikely that Custer did not attempt to communicate with Reno. It appears that the break down in communications may have been caused, in part, by the reluctance of the two messengers sent to do their duty.

The main parties involved with Knipe described his actions as follows: Benteen testified:

"A mile or so from that tepee I met a sergeant coming back with instructions to the commanding officer of the pack train to 'hurry up the packs.' I told him the pack train was about 7 miles back, and he could take the order back as I had nothing to do with that; that Capt McDougall was in charge of the pack train and would attend to the order."[277]

To the question, "Did a sergeant come to you with any directions about the pack train, if so, to whom was he directed and what was done by you in regard to it?" He replied, "He simply had verbal instructions to the commanding officer of the pack train and I did not consider that an order to me."[278]

Edgerly, corroborating Benteen, testified:

"A sergeant of C Company came back from General Custer's command and gave General Custer's compliments to Captain Benteen and he wanted him to bring up the packs. Captain Benteen said he thought he made a mistake, that Captain McDougall was in charge of the pack train and showed him the place and he went."[279]

"After that a sergeant of C Company came to him with reference to the pack train and received his directions and rode back towards Captain McDougall."[280]

John Frett a civilian with the pack train testified:

" We were at the watering place near the tepee, the last tepee that was there before we got to the battlefield, the one with the dead Indian in it, when a sergeant came from some company of the 7th Cavalry, I don't know what company, and said we should hurry up, that General Custer was attacking the Indians."[281]

---

[277]Nichols, *The Reno Court of Inquiry*, 404.
[278]Ibid., 463.
[279]Ibid., 441.
[280]Ibid., 459.
[281]Ibid., 503.

Lieutenant Edward Godfrey testified:

"*...just after we passed the tepee with the dead Indian in it we met a sergeant who came back going towards the pack train, and he called out to some of the men in the company, 'We've got 'em,' leaving the inference they had captured the village. I did not understand anything more he said to the men, he passed on to the rear.*"

To the question, Do you know where that sergeant went after passing back, Godfrey added, "*I did not watch him. I supposed he was going back to the pack train.*"[282]

Mathey testified:

Question - Did you receive orders from General Custer or Major Reno or Captain Benteen on that march?

Answer - "No, sir, only such as I received from Captain McDougall."

Question - Did any sergeant report to you with orders?

Answer "No, sir."[283]

McDougall testified:

Question - Did you receive any orders during that march from the place where you received General Custer's orders till you reached Major Reno's command on the hill?

Answer - "No, sir, the only thing was Lieutenant Mathey said the engagement was going on."

Question - "You received no notifica-

tion to hurry up the pack train?"

Answer - "No, sir, I think Lieutenant Mathey got that order. He told me about it, and I told him to hurry up, I was very anxious about it."

Knipe's statements included:

Knipe (June 16&17 1908 to Walter Camp) "*A little beyond this Tom Custer verbally gave Sergeant Knipe orders from General Custer to go back and order McDougall to follow him with the pack train and to hurry up. Knipe met Benteen a little west of burning tepee and on to McDougall a little further east.*"[284]

Knipe in the Greensboro, *NC Daily Record* 4/27/1924[285]

"*Just then the captain told me to go back and find McDougall and the pack train and deliver to them orders that had just been issued by General Custer.*

"*Tell McDougall,*" he said, "*to bring the pack train straight across to high ground-if packs get loose don't stop to fix them, cut them off. Come Quick. Big Indian camp.*"

I went back. I thought then that was tough luck, but it proved to be my salvation. If Sergeant Finkle had not dropped back a few minutes before he would have got the orders-and I would not be

---

[282]Ibid., 480.
[283]Ibid., 513.
[284]Hammer, *Custer in 76*, 93.
[285]Graham, *The Custer Myth*, 249.

telling this story.

Away off in the distance, the dust rolling up like a little cloud, I saw the pack train. I went toward that. My company and the others went on down toward the Indian camp. I remember the last words that I heard General Custer say; the men were on the hill, we all gave them three cheers riding at a full gallop, some of them couldn't hold their horses, galloping past General Custer. He shouted at them, 'Boys, hold your horses, there are plenty of them down there for us all.' They rode on. I rode back.

Reaching the pack train, I gave Captain McDougall the orders sent him, and went on toward Captain Benteen as I had been told to take them to him, also. McDougall and his outfit rode on to the top of the hill and reinforced Major Reno as he retired from the bottom of the bluffs."

Lieutenant Mathey was in command of the pack train while McDougall commanded troop B the pack train guard. It is likely, that, Mathey was at the head of the column leading the train and McDougall was following behind it as the rear guard. McDougall was assigned this role, by Custer that morning, as punishment duty for being the last troop to report as ready for duty. If Knipe went back to the train it is more reasonable to assume that he would meet Mathey first. However, both are adamant about not receiving an order via Knipe.

Knipe contradicts himself in 1908 saying he met Benteen first then went to McDougall and in 1924 saying he met McDougall first and then went to Benteen. The 1924 contradiction may be the result of time, but still neither Mathey nor McDougall acknowledged ever receiving an order via Knipe. His story does not sound credible as he stated he was told to tell McDougall *"...to bring the pack train straight across to high ground-if packs get loose don't stop to fix them, cut them off. Come Quick. Big Indian camp."* The words sound too much like a paraphrase of the written order Martin delivered to Benteen and the contents of which Knipe could have become privy to in the 48 years between the battle and the interview.

Benteen, Edgerly and Godfrey insist Knipe met them first and then went on to McDougall and Mathey. In 1908 Knipe stated the same, however in 1924 he stated he went to McDougall first and then to Benteen. The only source that verifies that Knipe reached the pack train is John Frett, but he does not corroborate that Knipe delivered any orders. It appears unlikely that Knipe reached the pack train prior to its arrival on Reno Hill and even more unlikely that Knipe was either a messenger to the pack train or delivered any orders to the officers with the pack train.

Knipe's story is suspect. Custer had received two urgent messages from Reno, to which he should have responded. When he sent Martin back, the packs were secondary to Benteen's coming in haste. Why then would the first messenger that Custer sent back, be to the pack train and not to Reno? Most likely, Knipe was a messenger to Reno, and he decided not to deliver the message and was heading towards parts unknown when he inadvertently ran into Benteen's battalion. Utilizing quick thinking, he invented the message for the pack train to explain his presence and to give him an excuse for leaving Benteen. He then got caught up in the confusion created by Reno's rout and wound up on Reno Hill. Custer was wiped out, and there was no one left to contest Knipe's story, so he became a hero, a surviving messenger from Custer.

SURVIVOR NATHAN SHORT - C TROOP

The name Nathan Short of C Troop appears on the monument. He was born 1854 in Lehigh, PA and enlisted October 9, 1875. If one follows the Custer trail from the mouth of the Rosebud to Little Bighorn there is a monument approximately 6 to 8 miles up from the mouth which states:

"In 1886, ranchers buried near here what many believe to be the remains of Private Nathan Short, Co. C, 7th U.S. Cavalry, Short was believed to be carrying a message from General Custer at the Battle of the Little Big Horn, 70 miles SW of this point on June 25, 1876. Erected by: The 7th Cavalry Regiment Association and the 1st Cavalry Division Association in cooperation of local residents 1983."

While there are many comments available, from survivors of the battle or eyewitnesses to the remains, there

appears to be no one who can account for why or how the remains of Nathan Short wound up where they did. Nathan Short's role will probably be forever unknown. Whether he was a messenger, escapee or deserter will be a matter for continuing conjecture.

James P. Boyle related to Walter Mason Camp:[286]

"James Boyle heard the Nathan Short story and told me without prompting that he heard he was C Co man. Heard it was on a high hill near the Rosebud."

Walter Mason Camp notes[287]

"Private Nathan Short, C Company whose remains were discovered by White Man Runs Him, a Crow scout, on the divide between the Rosebud and the Yellowstone, in August 1876.

Camp in a letter to Daniel Knipe 11/10/1909 Little Big Horn National Monument:

I have for some time been following up a line of investigation regarding Nathan Short of your Company, and I am beginning to get some results. George Herendeen writes me that the body was found pinned under the horse as though the horse had fallen and the man was too weak to extricate himself. The supposition is, of course, that both the man and the horse had been wounded and that both were so weak when the horse fell that

---

[286]Hardorff, *Camp, Custer and the Little Bighorn*, 79.
[287]Ibid., 80.

neither of them could get up. Herendeen said the Crows found the dead man and the horse near the Rosebud and down near the Yellowstone. He also states that the man had a light colored hat with crossed sabers drawn on the front of it with pen and ink and the number seven between the sabers."

Camp concludes in a letter to Charles Booth.[288]

"It now occurs to me more clearly than before that if there were two finds at about the same time a man and a horse in one place and a horse in another-it would have been an easy matter for the accounts of the two incidents to have become more or less mixed or confused in subsequent recitals."

John C Creighton[289]

"Heard of Nathan Short's white hat with "C 7th" marked on it."

Alfred Dale 3/2/1912[290]

"Saw lots of men who saw Nathan Short's remains and they wanted to know if I was going out with the ambulance to get it. A party went out and buried the remains. Sorrel horse and supposed to be one of Tom Custer's men. Found by flankers of the 20th Infantry on right flank while marching up to meet Crook in August. Was a very warm day and Gen. Otis let his men put baggage on wagon train. Remains were found of both man and horse. The man's whole equipment was with him,

including carbine and was supposed to be one of Tom Custer's men," in foot note below he goes on."[291]

George W. Glenn told Walter Camp, on January 22, 1914:

"On our way up the Rosebud to meet Crook, a cavalryman's hat was found near the Rosebud. I saw the hat. It was a white wool hat, with brass covered sabers and a brass letter 'C'. It was passed around among the men to see if any one could identify the owner of it. I do not recall that there was any report about a dead man or a dead horse being found with it."

Daniel Knipe to Walter Camp in a letter dated July 29, 1908[292]

"...in regard to the dead trooper with his gun and dead horse still lariated to the picket pin [which] was found a few days journey from Custer's Hill. It was not six months before his body was found, but somewhere about three or four weeks. General Crook's command found him, He was over in the Rosebud Country. He was in the direction of about east or southeast [northeast] from the battle field where Custer was found. I knew the man well. His name was Short, I do not remember his given name. He belonged to 'C' Troop, my

---

[288]Ibid., 114.
[289]Ibid., 71.
[290]Ibid., 109.
[291]Hammer, *Men With Custer*, 137.
[292]Ibid., 319.

company. How I came to know it was Short of my company was that he had his stuff numbered 50 and General Crook reported the man's number was 50. He was with the company when I left it, on Reno's Hill."

John Maguire noted about Nathan Short that:

"Heard of Nathan Short. He got good distance toward Rosebud. Had bobtailed horse. Only bobtailed horse in co. Had initials on cartridge belt."[293]

Peter Thompson heard of Nathan Short the C Company carpenter.[294]

"He was found over on the Rosebud. The horse had been mortally wounded and had fallen and pinned the soldier to the ground, who also was supposed to be so badly wounded as not to be able to extricate himself. He had a white hat with crossed sabers and 'C' 7 on the front in black letters on lining of white hat."

Richard E. Thompson, on February 14, 1911, told Walter Camp that:

"He personally saw Nathan Short's horse and carbine but not the body of man. They lay in some brush near Rosebud and Yellowstone, and not at the time it was supposed that this man had escaped from the Custer fight."[295]

Ferdinand Widmayer gave the following story to Walter Camp, on October 7, 1910:

"Saw Nathan Short. Heard that a dead soldier was found and went to see him. Bones of man and horse and carbine were found. Sling belt still on the skeleton. Says was near the Rosebud. Body lay out in open space near some brush but not in brush. No log near the remains. A good many went to see it. Sure this was before met Crook. Sure the bones of a horse also there. Says body had been dead a long time and clothing rotted. If this is correct could not have been Short, but he says the talk at the time was this was supposed to have been one of Custer's men who got away. Says the remains of the man were buried there."[296]

The remains of Nathan Short are a true mystery of the Battle of the Little Bighorn. The how, when and why he reached the point where his remains were found will probably never be answered. He either was a messenger, escapee or deserter from the battlefield. He and/or his horse were wounded at some point in their travels, the horse eventually gave out and collapsed on Short, trapping him between the horse and the ground. Short's death was probably caused by him being too weak to extricate himself from the vise formed by the horse and the ground. He died where and as his remains were found.

It appears highly likely, that the remains of Nathan Short have been confused in the memory of some people, with other finds of human and

---

[293]Ibid., 126.
[294]Ibid., 109.
[295]*Hammer, Custer in '76,* 248.
[296]Ibid., 146.

horse remains. Walter Camp's conclusion that there were at least two finds of remains is most probably correct. It is even quite possible that there were three finds as the stories told do not reduce to one of two possibilities and appear to blend together more information. There is the tale of Short which includes the remains of a man, a horse and a hat with the number 50 inside [this would appear to be an accurate description of Nathan Short, the finding of a hat without the accompanying body of a man and the remains of a horse and a carbine without the remains of a human.] One or more sets of remains were found by the 7th Cavalry, and one set was found by Crook's troops. One set was found three to four weeks after the battle, and one set was found approximately six months after the battle. The distillation of all this is that it appears that the remains of Nathan Short and his horse, with his hat, were found some three to four weeks after the battle by the 7th Cavalry. Some six months after the battle, Crook's troops found the skeleton of a 7th Cavalry horse and a carbine and either in conjunction with these finds, or somewhere in between, a hat by itself was found.

There is sufficient conclusive evidence to state that the remains of Nathan Short and his horse were recovered. The remains of another trooper appears doubtful. One or more other horses and a hat appear to be possible finds. As the second set of horse remains recovered was far too decomposed to have been in the Custer fight, they may well have been the remains of a soldier or deserter from another day.

THE OTHER SURVIVORS

John Brennan and **John Fitzgerald** were in all likelihood deserters, who were open in their admission of their refusal to fight that day. **Peter Thompson** and **Joe Watson** may actually have been legitimate stragglers whose horses did in fact give out. A certain amount of credibility is awarded Thompson, as he was awarded a medal of honor for his actions as a water carrier during the hilltop fight. It is doubted that a man would drop back out of cowardice and then exhibit extreme bravery moments later.

Walter Camp's notes contain:
"I believe that he [Thompson] and Watson actually straggled back from Custer's command, for I have good evidence that neither he nor Watson were with the pack train that day [June 25]. They did not fall out from Custer's command at the lone tepee, but between Reno Hill (where you made the stand two days) and where Custer was killed."[297]

Richard P. Hanley on October 4, 1910 told Walter Camp:
"...that Peter Thompson, John Fitzgerald and John Brennan were not with the packs on 6/25/76 but were with their company and straggled back from Custer after the packs reached the bluff at river. He does not know just when they got back."[298]

---

[297]Hardorff, *Camp, Custer and the Little Bighorn*, 98.
[298]Hammer, *Custer in 76*, 127-128.

"John McGuire says that among C troop it was always the opinion that John Brennan and John Fitzgerald fell back from Custer's 5 troops out of cowardice and in that way did not get into the fight says that they...often joked about it afterward. Was there any particular reason for Thompson and Watson keeping still about their manner of escape? Yes, the company filled up with new men in the fall who would not understand such discussions, and the old men never said much about questions of this kind."[299]

Gustav Korn of L claimed his horse bolted, ran wild, carried him through the village and brought him to Reno Hill. Korn rose to the rank of sergeant, was I Company's farrier and became Comanche's care taker. He was killed at Wounded Knee, and it is said that Comanche died shortly afterwards of a broken heart.

Camp's notes show *"Korn claimed to have rode through village, past skirmish ground, and up the bluffs. Korn told this to Hardy at the time."*[300] *'We saw Korn coming towards us very much excited, his horse foaming at the mouth. Sergt. Delacey, who was in charge of I troop's packs asked him how it was he left the troop: He said his horse ran away with him. His case was investigated and [he] was exonerated afterwards.'"*

Morris Farrar was most likely a deserter. It is claimed he straggled from Custer's column to the hilltop. There is no known explanation for his

presence on the hilltop. His service record indicates he deserted the Army for good on November 21, 1881. For **William Shields of C, William Reese of C, Bernard Lyons of F, John Sweeny of F and Philip Mc Hugh of L,** there appears to be no explanation as to why they were on the hilltop, how they got there and how or why they detached themselves from Custer's battalion... Shields was wounded during the fight.[301]

So much for the fable that "NO OFFICER OR MAN OF 5 COMPANIES LEFT TO TELL THE TALE." The five Crow scouts told varied conflicting versions of the battle and how, when and where they were released by Custer. Knipe was interviewed and wrote letters and articles continually contradicting himself. Thompson wrote a book with incredulous tales in it. Several of the enlisted were interviewed by Walter Mason Camp. Billy Cross was probably not with Custer subsequent to the turn to the right, but he is mentioned here as it has been inferred, by some, that he did ride with Custer. In addition to the 19 men mentioned above John Martin served as Custer's orderly until he was sent back with an order to Benteen.

Other than Martin none of the men listed above testified at the Reno Court of Inquiry. The exclusion of Knipe from the witness list for the Inquiry indicates the Army thought very little of his claim to be a

---

[299]Ibid., 125-126.
[300]Hardorff, *Camp, Custer and the Little Bighorn,* 82.
[301]Hammer, *Men with Custer,* 318.

messenger. The absence of the other 18 suggests they either had spurious reasons for surviving or were believed to have no useful knowledge to share. Perhaps, with the exception of Martin, the headline should have read "ONLY ONE MAN LEFT WITH A CREDULOUS TALE TO TELL, NINETEEN OTHERS WITH INTERESTING FABLES."

CHAPTER 17
The Missing, Mutilated and Dead

"The scene at Custer's battlefield was beyond description, and it filled us with horror and anguish. The dead had been mutilated in the most savage way and they lay as they had fallen, scattered in the wildest confusion over the ground, in groups of two or three, or piled in an indiscriminate mass of men and horses. They had lain thus for nearly three days under the fierce heat of the sun, exposed to swarms of flies, and flesh eating crows, and the scene was rendered even more desolate by the deep silence which seemed to hang like a weird mystery over the battlefield. Custer lay as if asleep but all the other men had been most brutally mangled and stripped of their clothing. Many of their skulls had been crushed in, eyes had been torn from their sockets, and hands, feet, arms, legs and noses had been wrenched off. Many had their flesh cut in strips the entire length of their bodies, and there were others whose limbs were closely perforated with bullets, showing that the wretched victims were still alive." So Major Marcus Reno described the conditions of the dead on the battle field, a few days after the carnage was over.[302]

Daniel Knipe added,
"You could tell what man had been wounded, because the little Indians and the squaws would always, after taking the clothes off the men, shoot them full of arrows or chop them in the faces with tomahawks. They never hurt a dead man, just those what were wounded."[303]

Private Thomas Coleman corroborated this with,
"My Company buried 30 men of E Company the [y] were in line not 10 feet apart the [y] were so disfigured by those female Monsters the squaws that I could not recognize one of them."[304]

Frederic F. Gerard related to Walter Camp that,

---

[302]Hardorff, *The Custer Battle Casualties*, 97.
[303]Graham, *The Custer Myth*, 250.
[304]Liddic, *I Buried Custer The Diary of Pvt. Thomas Coleman 7ᵗʰ US Cavalry*, 124.

"The horror of sight and feeling over the bodies of all these brave men after lying in the hot sun for three days I will not attempt to describe. The eyes of surviving comrades filled with tears, and throats were choked with grief. The stench of the dead men was nauseating.[305]

The carnage on Custer's battlefield, when the burial squads arrived was horrific and beyond the ability of the average individual to describe or comprehend. The Indians, primarily the squaws and youths, performed the most dastardly and disfiguring mutilations imaginable on the wounded. The warriors had counted coup and mutilated the dead.

The majority of the corpses were in advanced stages of decomposition. The parts of the bodies which were exposed to the burning sun for three days had blackened. The parts of the bodies that rested on the ground had swelled and turned reddish from the settlement of blood. The chest and abdominal cavities of the bodies had become swollen and bloated from the expansion of trapped gasses.

Most were so severely mutilated that they were rendered unidentifiable. Bodies were hacked into pieces, there were mass decapitations, heads were mashed flat with clubs and stones eliminating the facial features. The bodies on the field had been a huge buffet for wildlife such as flies, maggots, crows, wolves and coyotes that feed on carrion.

There was neither means of identifying a specific body nor great desire to do so. The stench of the dead was nauseating and the risk of contamination and disease great to the burial details. In some cases there were co-mingled parts of multiple human bodies, in other instances there were co-mingled human and horse remains. Thus for the most part the enlisted were not identified. The remains of only ten officers and four civilians were publicly deemed to be identified as well as positively identified.

HARRINGTON, STURGIS AND PORTER

The bodies of Lieutenants James Porter of I Troop, James Sturgis of E Troop and Henry Harrington were allegedly never recovered.

A true mystery of the Battle of the Little Bighorn is the final disposition of **Second Lieutenant Henry Moore Harrington**, an 1872 graduate of West Point, also field commander of C Troop. His body was neither found nor identified. Could it have been so wretchedly disfigured that it was not recognized, or it is possible that he escaped from the battlefield? The Indians said that a man on a sorrel horse raced back in the direction from which the troops had come, that he was chased a long way by two Cheyennes and a Sioux and was hit between the shoulders and killed. This could either apply to Lieutenant Harrington or Nathan Short.[306] As noted in the text regarding Nathan Short, Walter Mason Camp concludes in a letter to Charles Booth,

---

[305]Hammer, *Custer in 76*, Page 236-237.
[306]Connell, *Son of the Morningstar*, Page 312.

*"It now occurs to me more clearly than before that **if there were two finds at about the same time a man and a horse in one place and a horse in another-it would have been an easy matter for the accounts of the two incidents to have become more or less mixed or confused in subsequent recitals.**"*[307]

It appears from Walter Camp's notes and research that there were in fact two finds of remains. One was the remains of only a 7th Cavalry horse and the second the remains of both a 7th Cavalry horse and a 7th Cavalry trooper. The horse and trooper appear to have been definitely identified as Nathan Short. The horse alone may pertain to Harrington. This many years after the battle and with no definitive information ever being uncovered regarding his final disposition, we must defer to the words of Lieutenant Francis Gibson that no trace of him was ever found.[308] It is quite possible that he was an escapee of the battle who perished elsewhere.

Second Lieutenant James Garland Sturgis, West Point Class of 1875 of M Troop serving with E Troop, was the son of the regiment's commanding officer Colonel Samuel D. Sturgis who was on detached service from the regiment. While there is the quite famous photograph of a freshly dug grave, a soldier kneeling by it, and a cross implanted into it bearing the name Jack Sturgis, his body was allegedly never found, identified or buried. In deference to Colonel Sturgis and his wife the gruesome fate that befell their son was concealed and he was deemed missing. Gibbon's Surgeon Dr. Holmes Paulding recovered the under-clothing of Jack Sturgis, with his spurs.[309] Gibbon wrote, "Some one had picked up a pair of bloody drawers, upon which was plainly written the words, 'Sturgis's 7th Cavalry.'" The most horrid of findings was well hidden from the Sturgis family, when Sturgis' shirt was found, the collar was blood soaked and still buttoned, he had been decapitated. Decapitation was a popular form of mutilation used by the Santee Sioux, the Cheyenne preferred cutting arm flesh to the bone, and removing hairy skin, nose slits were used by the Arapahoes, and throat cutting was used by most Sioux tribes.[310] It is highly probable that he was the "Custer" of Indian narratives was shot at the river. When E Troop began its charge out of Medicine Tail Coulee and reached the river, it is most likely that it was Sturgis who was shot at midstream, and either he or his body was recovered by the Sioux and dragged into the village. This would explain why both Sturgis' body was neither recovered or identified, and some Indians thought Custer was shot at the river. The act of Sturgis being shot and increasing Sioux pressure forced E Troop back to the river bed and then towards Ford C.

---

[307]Hardorff, *Camp, Custer and the Little Bighorn*, 114.
[308]Hardorff, *The Custer Battle Casualties*, 105.
[309]Koury, *Diaries of the Little Bighorn*, 77.
[310]Connell, *Son of the Morningstar*, 161.

First Lieutenant James Ezekiel Porter, West Point class of 1869, field commander of I Troop was the third officer whose body was never identified or buried. With Porter also, there is no doubt what happened to him and how he met his demise. When Dr. Holmes Paulding found Sturgis's underwear, he also noticed Lt. James Porter's buckskin shirt. "Poor fellow, there was a hole under the right shoulder and blood over the rest."[311] Lieutenant Francis Gibson, in a letter to his wife dated July 4, 1876, wrote that - Porter's coat with his name in it was found with a bullet hole through the back.[312] Godfrey's description of Porter's wounds and remains was that he was wearing a buckskin jacket that day, his body was never recovered. Godfrey stated he found Porter's jacket in the village during the course of destroying Indian property. He described the wound as a chest shot entering the rear and exiting the front in the general heart area.[313]

First Lieutenant William Winer Cooke, a Canadian national who served in the Civil War, was the regiment's Adjutant. He was found on the top of the knoll near Custer. Cooke had attracted the attention of the Indians due to the unusual sideburns he wore. Privates Jacob Adams of H Troop and William Slaper of M Troop described Cooke as being scalped and having his sideburns removed.[314] De Rudio, in a February 2, 1910 interview with Walter Mason Camp, added this information about Cooke, "...his thighs were cut open in several places."[315]

Captain Thomas Ward Custer, a two time Medal of Honor winner, was the most horribly disfigured officer. He, too, was found on the top of the knoll near his brother George. He was the commanding officer of C Troop but on June 25, 1876 he was serving as his brother's Aide-de-Camp. His disfigurement was so massive that he could only be identified by a tatoo on his right forearm. His facial features had been mashed into a mush of flesh, blood and gore, while his skull was pounded nearly flat.

Frederic F. Gerard:
"...Tom Custer had the back of his head smashed in with a stone hammer, and an arrow had been shot into the top of his skull. The arrow point had penetrated his brain and it had turned in such a way that it could not be pulled out."[316]

John Ryan:
"His body, when found, lay on its face and hands, and it was terribly mutilated that it was not recognized until I recalled that I had seen the letters T. W. C. on his arms when he was the first lieutenant of my troop. He was split down the center of his body, his throat was cut, his head smashed flat, and he was also split through the muscles of his arms and thighs."[317]

---

[311]Koury, *Diaries of the Little Bighorn*, 77.

[312]Hardorff, *The Custer Battle Caualties*, 105.

[313]Graham, *The Custer Myth*, 347-348.

[314]Hardorff, *The Custer Battle Casualties*, 99-100.

[315]Hammer, *Custer in 76*, 87.

[316]Ibid., 98.

[317]Ibid., 98.

Edward S. Godfrey:

"The identification of Captain Tom Custer was very difficult and would not have been possible except that we finally found the initials T. W. C. on his shattered arm. His whole scalp had been removed, his skull was crushed in, his head and body shot full of arrows, while his abdomen had been slashed which caused the bowels to protrude"[318]

That Tom Custer was so massively disfigured leads to the conclusion he might have been either the last to die or recognized by an old enemy Rain-In-The-Face. If he were the last to die, a great number of Indians might have wanted to count coup on his remains and each who did so added one or more mutilations to the remains, as a final release that the battle was over. Rain-In-The-Face may have exacted a terrible revenge on a dead Tom Custer, for once being imprisoned by a living Tom Custer.

First Lieutenant Algernon E. Smith commanded E Troop. Smith, wearing a buckskin jacket on June 25, 1876,[319] was found on the knoll near Custer. As E Troop figures significantly in the action at Medicine Tail Ford, and he was wearing a buckskin jacket, he may have been the officer wounded there. This would explain why his body was not found in Deep Ravine with the majority of E Troop, but instead on Last Stand Hill. If he were wounded early on, he would have been moved to the hospital area, which would have been located on Last Stand Hill.

Second Lieutenant William Van Wyck Reily, of E Troop, was found at the base of the knoll, his body was riddled with arrows, he was identified by Lieutenant Winfield Scott Edgerly.[320]

Captain George Wilhelmus Mancius Yates, commanding officer of F Troop was found on the base of the knoll. Yates' finger had been cut off to get his ring, per Captain Henry B. Freeman.[321] His gloves were found in the same tepee containing Sturgis' possessions and Porter's jacket, by Dr. Holmes Paulding.[322] This creates the possibility that the belongings of Sturgis and Porter were merely brought into the village and their bodies were left on the field and not identified. This is somewhat likely in Porter's case and unlikely in Sturgis's case. There were multiple possessions of Sturgis, including his bloody underwear found in the village, while only Porter's jacket was found, much like only Yates' gloves. It is possible that Sturgis' head was found as well in the village. This is discussed in the "Three Heads on Poles" discussion in subsequent paragraphs.

Captain Myles Walter Keogh, commanding officer of I Troop was a battalion commander under Custer. Lieutenant Winfield Scott Edgerly noted that "One of the shots that went through Comanche broke Keogh's leg." Captain Edward Luce was more graphic in saying "Keogh's left leg and

[318]Ibid., 99.
[319]Graham, *The Custer Myth,* 345.
[320]Hardorff, *The Custer Battle Casualties,* 34.
[321]Ibid., 100.
[322]Koury, *Diaries of the Little Bighorn,* 77.

knee were badly shattered by a gunshot wound, and Comanche had suffered a severe bone-hit, the bullet entering the right shoulder and emerging from the left, exactly where Keogh's knee would have been if he had been mounted."[323]

First Lieutenant James Calhoun, married to Custer's sister Margaret, commanded L Troop. Edgerly and others stated that his body was not mutilated. There are no known statements to the contrary. These descriptions may be in deference to Victorian sensibilities.

Second Lieutenant John Jordan Crittenden, Twentieth Infantry, was second in command of L Troop. He was described by Edgerly as having numerous arrows sticking in his body.

Dr. George Edwin Lord, Assistant Surgeon, was identified by Colonel Richard E. Thompson in a February 14, 1911 interview with Walter Mason Camp as, "He lay 20 ft. Southeast of Custer's body on side hill. Lord had on a blue shirt and lay near Custer."[324] Dr. Lord's surgical case was found in the village, as related by DeRudio in 1910.[325]

Boston Custer, George and Tom's younger brother, was found fully clothed alongside the fully clothed body of **Armstrong Reed**, the nephew of the Custer brothers. They were 100 yards southwest of the Custer group on the knoll. Boston was shot several times and was somewhat mutilated. Autie Reed was shot in the body and did not appear mutilated.[326]

Mitch Boyer, the half-breed scout, was found near the river, badly mutilated. A recovered skull has since been forensically identified to pictures of him.

Mark Kellogg's body was found by Colonel John Gibbon. His description of finding Kellogg, was: "We proceeded up the valley, now an open grassy slope, we suddenly came upon a body lying in the grass. It was lying upon its back, and was in an advanced state of decomposition. It was not stripped, but had evidently been scalped and one ear cut off. The clothing was not that of a soldier, and, with the idea of identifying the remains, I caused one of the boots to be cut off and the stocking and drawers examined for a name, but none could be found. On looking at the boot, however, a curious construction was observed. The heel of the boot was reinforced by a piece of leather which in front terminated in two straps, one of which was furnished with a buckle, evidently for the purpose of tightening the instep of the boot. This led to the identification of the remains, for on being carried to camp the boot was recognized as belonging to Mr. Kellogg, a newspaper correspondent who accompanied General Custer's column."[327]

As the officers and civilians of Custer's column are thus described, as

---

[323]Hardorff, *The Custer Battle Casualties*, 102.
[324]Hammer, *Custer in 76*, 248.
[325]Ibid., 87.
[326]Hardorff, *The Custer Battle Casualties*, 121-122.
[327]Gibbon, *Gibbon on the Great Sioux Campaign of 1876*, 39.

being found in the most ghastly of condition, it is no wonder that so many of the enlisted could not be identified. The severity of the mutilations increased in direct proportion to the body's proximity to the village. Reno's troops were severely mutilated as were Custer's. Those with Calhoun and Keogh were still mutilated, but to a lesser degree. The Calhoun and Keogh mutilations appeared to be mainly the handiwork of the warriors who did not have time to complete the job, as they had to move on to Custer. While Custer's dead fell victim to both the warriors, the squaws and the young. Some examples of the mutilations to enlisted men are:

Corporal John Briody of F Troop
"had his right leg cut off and laid under his head. The supposition was that he was trying to get to Reno's command. Briody had one of the fastest horses in the troop," as per James Rooney to Walter Camp, July 19, 1909.[328]

Private James M. Rooney, related that:
"William Brown and his horse lay dead in the village. Brown's body lay about 250 yards from the river and his horse farther. They lay opposite Deep Ravine."[329]

Godfrey stated that
"Sergeant Butler was not entirely stripped; but he had several wounds and was scalped and otherwise mutilated."[330]

Private Henry Petring said that
"Trumpeter Henry Dose, orderly

for Custer on June 25, 1876, was found halfway between Custer and Reno with arrows in his back and sides."[331]

Thomas L Tweed of L troop
"had his crotch split with an ax and one of his legs was thrown over his shoulder. He was shot with arrows in both eyes. A wounded horse lay near him still groaning which we knocked in the head with a bloody ax", as per Private George W. Glenn.[332]

THREE HEADS ON POLES

Approaching the center of this huge encampment, the advance guard discovered three poles standing upright in a triangle each covered by an inverted camp kettle. Reno related a "ghastly find" as three lodge poles in the form of a triangle "on top of each were inverted camp kettles while below them, on the grass, were the heads of three men whom I recognized as belonging to my command. These heads had been severed from their trunks by some very sharp instrument, as the flesh was smoothly cut, and they were placed within the triangle, facing one another in a horrible sightless stare."[333]

Further investigation revealed that the kettles were inverted over the decapitated heads of Troopers John McGinnis, John Armstrong and

---

[328]Hardorff, *The Custer Battle Casualties*, 108.
[329]Ibid., 109.
[330]Ibid., 110.
[331]Ibid., 111.
[332]Ibid., 116.
[333]Connell, *Son of the Morningstar*, 317.

an unknown, facing each other in an endless stare. On the river bank lay another soldier his facial features obliterated, making identification impossible.[334] Henry Jones claimed John Armstong's headless body was found closest to that of Isaiah Dorman's and his head found in the lower part of the village. William Nugent said Armstrong's head was found on a pole.[335] John McGinnis, of G troop, lost control of his horse and it bolted into the village. His head was later found in the village, as one of the three heads on poles. Corporal John E. Hammon and Private James P. Boyle both identified McGinnis' head on one of the poles.[336]

Lt. Porter commanded I troop, Lt. Sturgis was with E troop, and Lt. Harrington commanded C troop. Two of these officer's three troops figure prominently in the battle tales of Medicine Tail Ford, and their bodies are the ones which were never found or positively identified. Sturgis's clothing, underwear and shirt was found in the village. His shirt collar was blood soaked and still buttoned - graphically indicating his fate. Porter's Buckskin jacket was found in the village with a bullet hole in the back over the heart area.

The three heads, allegedly unidentifiable, were found charred and hanging from poles. Two of the heads were identified as belonging to Troopers Armstrong of A Troop and John McGinnis of M Troop. The third head was believed to be that of Jack Sturgis, but this could not be admitted as it would have devastated his parents, so the third head officially

became unidentified. Another head was found under a camp kettle and was identified as a Corporal from G Troop, either Otto Hagermann or James Martin.

At least Sturgis and possibly Porter were among the captives who were dismembered and burned to provide the entertainment at the post battle festivities. What remained of their bodies were either consumed by the fires or thrown into the river. Hopefully, they were all long dead before their capture and being brought to the village.

CUSTER

With the mutilations of the officers, civilians and enlisted described so graphically, telling the story of mutilations, it is incredulous to conceive that Custer was untouched as Bradley and others stated:

"His expression was rather that of a man who had fallen asleep and enjoyed peaceful dreams, than one who had met his death amid such fearful scenes as the field witnessed, the features being wholly without ghastliness or any impression of fear, horror, or despair."[337]

but closer to Godfrey's description of:
"General Custer was stripped with the exception of his sox. He had a gunshot wound in his head

---

[334]Hardorff, *The Custer Battle Casualties*, 16.
[335]Hammer, *Men with Custer*, 7.
[336]Hardorff, *The Custer Battle Casualties*, 140.
[337]Bradley, *The March of the Montana Column*, 173.

and another in his side, and in his left thigh, there was a gash about eleven inches long that exposed bone. Custer was not scalped nor otherwise mutilated, and I am sure that he did not commit suicide...There were no powder burns on Custer's face and, in those days of black powder, it would have been next to impossible for a man to hold a gun far enough away from his face to escape such burns when committing suicide."[338]

Sergeant Ryan is quoted, in an undated note in the Walter Camp papers, of saying:

"Under Custer's body lay some empty shells of special make from his carbine."[339]

Such a reference would pertain to the unique 50 caliber brass shells for ammunition used in Custer's Remington Sporting Rifle with an octagonal shaped barrel. He was the only person in the command to have such a weapon, and it required unique ammunition. This would indicate that Custer was alive and capable of fighting, at least part of the time, while he was on Last Stand Hill.

If a composite is created from all the descriptions of Custer's wounds and the mutilations inflicted, his remains would have appeared this way:

Custer was found in a half sitting, half lying position, the lower half of his body reddened from the settling of his blood, the upper half blackened from decomposition and exposure to the sun, the body severely bloated and infested with flies and other vermin. The body exhibited the following wounds and mutilations:

- A head wound behind the temple that bled, entering on the left side and exiting on the right side, probably the fatal wound
- A chest wound on the left side that did not bleed, probably non fatal and inflicted postmortem
- A gash or bullet wound on the right forearm
- A gash in the left thigh from 6 to 11 inches long down to the bone
- An arrow in his penis
- He was not scalped as his receding hair line made the scalp undesirable
- He was completely stripped except that his socks were still on

CUSTER'S BULLET WOUNDS

John Hammond, who signed Custer's death certificate, said there were three bullet holes found on his person, one on the left under the heart, one in the left side of the head in the ear, one in the right forearm.[340]

Dr. Henry Porter took locks of hair of all the officers. His description of Custer's wounds tallies with Hammon's.[341]

---

[338]Hardorff, *The Custer Battle Casualties*, 19.
[339]Hardorff, *On The Little Bighorn With Walter Camp*, 182.
[340]Hardorff, *The Custer Battle Casualties*, 27.
[341]Ibid., 28.

Ryan adds to the confusion,

"...*one bullet having struck him in the right side of his face and passing through to the other side, the other in his right side of his body, passing through to the left side, and which I understood at the time, one of the soldiers took from his body.*" Ryan's participation in Custer's burial is in dispute.[342]

Hardoff summarized the condition of the body as,

"*One bullet crashed into the left temple, halfway between the ear and the eye, while the second projectile had entered the rib case just below the heart. A number of eyewitnesses indicated that the bullet in the head had traveled through either both temples or both ears. However, considering the impact of the projectile, the pressure might well have bursted the eardrums, causing drainage to ooze through both ear passages. This drainage, and according to Jacob Adams, that from the right temple wound, oozed down the face and right arm, its crust probably being mistaken by John Hammon for the third bullet wound.*"

Custer's body was found in a sitting position, therefore his head was higher than his heart, for this wound to have bled it had to occur first, otherwise there would not have been any seepage found. If it was a postmortem wound it would not have bled at all due to the position of the body and the wound. The chest wound did not bleed and there is no known description of it, as being bloody. Therefore, this was definitely a post-mortem wound likely occurring when the Indians were seen shooting into the dead and wounded on the ground. The head wound based upon descriptions of it, had to be instantaneously fatal.

THE WOUND IN CUSTER'S RIGHT FOREARM

The arm wound was mentioned by Corporal John E. Hammon of G troop. He was the one who signed Custer's insurance papers as a witness to his death. This is from an 1898 deposition to Charles De Land.

"*His left hand was lying natural, his right lay out at right angles from the body at full length, the hand twisted as if something had been wrenched out of it. There was a dead soldier lying under the calf of his right leg alongside a dead horse. Three bullet holes were found on his person: one in the left under the heart in the ribs; one in the left side of the head in the ear; the other in the right forearm. He was not scalped or mutilated a particle.*"[343]

THE GASH IN CUSTER'S LEFT THIGH

Jacob Adams described Custer's wound as an eleven inch gash in the left thigh, no powder burns, gunshot wounds to the head and breast, the

---

[342]Ibid., 25.
[343]Ibid., 27.

wound in the temple bled and trickled down his face, the other wounds did not bleed. Jacob Adams said,

"General Custer was stripped with the exception of his sox. He had a gunshot wound in his head and another in his side, and in his left thigh there was a gash about eleven inches long that exposed the bone."[344]

Adams later said in a letter to Godfrey,

"...he had two wounds-one in the right temple and one in the right breast and a knife wound about 6 inches long in the thigh. I think the wound in the temple killed him as it had bled and run down his face, and the other wounds had not bled any..."[345]

THE OTHER MUTILATIONS TO CUSTER'S BODY

Godfrey in an interview with his friend Colonel Charles F. Bates adds the disclosure of the genitals being mutilated by an arrow which had been forced up his penis.[346] This was a mutilation that was kept secret during Mrs. Custer's lifetime.

Hardorff described Custer's remains in this manner,

"The mutilation of Custer's corpse was nihil. In addition to the disfigurement of the genitals, the left thigh had received a knife slash which exposed the bone. No other signs of mutilation were found on the body. It should be noted further that the top of the corpse had turned black from exposure to the sun, while the bottom parts had reddened by the settlement of blood. Both the chest and stomach cavities were bloated from the expansion of trapped gasses. Decomposition had set in, while the maceration was accelerated by the myriad of flies attracted by the fetid odor. Thus was the sight beheld of Custer, whose face failed to reflect any inner turmoil."[347]

It was the Victorian Era, a period of time that stressed chivalry and honor. The survivors and rescuers all modified their versions of the condition of the dead, especially Custer to protect the feelings of Mrs. Custer and the other widows and relatives of the deceased. The reason most stories do not correlate is that they were either sugar coated or omitted details, in the name of propriety, thereby bearing little semblance to the horror that in reality was known as Custer Battlefield.

The reinterments were done under the supervision of Captain Michael Sheridan. His philosophy is summed up by the following paragraph:

"There was a dispute about the remains of Custer as to whether the bones were Custer's. The first two sets of bones were taken from the box and the third put in."

Michael Sheridan, a brother of Gen. Sheridan, who was detailed to go

---

344Ibid., 19.
345Ibid., 20.
346Ibid., 21.
347Ibid., 31.

with Captain Nowlan, made the remark: *"Nail the box up; it is alright as long as the people think so."*[348] The locks of hair of the officers, that were sent to the relatives, to prove identification of the deceased, were most likely the locks of hair that Dr. Porter removed from the bodies the year before. Perhaps Dr. Porter anticipated that the remains would not be identifiable in a year and the Army would require something to comfort the relatives and friends of the 7th Cavalry's gallant dead.

It must be assumed that if this was the lack of concern that Michael Sheridan exhibited for Custer's remains, that far less was exhibited for the other officers and nil for the enlisted. It is doubted that anything of historical value can be gleaned from the location of the markers that Sheridan supposedly put in place and unlikely that many of the officers' bodies, as recovered by him, were correctly identified.

CUSTER'S WEAPONS

According to Godfrey: "General Custer carried a Remington Sporting rifle, octagonal barrel; **two Bulldog self-cocking, English, white handled pistols, with a ring in the butt for a lanyard**; a hunting knife, in a beaded fringed scabbard; and a canvas cartridge belt."[349] While Godfrey appears correct about the rifle, as shells for this weapon were recovered under Custer's body, as noted elsewhere herein, and there is nothing to refute the knife or state what kind of knife it was, he is totally incorrect about the pistols. As none of the weapons were ever recovered, all that exists to support their physical existence is the forensic evidence of the rifle shells. The British Bulldog revolvers, to which Godfrey alludes, could not have been in Custer's possession, at the battle, because Webley did not introduce this style of pistol until 1878.

"The earliest Bulldog revolvers were designed, produced and marketed by the Birmingham firm of P. Webley and Son. Although a few were adopted for the military or police use, the great bulk of them were sold on the civilian market, as house or self-defence weapons, in the period 1878 to 1914."[350]

"The period of production of 'The British Bulldog,' as this pocket revolver is called, was from 1878 to 1914."[351]

Even if the "The Webley Bulldog were available in 1876, it is highly doubted that Custer would have carried it for Indian fighting as it is a puny 5.5 inch weapon with a 2.1 inch barrel, holding either five rounds of 32 or 38 caliber ammunition and weighing 11 ounces. See page 144 for a picture of two - 38 caliber British Bulldogs from the author's collection.

The appropriate question, now, is what type of pistols could Custer have carried, as the Bulldog is eliminated as a possibility. Custer did own: "A pair

---

[348]Ibid., 46.
[349]Graham, *The Custer Myth*, 345.
[350]Myatt, *The Illustrated Encyclopedia of Pistols and Revolvers*, 118.
[351]Dowell, *The Webley Story*, 68.

of superb No. 2 [Colt] 32 calibre revolvers presented to him by J. B Sutherland in 1869. Finely engraved and fitted with pearl grips, they were much prized by the General."[352] Though these guns match Godfrey's description of having white handles and being a pair, they could not be the guns he carried as Custer left these behind and they exist today.

Though it is not known if Custer owned one of these pistols, there are two likely candidates for the pistol(s) he could have carried. The first is the 1867 Webley, which in 1868 was adopted for use by the Royal Irish Constabulary and became known as the R.I.C. model and remained in production until the early 1900's.[353] This pistol was 9.25 inches long, with 4.5 inch barrel, double action, held six rounds of 45 caliber ammunition, had a lanyard ring and weighed a hefty 30 ounces.[354] It was very suited for Indian fighting. See page 144 for a picture of an early model R.I.C. in the author's collection.

The second and more likely candidate is the Belgium made modification of the R.I.C. known as the "Frontier Bulldog." It was 9.5 inches long, with a 4.5 inch barrel, double action, held 6 rounds of Winchester 44 caliber ammunition, had a lanyard ring, and weighed 31 ounces. It was stamped "Frontier Bulldog" along the head strap. See page 144 for a picture of an 1875 model of the "Frontier Bulldog," in the author's collection.

As Godfrey gave his description of Custer's weapons on January 16, 1896, it is quite possible that his memory had blurred a bit and created a composite weapon that never existed in reality. Perhaps he had a vivid memory of the white handles of the Colts and placed them on either an R.I.C., or a "Frontier Bulldog." The most reasonable scenario is that the white handles wound up on a "Frontier Bulldog," the only weapon that fits all criteria of Godfrey's description except the color of the handles, which easily could have been a post manufacturing change or addition.

COMANCHE THE SOLE SURVIVOR?

One of the more popular legends of the Battle of the Little Bighorn is that Myles Keogh's horse Comanche was the sole survivor. This appears to be refuted by the Journal of Sergeant Alexander Brown of Troop G of the 7th Cavalry. In the Journal Sergeant Brown notes that 23 horses were killed in the battle and 25 were abandoned on the field.[355] He gives this list of the horses killed: Puff (Lt. McIntosh's), Goat (Sergeant Botzen's), Wild Bill (Turner Wells'), Gray (Trumpeter Dore's), Considine Bay, Martin, Hagemann, Moore, Small (Horse shot by the rear guard), Stanley, McGonigle (Horse shot on the 29th June), Beafferman, Rogers, Rapp, Lattmann Bay, Goldin, McCormick, Selly, Loyd, Weiss, Robb, O Neill, Taylor, Sevenson, and Johnson. Sergeant Brown fails, however, to name the 25 horses

[352]Rosa, *Guns of the American West*, 117, with a picture of the guns.
[353]Dowell, *The Webley Story*, 62.
[354]Myatt, *The Illustrated Encyclopedia of Pistols and Revolvers*, 124.
[355]Koury, *Diaries of the Little Bighorn*, 38.

abandoned on the field which we must assume were wounded and beyond treatment. This intimates that the number of survivors, at least among livestock, was far more than one.

CHAPTER 18
The "Ammunition Enigma"

It is incredulous to believe that the combined Reno/Benteen force engaged in a prolonged fight with the Indians for the two days it is alleged they were under siege. It is much more likely that the Reno/Benteen force was pinned down by a relatively few warriors who took pot shots at them and not by the overwhelming number of Indians who annihilated Custer. It was instead Reno's and Benteen's total unwillingness to engage in battle that kept two thirds of the vaunted Seventh Cavalry trapped for two days. To the extent they were engaged by Indians, the pressure came from their front and part of their flanks. There is no doubt there were Indians in their front coming from the valley, the west. There was sniping fire from the north and northwest, coming from Sharpshooter's ridge. There were Indian positions to the south and southwest. There were, however, no reports of warrior positions to the northeast, east and southeast.

Indians were not siege fighters, they were individual fighters who occasionally banded together. They did not engage as a fighting force in an organized siege of a specific position.

Custer described the Indians ability to attack fortified positions, in his autobiography, as:

"This successful defence against the Indians was in great measure due to the presence of the wagons, which, arranged in the order described, formed a complete barrier to the charges and assaults of the savages; and, as a last resort, the wagons could have been halted and used as a breastwork, behind which the cavalry, dismounted, would have been almost invincible against their more numerous enemies. **There is nothing an Indian dislikes more in warfare than to attack a foe, however weak, behind breastworks of any kind. Any contrivance which is an obstacle to his pony is a most serious obstacle to the warrior."**[356]

---

[356]Custer, *My Life On The Plains*, 166.

There was no grand charge. The terrain around the Reno/Benteen position did not allow for large numbers of an opposing force to attack the fortified defenders. There are no stories of large bands of Indians fording the river and attacking the defenders in mass numbers. No, it is quite evident that the Reno/Benteen defenders were merely surrounded by isolated bands of "good shooters" who attempted and succeeded in pinning them down with sniping fire. It is logical then to conclude that Reno could have broken off the engagement whenever he desired, just as Crook did.

This theory is easily proved by what can be called the "ammunition enigma." Seventh Cavalry Soldiers received a specified supply of ammunition for the campaign. Each Officer and Trooper was issued 25 rounds of revolver cartridges and 100 rounds of ammunition per carbine, of which 50 rounds of carbine ammunition was kept on the trooper's person and 50 rounds in his saddle bags. In addition the regiment carried 25,000 extra rounds in the pack train. Thus, the ammunition available to the Seventh Cavalry was in the range of 105,000 to 110,000 rounds. This is a large amount for soldiers who were well trained to shoot straight, using single shot carbines, but the 7th Cavalry troopers were poorly trained, if at all. An average trooper was trained to fire one shot every six seconds from his carbine, approximately ten rounds per minute. The poorly trained 7th exhibited little fire control on June 25, 1876, and

consumed its ammunition at a much higher rate.

In most battles, of any duration, soldiers of the period quickly expended their personal allotment of ammunition.[357] This was demonstrated in both the Reno valley fight and Crook's Battle of the Rosebud. The Battle of the Rosebud is most aptly described by Robert M. Utely as: "The conflict raged back and forth across the valley throughout the afternoon, but the Sioux finally abandoned the field. Crook had used up his ammunition and had also discovered that there were a lot more warriors than anyone dreamed. He therefore pulled back to his supply base on Goose Creek, near the present city of Sheridan, Wyoming."[358] Crook had approximately 1100 men under his command, if each were issued the same 125 rounds of ammunition as the 7th Cavalry, his expedition had approximately 137,500 rounds on the soldiers' persons and a reserve, estimated at 25,000 to 50,000 rounds. Crook's force used up its ammunition in a six hour battle with 1,500 Indians.

Reno's charge into the Sioux village was much more short lived, it commenced approximately 3:00 PM and ended approximately 4:00 PM when Reno reached siege hill. Based upon testimony at the Reno Court of

---

[357]Custer was well aware of this fact and that is why he requested the packs be brought up on sighting the village and before he ever engaged the Indians. He knew the ammunition carried by the command would only last 20 to 30 minutes under intense battle conditions.
[358]Utley, *Custer and The Great Controversy*, 22.

Inquiry and various time motion studies, it appears that Reno deployed to a skirmish line approximately 3:20 PM and commenced his retreat by 3:45 PM. This equates to approximately 25 minutes for actual fighting time, fifteen minutes on the skirmish line and ten minutes in the timber. When Benteen's column arrived on siege hill by 4:10 PM he found Reno's troops virtually devoid of ammunition. Reno's command consisted of 11 Officers and 140 Enlisted Men, each allotted 125 rounds of ammunition, or 18,875 rounds in the aggregate. Virtually this entire supply of ammunition was entirely expended in a rather light fire fight, with poor fire control, lasting 15 to 20 minutes. Some of this ammunition was either lost or abandoned to the Indians during the rout.

The mathematics of this scenario is analyzed quite easily. The average trooper was trained to fire one round every six seconds from a carbine and six rounds per minute from a revolver. There were minimal losses until the rout commenced. It can be assumed that 130 men on the skirmish line might have dispensed approximately 11,700 rounds [130 x 6 x 15 = 11,700] of carbine ammunition, from an available supply of 13,000 rounds. This constitutes a fair estimate of the rate of consumption of ammunition of Reno's Battalion, on the skirmish line, considering the fire control was very lax and the shooting wild. With approximately 30 horses lost in the rout, it can be assumed that the saddle bag ammunition of 50 rounds of carbine and 25 rounds of revolver ammunition, per horse, was lost, too.

Another 2250 rounds in the aggregate was lost in the saddle bags. The remaining 110 men wildly fired their revolvers during the rout consuming another 660 rounds. All together, during the valley fight and rout, Reno's battalion may have consumed or lost approximately 16,000 rounds of combined carbine and revolver ammunition. On the hill, more shots were fired, leaving very little of the possible 2,875 rounds, that could have remained, available, by the time Benteen and his battalion arrived.

When Benteen's Battalion was combined with Reno's survivors and the troops guarding the pack train, the aggregate force consisted of approximately 15 Officers and 330 enlisted men who would have had approximately 33,000 rounds of ammunition on their persons[359] and saddle bags, plus the 25,000 rounds of extra ammunition in the pack train, or an aggregate of approximately 58,000 rounds available. Assuming the same rate of fire for Reno's column during the "charge, valley fight and rout," 330 soldiers could have expended 2,640 rounds per minute. This could allow the remaining 58,000 rounds to last a mere 20 to 30 minutes. The simple and inescapable question arises, "How were the combined survivors able to

---

[359]Benteen's column contained 129 officers and men and McDougal had 111 officers, men civilians with the pack train. They had not yet fired a shot. This force of approximately 240 men had their 125 rounds intact, or 30,000 in the aggregate. It may be assumed that Reno's surviving 110 men had 25 rounds left each, or approximately 3,000 rounds, in total. The total combined force, thus, had 33,000 rounds of ammunition.

sustain an *intense* fire fight for two days with only enough ammunition for 30 minutes intense firing?"

It is accepted that Reno departed for Weir Point by 6:30 P.M. and had not been engaged since achieving the hill. It is fair to assume that his force returned to and was entrenched by 7:30 P.M. on the hill. Sundown was approximately 9:30 P.M. on June 25, 1876. There was a light exchange of fire at long range, for perhaps two hours, until sundown, and then nothing. The firing commenced at sun rise and continued until late morning. Again the firing was light and at long range, most of it done with judicious fire control by sharpshooters. By noon all that remained of the Indian force was a small group of sharpshooters giving rear guard covering fire as the village prepared to withdraw. The village commenced withdrawing at 3 P.M. on June 26, 1876, with a small group of warriors left behind to cover the withdrawal. From 3 P.M. on June 26, 1876, until Gibbon's arrival approximately midday of June 27, 1876, Reno was neither engaged, under siege nor on the offensive.

It is an irrefutable fact that from the time the village withdrew, until Gibbon's arrival Reno did absolutely nothing offensively, made no attempt to find Custer, was not under siege and was not engaged by the Indians. He made no effort to find Custer, which he was under a military duty to do. An officer is under a duty to report to his commanding officer as soon as possible after the completion of his mission. When Terry and Gibbon arrived, the 7th Cavalry had ample ammunition for its troops, as there were no reports of the 7th asking for or receiving any ammunition from Gibbon's force. It would appear that Reno was not under intense attack by large numbers of warriors, but merely harried and pestered by small scattered bands, and this stopped by mid afternoon of the 26th. He could have made a movement east any time he wanted to and was free to move in whatever direction he chose from 3 P.M. of June 26, 1876, but instead the drunken coward chose to do nothing and waited on the hill to be rescued!

CHAPTER 19
Custer's Performance

One of the more significant challenges put towards Custer's performance at the Little Bighorn is: whether or not he should have accepted the offer of the four troops of the Second Cavalry to accompany his column, which he had refused. Custer believed the Seventh Cavalry was capable of defeating any foe it might encounter, by itself. This was based upon the intelligence estimates available of 800 to 1500 warriors being anticipated in the area and Sheridan's theory of invincibility. Major Brisbin claimed he had previously informed Custer of the possibility of 3,000 warriors being in the area, and...he should use caution. Terry and Custer knew the approximate number of Indians actually massed exceeded the estimates based upon Gibbon's observations and Reno's scout. Terry and Custer both believed that the Seventh Cavalry could handle anything it might encounter, by itself. This was in part due to Sheridan's pronouncements that any of the three forces could handle any number of Indians, as they would not stand and fight, but instead scatter and run.

The strategy for the Little Bighorn Campaign was constructed on the night of June 21, 1876 aboard the steamer Far West. In attendance were most of the ranking officers from Gibbon's and Custer's columns, including: Terry, Gibbon, Brisbin, Custer, Reno, and Benteen.

It was at this strategy session that Major James S. Brisbin, commanding officer of the Second Cavalry troops with the Montana Column, initiated the idea of combining the cavalry forces into one unit and proposed it to General Terry. When Brisbin put the proposal to Terry he did add one very strong qualification, that Terry only combine the cavalry units if Terry rode with them in command, as Brisbin feared and distrusted Custer. The entire conversation was restated by Brisbin in a letter to General E. S. Godfrey dated January 1, 1892.[360] According to Brisbin the conversation was:[361]

---

[360]Brininstool, *Troopers With Custer*, 275-286.
[361]Ibid., 278-279.

I said to Terry: *"Why not put my cavalry with Custer's and go yourself in command?"* He replied: *"Custer is smarting under the rebuke of the President, and wants an independent command, and I wish to give him a chance to do something."* Terry seemed troubled , and asked: *"Don't you think Custer's regiment can handle them?"* *"No,"* I said, *"there is enough for all of us-possibly Custer can whip them with the 7th Cavalry, but what is the use in taking any chances? Put all the cavalry together, and go yourself in command of it."* He said, *"I have had but little experience in Indian fighting, and Custer has had much, and is sure he can whip anything he meets."* *"General,"* I said, *"You underrate your own ability and overrate Custer's."* He laughed and said, *"I'll tell you what you may do; go to Custer and offer your cavalry, and if he says 'No', we will put the Montana Battalion of the 2nd and the 7th together."*

"And you will go in command of the combined force?" I inquired. He hesitated and seemed to be thinking, turning the matter over and over in his mind. Seeing that he did not reply, and fearing he might send me with Custer, I made haste to say: *"You will pardon me, General, if I speak plainly, but my affection and respect for you, as well as the care of the lives of my men and officers, always prompts me to do so in perilous times."* He said, *" I thank you, and you may always speak plainly to me, as it gives no offense to have my officers frank with me."* *"Then,"* said I, *"if I go with Custer, I want you to go in command, or not to send me and my battalion."*

"Well, speak to him anyway about going with him, if you like, and see what he says." *"And if he thinks well of it, and the columns are united, you will go in command of both?"* I said. *"Yes, I will,"* he replied.

This was how Custer came to be offered the battalion of the 2nd Cavalry.

In the evening he came on the boat, and was on the front deck, talking to John Carland, 6th Infantry, when Brisbin went up to him and said: *"General, do you feel quite strong enough with your 7th Cavalry to handle all the Indians you may meet? If not, myself and officers will be most happy to take service with you."*

He replied quite briskly, *"The 7th can handle anything it meets."*

I was glad to hear him say so, and turned on my heel and went away at once. After I had gone, as Carland told me after Custer's death, the General said, *"That was very clever in Brisbin to offer to go with me, but you know, Carland, this is to be a 7th Cavalry battle, and I want all the glory for the 7th Cavalry there is in it."*

Clearly Brisbin was a conniving officer who put his ego first. He couched the offer in such a way that it appeared neither real nor necessary, and Custer would naturally refuse it. Brisbin asked Custer if he thought he could handle all the Indians he might meet, not telling him there were probably 3,000 warriors on the loose. Of course, Custer would answer without knowing the true size of the opposition, he could handle what he would meet. This method of asking and the answer derived, got Brisbin off the hook of possibly serving under Custer, who he did not care for. Custer may have feared that the adding of the Second Cavalry troops to his Seventh Cavalry would effectively eliminate the offensive capabilities of the Montana Column, and Terry would be forced to totally combine the two columns. Custer would then lose his independent command.

Brisbin also stated in his letter that the Gibbon column had scouted a large Indian camp some seven miles long, containing 5,000 Indians of which 3,000 were fighting men, and that he personally made Custer aware of these facts: "All this Custer knew, for I told him all about it and cautioned him to be careful."[362] Yet he does not relate the substance of the conversation, though he remembers everything else so well. Custer was correct in foregoing the offer of the Second Cavalry troops as he rightly believed the Seventh Cavalry could handle anything it came up against. Of course, Custer predicated his premise on the concept he had junior officers who would follow orders when the need arose. The real benefit that Custer might have gained if he accepted the offer of the Second Cavalry troops was the addition to his staff of an officer who would follow orders and not be afraid to engage the enemy.

Until the latter part of 1878 the basic course and conduct of the battle was known and rather openly discussed and written about. Reno was viewed as the shame of the 7th by his contemporaries and was besmirched both behind his back and to his face. His actions at the Battle of the Little Bighorn supplied many a sutler's store with an evening full of good jokes. Reno was inspired by elements both within the Army and outside to seek an Inquiry to "clear his name." These groups needed a scapegoat to blame for the disaster and it is well established that dead men make the best targets. The Inquiry of 1879 was the first major effort to rewrite the history of the battle and white wash its sordid events. The Maguire Maps had been edited and redrawn in September, 1876, pursuant to the orders of Major George Elliott. The officers who testified apparently suffered from temporary loss of memory. The methodology for recording the testimony was near comical. Numerous scribes quit, as they could not keep up with the testimony. There were days when no notes were taken as there was no scribe available, so newspaper columns were inserted into the official record. Lastly, there were days when the testimony was not

---

[362]Ibid., 278.

recorded at all. From these shambles came an "official record" that generations would labor over trying to determine fact from fiction.

Edward Settle Godfrey, with one gallant sweep of his memory eraser, removed what little remained of the true story of the battle and Custer's movements. He based his revised thinking on an 1886 conversation he had with Gall at the battlefield. As was noted elsewhere, Indians only knew what they saw, and Gall was a late comer to the battle as he had been involved with the Reno fight. When Gall arrived at the scene, Custer had already made his assault down Medicine Tail Coulee and was now in retreat. Gall never saw the attack only the retreat, so he believed what he said when he told Godfrey that Custer never got to the river. Why Godfrey would base his whole theory on this one, out of context, unsubstantiated, uncorroborated conversation is quite suspect.

It has taken over 100 years to correct the damage Godfrey caused and to recreate the historical record he erased. In his 1892 Century Magazine article, he presented a map which showed that Custer's route from Reno Hill to Last Stand Hill was "unknown." Far too many subsequent historians bought into this nonsense, with gusto. Many of the writings, thereafter, all echoed the same theme that Custer's route to Last Stand Hill was unknown, and he never got near the river. It was never unknown to the Indians who won the battle, or to all the soldiers who followed Custer's trail days after the battle. The story

was told by where the dead fell and were found. It was told by the colors of the dead horses and their location on the field. It was told by the litter and debris that remained on the field after the battle and found in the village afterwards. It is as much nonsense that the Indians took everything of value, as Custer died with a smile on his face.

The battlefield fire of 1984 opened up areas to archeological study that were heretofore prohibited. The so called revelations of these archeological studies provided no new information, but merely a redirection of the story back to the true facts which were known prior to 1879. The archeological discoveries, when overlaid on the primary source material available from prior to 1879, tell almost the entire story. It isn't pretty, it is contrary to most twentieth century writings and it finally corrects the lies told at the Inquiry and the fog created by Godfrey's giant memory eraser.

The question then arises, after recreating the data lost by Godfrey and others, what did Custer do and what was the flow of the battle? If primary sources exist which relate the story, do they allow us to piece together the flow of the battle? These primary sources do exist, they are the narratives of the Indians who fought and prevailed against Custer. As previously noted, some Indians, when telling a story, only relate the part of the story that involved them or what they saw. The sequence of events, whether chronological or geographical, seem insignificant. The only recourse is to take the various Indian statements, identify the significant point or points within their statements and then put the statements in chronological and geographical order. After this is accomplished, the story of Custer's last battle becomes:

Custer descended Medicine Tail Coulee with the intent to ford and attack there. Part of the way down, he came under fire from Indians on the bluffs on the east of the coulee. He dismounted as skirmishers of one platoon of C Troop on the Lower part of Calhoun Ridge to handle this opposition and to cover his intended crossing. When he reached the river bank, he found the opposition too strong to ford there, so he turned right, heading towards Ford C. The Sioux crossed at Ford B, splitting his column, driving F Troop back up Medicine Tail Coulee. F Troop retreated across the bluffs towards Last Stand Hill. Custer, now, was at Ford C with the Headquarters Group and E Troop. He found heavy Cheyenne opposition to a crossing and ordered a dismounted retreat up Deep Coulee. E Troop dismounted and started walking backwards towards Deep Ravine, acting as a rear guard. E and C Troops started to merge near Deep Coulee, and the E horses stampeded. When most of the Gray horses ran off, E Troop sought shelter in, and subsequently became trapped in Deep Ravine. F Troop and one Platoon of C made it to Last Stand Hill. L Troop was overwhelmed by Sioux coming up from Medicine Tail Coulee. Crazy Horse finally joined the battle, separating Custer's group on Last Stand Hill and the remnants of Keogh's battalion. Keogh was overwhelmed, and Custer was now surrounded. The Indians kept advancing towards Custer's diminishing position until his force ceased to exist.

The following are the Indian statements which produced the above story of the battle:

Flying Hawk to Ricker 1907:[363]

"Flying Hawk was with the leaders and could see [all]. The Indians had crossed the river above Calhoun Hill before Custer left the second ridge. The soldiers saw the Indians in the creek leading to the river and then **Custer came down off the second ridge and went up onto Calhoun Hill, leaving a detachment there, and he went right on over to Custer Hill and made a stand there."**

Good Voiced Elk to Camp 1909:[364]

"Custer got close enough to river to fire into and over the tepees. As he was going down the right side of river, the Indians who had fought Reno were coming down the left side, but Custer had somewhat the lead. Custer was making direct for the village as though to cross

---

[363]Hardorff, *Lakota Recollections of the Custer Fight*, 51-52.
[364]Hardorff, *Markers, Artifacts and Indian Testimony*, 26.

river and come into village, when Indians went over and drove him back."

He Dog to Walter Camp 1910
"I went back to the Uncpapas camp, and we looked and saw other soldiers coming on the big hill right over east. They kept right on down the river and crossed Medicine Tail Coulee and onto little rise...Here Custer's line was scattered all along parallel with river from Foley and Butler. When Custer passed near to Ford B he was moving as though to reach the lower end of our camp."[365]

"The Indians had left the camp over west to get ready. There was no fighting while Custer down near river but a few shots down there. No general fighting; fifteen or twenty Sioux on east side of river, and some of soldiers replied, but not much shooting."[366]

Foolish Elk to Walter Mason Camp 1908:[367]
The Indians were now getting their horses in from the hills and soon came up in large numbers. Some crossed the stream farther down and others crossed the ford and followed on after Custer in overwhelming numbers. They could not see how such a small force of soldiers had any chance to stand against them. The Indians were between Custer and the river and all the time coming up and getting around to the east of him,

passing around both his front and rear. Custer was following the ridges, and the Indians were keeping abreast of him in the hollows and ravines. Personally, he, (Foolish Elk), was with the Indians to the east, or on Custer's right. Custer charged the Indians twice but could not drive them away, and then the battle became furious. It did not appear to him that a stand was made by Custer's men anywhere except at the monument. He was in the gully and saw the soldiers killed on the side hill [Keogh] as they "marched" toward the high ground at the end of the ridge [monument]. They made no stand here, but all were going toward the high ground at end of ridge. The gray horses went up in a body; then came bay horses and men on foot all mixed together. The men on the horses did not stop to fight, but went ahead as fast as they could go. The men on foot, however, were shooting as they passed along. When the horses got to the top of the ridge the gray ones and bays became mingled, and the soldiers with them were all in confusion. The Indians were so numerous that the soldiers could not go any further, and they knew that they had to die...He then laughed and said that had I seen the amount of firing that was done on the battlefield I would never suppose

---

[365]Hammer, *Custer in 76*, 206-207.
[366]Hardorff, *Markers, Artifacts and Indian Testimony*, 26.
[367]Hammer, *Custer in 76*, 198.

that any of the soldiers could come out alive.

Standing Bear to Walter Mason Camp 1910:[368]

Says as soon as Custer came in sight and halted, some of the Indians crossed over, but he advanced against this resistance nearly to the river before it became strong enough to check him.

Two Moon to Throssel 1907:[369]

Considerable numbers of Sioux had already gone over the river at Ford B and as Custer drew near they disappeared into ravines to the northward. **Custer and his men rode nearly to the river on their horses and were being fired upon by the Sioux posted along the west bank. Here Custer stopped momentarily, and supposing that he would cross, the Sioux began to appear on his right and rear. He says that here some soldiers were killed and were afterward dragged into the village, dismembered and burned at big dance that night.**[370]

Standing Bear to Walter Mason Camp 1910:[371]

Keogh is the first place where any of the soldiers stopped to fight. Those between Custer and the river were soldiers running toward river on foot. Between Calhoun and monument there Indians on both sides of river as soldiers went along. **The soldiers killed between Custer and river were men on**

foot trying to make the river, and they were killed in the deep ravine.

He Dog to Walter Mason Camp 1910:[372]
The Indians had left the camp over west to get ready. **There was no fighting while Custer down near river but a few shots down there. No general fighting; fifteen or twenty Sioux on east side of river, and some of soldiers replied, but not much shooting there.**

Before the fight started, we drove him up a slope to a ridge (Keogh) and over to the other side of it. Soldiers mounted all the time and kept right along. All together all time. Did not fight by companies. *Indians all along Custer ridge, and Custer went down along hollow by Keogh.*[373]

At this time Indians all around. **At first gray horses all together but after go on hill mixed up with other horses. Fighting**

---

[368]Ibid., 215.

[369]Hardorff, *Markers, Artifacts and Indian Testimony,* 27.

[370]It is most likely that this is how, where and why Second Lieutenant James Sturgis of E Troop and Second Lieutenant Henry Harrington of C Troop disappeared, being captured in the fighting at the river and after horrific torture their bodies were burned in the huge bonfires made on the night of June 25, 1876. It is most probable that their bodies were totally consumed by the flames of the Indian fires and that is why no trace of their remains were ever found.

[371]Hammer, *Custer in 76,* 215.

[372]Hardorff, *Markers, Artifacts and Indian Testimony,* 26.

[373]Hammer, *Custer in 76,* 207.

started at Finley and kept up all along. At Keogh is where Crazy Horse charged and broke through and split up soldiers into two bunches. **Horses stampeded toward river, getting away from soldiers. There was no charge by Custer's [men] on ridge during fight. Custer's men at end of ridge.** Did not run out of ammunition. Found ammunition on dead soldiers.[374]

Two Moon to Throssel 1907:[375]

Custer now turned and charged down the river at Indians who were opposing him, and his [Two Moon's] warriors had by this time arrived in large force with their horses. He therefore forded and followed in Custer's rear, the soldiers fighting on foot, in two wings, with the lead horses between them. As Custer passed onto high ground the Cheyennes split and passed into ravines surrounding the soldiers. Heavy firing was poured into the soldiers from all sides, and as successive charges were made, some part of the troops was wiped out. The soldiers with the gray horses were the last to fall.

Flying By to Walter Mason Camp 5/21/1907:[376]

The soldiers had four or five flags [means four or five groups of troops] Custer acted as though would cross and attack the village. When I got to Custer, Indians had been fighting quite awhile. **Some of soldiers let horses go early in fight. Soldiers did not charge after I got there.** *We crossed over at all points along the river as quick as we could and found Custer already fighting Indians and driving Indians back toward river, but when we got over in great numbers, Custer was soon surrounded. The soldiers then got off their horses and some let them go, and we captured a lot of them. I captured one myself. I took some of the horses to village before battle was over and then came back. Got ammunition from saddles of horses. After came back from taking horses to village, I came to gully east of long ridge and many soldiers already killed.*

Tall Bull to Walter Mason Camp 7/22/1910:[377]

By the time I got there [Indians] had driven soldiers to first rise [where Foley lay], and they were going up the ridge to the right of Custer coulee and Indians driving them.

The men who had not horses to go to Reno first began the attack on Custer, and I did not see the first of it. Soldiers did not make any charge on Indians during the Custer fight. He is very clear that Custer was driven farther and farther back from the river. Soldiers fell back from river. Some mounted and some on foot

---

[374]Ibid., 207.
[375]Hardorff, *Cheyenne Memories of the Custer Fight*, 126-127.
[376]Ibid., 209-210.
[377]Ibid., 213.

*and not in very good order. Heard the volleys. The first was at the beginning of fight at C [Finley marker]. The last was at G. **Gray horses all mixed up with bays.***

*I was near H and heard a big war whoop that soldiers were coming. **Soldiers came on foot and ran right through us into deep gully, and this was the last of the fight, and the men were killed in this gully.***

Standing Bear to Walter Mason Camp 7/12/1910:[378]

*Custer's men did not fight by companies but were together all the time. Could not make him say different. His recollection clear on this point. **The gray horses mixed up in with rest and but few horses got beyond Keogh. Nearly all killed or captured before got farther than this.***

Turtle Rib to Walter Mason Camp 9/22/1908:[379]

When he got up with the soldiers, there was a running fight with some of the soldiers on foot. Those who kept their horses seemed to be stampeded. Some were going toward the monument, and some were trying to ride back the way they came. Those on foot seemed to be the coolest and fought the hardest. No stand was made except at the end of the long ridge [where Custer fell] and here the bay and gray horses were all mixed together.

If we extract the highlighted text and put it in rough narrative form,

sorted by geographical location and chronological order we obtain a parallel version to the one above. The Indian story of the battle is:

Custer descended Medicine Tail Coulee with the intent to ford and attack there. Part of the way down, he came under fire from Indians in the bluffs on the east of the coulee. He deployed and dismounted a platoon from C Troop on the Lower part of Calhoun Ridge to deal with this opposition and to cover his intended crossing. When he reached the river bank, he found the opposition too strong to ford there, so he turned right heading towards Ford C. Sioux crossed at Ford B splitting his column, driving F Troop back up Medicine Tail Coulee. F Troop, mounted, retreated across the bluffs towards Deep Ravine and Last Stand Hill.

Flying Hawk:

Custer came down off the second ridge and went up onto Calhoun Hill, leaving a detachment there, and he went right on over to Custer Hill and made a stand there

Good Voiced Elk:

Custer got close enough to river to fire into and over the tepees. As he was going down the right side of river, the Indians who had fought Reno were coming down the left side, but Custer had somewhat the lead. Custer was making direct for the village as though to cross river and come into village, when

[378]Ibid., 215.
[379]Ibid., 201.

Indians went over and drove him back.

He Dog:

They kept right on down the river and crossed Medicine Tail Coulee and onto little rise...Here Custer's line was scattered all along parallel with river from Foley and Butler. When Custer passed near to Ford B he was moving as though to reach the lower end of our camp. The Indians had left the camp over west to get ready. There was no fighting while Custer down near river but a few shots down there. No general fighting; fifteen or twenty Sioux on east side of river, and some of soldiers replied, but not much shooting.

Foolish Elk:

Custer charged the Indians twice but could not drive them away, and then the battle became furious. It did not appear to him that a stand was made by Custer's men anywhere except at the monument.

Standing Bear:

Says as soon as Custer came in sight and halted, some of the Indians crossed over, but he advanced against this resistance nearly to the river before it became strong enough to check him.

Two Moons:

Custer and his men rode nearly to the river on their horses and were being fired upon by the Sioux posted along the west bank. Here Custer stopped momentarily, and supposing that he would cross, the Sioux began to appear on his right

and rear. He says that here some soldiers were killed and were afterward dragged into the village, dismembered and burned at big dance that night.

Custer was, now, at Ford C, with the remaining platoon of E Troop, and the Headquarters Group, where he found Cheyenne opposition to a crossing. He ordered a retreat. E Troop dismounted to cover the retreat and started walking backwards towards Deep Ravine. C and F Troops started to merge near the top of Deep Coulee. Most of the Gray horses stampeded and E Troop was trapped in Deep Ravine.

Standing Bear:

The soldiers killed between Custer and river were men on foot trying to make the river, and they were killed in the deep ravine.

He Dog:

There was no fighting while Custer down near river but a few shots down there. No general fighting; fifteen or twenty Sioux on east side of river, and some of soldiers replied, but not much shooting there. Before the fight started, we drove him up a slope to a ridge (Keogh) and over to the other side of it. Soldiers mounted all the time and kept right along. At first gray horses all together but after go on hill mixed up with other horses. Fighting started at Finley and kept up all along.

Two Moons:

Custer now turned and charged down the river at Indians who were opposing him, and his [Two Moons] warriors had by this time arrived in large force with their horses. He therefore forded and followed in Custer's rear, the soldiers fighting on foot, in two wings, with the lead horses between them. As Custer passed onto high ground the Cheyennes split and passed into ravines surrounding the soldiers. Heavy firing was poured into the soldiers from all sides, and as successive charges were made, some part of the troops was wiped out. The soldiers with the gray horses were the last to fall.

Flying By:

Some of soldiers let horses go early in fight. Soldiers did not charge after I got there.

Tall Bull:

Gray horses all mixed up with bays. Soldiers came on foot and ran right through us into deep gully, and this was the last of the fight, and the men were killed in this gully.

Standing Bear:

The gray horses mixed up in with rest and but few horses got beyond Keogh. Nearly all killed or captured before got farther than this.

F Troop and one Platoon of C made it to Last Stand Hill. L Troop was overwhelmed by Sioux coming up Medicine Tail Coulee. Crazy Horse finally joined the battle, separating Custer's group on Last Stand Hill and the remnants of Keogh's battalion. Keogh was overwhelmed and Custer was now surrounded. The Indians kept advancing towards Custer's diminishing position until his force ceased to exist.

He Dog:

At Keogh is where Crazy Horse charged and broke through and split up soldiers into two bunches. Horses stampeded toward river, getting away from soldiers. There was no charge by Custer's [men] on ridge during fight. Custer's men at end of ridge. Did not run out of ammunition. Found ammunition on dead soldiers.

Turtle Rib:

When he got up with the soldiers, there was a running fight with some of the soldiers on foot. Those who kept their horses seemed to be stampeded. Some were going toward the monument, and some were trying to ride back the way they came. Those on foot seemed to be the coolest and fought the hardest. No stand was made except at the end of the long ridge [where Custer fell] and here the bay and gray horses were all mixed together.

Clearly, Custer did his duty and attacked the enemy and provided the support he had promised Reno. Unfortunately, by the time he attacked Reno had already vacated the valley and was sniveling on the hill. Custer had the advantage of tactical surprise and an adversary which he could overcome if his second in command had followed orders and attacked the upper end of the village and his third in command had obeyed written orders to bring up the reserves and extra ammunition. When Custer attacked, he found himself facing not only the Indians of the lower end of the village, but the ones who had just defeated Reno in the upper end of the village.

Reno's timidity, and the Indians subsequent rout of his battalion from the valley, strengthened their will to resist and fight Custer. The Indians were instilled with courage to stand and fight, and utilizing their overwhelming numbers surrounded and annihilated Custer's force. Clearly, Custer fell victim to an overwhelming foe, which he was forced to fight alone because his two subalterns refused to engage the enemy. One vacated the field of battle a coward, the other delayed in following direct written orders and malingered until long after the real fighting was over and moved forward when his contribution would be meaningless. It should be noted here, that if Reno and Benteen had ever decided to go to Custer's aid they were merely fifteen minutes away from him, as noted by General Nelson A. Miles:[380]

"The distance from where the running Reno halted and kept the seven troops and reserve ammunition, to the extreme right of Custer's command was about four miles. A cavalry horse walked that distance in fifty-eight minutes. At a smart trot or gallop, as a cavalryman goes into action, fifteen minutes would have brought the whole command into the engagement and the result might have been entirely different. This we proved on that same ground by actual test of moving our horses over it, and timing them by the watch."

The best way to summarize Custer's battle performance is to defer to an impartial expert, General Nelson A Miles, a former Commanding General of the Army and vanquisher of Crazy Horse and most other Sioux leaders in the year following the Little Bighorn:[381]

"No commanding officer can win victories with seven-twelfths of his command remaining out of the engagement when within sound of his rifle shots."

---

[380]Miles, *The Personal Reflections of General Nelson A Miles*, 290.
[381]Ibid., 290.

CHAPTER 20
Benteen's Performance

On June 25, 1876, Benteen was still sulking and mad over an incident that occurred on the night of June 24. Mathey told Walter Camp that:

"...on the night of June 24 Custer asked him to report which company's packs were giving the most trouble. Mathey said that he remarked that he did not like to make comparisons, seeing that all were doing the best they could, but if required to do so he would have to name the packs of Companies G and H. McIntosh took the criticism good naturedly, but it made Benteen angry."[382]

With Benteen's personality, this incident must have infuriated him and contributed to his malingering and inactions, on June 25, 1876. Benteen's failure to perform in an exemplary manner stemmed directly from his personality deficiencies. He was a moody, sullen, abrasive individual who was capable of harboring grudges and ill feelings for years. Custer was on Benteen's short list of people he loved to hate. General James M. Bell, in notes found among Walter Camp's papers, described Benteen in this manner:

"Benteen's weakness was his vindictiveness, which was pronounced. He was indifferent to the minor matters of discipline and always had the poorest company in the regiment. He was not considered a good company officer, but was in fact a first-rate fighter. It always galled Benteen to serve in such low rank as captain after having been a colonel in the war. For this reason he never took the interest in his command that might have been expected of him."[383]

These ill feelings manifested themselves after the death of Major Joel Elliott during the battle of Washita. Major Elliott, in an act of bravado, disobeyed Custer's direct order not to leave the confines of the

---

[382]Hammer, *Custer in 76*, 78.
[383]Hardorff, *On The Little Bighorn With Walter Camp*, 189.

captured Indian village. Elliott took 18 men with him and left for his date with infamy proclaiming to Lieutenant Owen Hale, "Here goes for a brevet or a coffin."[384] Though Custer sent out search parties, his troops were soon subjected to counterattack by neighboring Indians. The searches had to be curtailed and Custer withdrew. Benteen claimed Custer abandoned Elliott, and from that point forward Benteen maintained a hatred of Custer that grew worse with the passage of time, festering like an open sore.

Whether Benteen allowed his hatred of Custer to affect his performance on June 25 is subject to conjecture. Benteen was, basically, a good soldier, who fulfilled his duty to his country and uniform. That Benteen would overtly dishonor his uniform out of hatred for Custer is doubtful, but it is certainly within the realm of reality that he would and did perform below the level of his ability, in order to frustrate and irritate Custer.

Benteen can be faulted for delaying and failing to move forward in a timely manner after watering his horses at the morass. There was a nexus between Benteen and the pack train at the morass. It is doubted that Benteen could not have co-ordinated the movements of both columns once he received orders to do so. It certainly appears that the columns were not the seven miles apart that he told Knipe and instead were very close together. Benteen could have conferred with McDougall.

Godfrey in an interview with Walter Mason Camp stated:

"When Benteen had watered his horses at the morass he waited there some time-in fact so long that some of his officers began to get uneasy, especially as they were hearing firing (which must have been Reno's) ...Weir said 'they ought to be over there' (where the fighting was going on) and, being at the head of the column, started out with his co. Benteen seeing this, immediately ordered the column to advance. At this time the pack train was coming up and the leading mules had reached the water and being very thirsty, they plunged in." [385]

When Benteen reached Reno on the Hill he came under Reno's immediate command. Benteen did promptly show Reno the written order he received from Custer. Compliance with this order was then Reno's responsibility. He either had to give Benteen leave to comply with Custer's written order, or be prepared to give Custer a superlative reason why he countermanded it, when next he would meet Custer. Reno did neither and simply ignored the existence of the order. Both Reno and Benteen testified to this at the Inquiry. Recorder Lee was so inept in interrogating Reno on this topic, that Lee may well have lost his case by failing to pursue this highly important issue:

Q- *"At the time you met Captain Benteen, were you informed of the order that had been sent by Lieutenant Cooke?*

---

[384]Connell, *Son of the Morningstar*, 195.
[385]Hammer, *Custer in 76*, 75.

A- *He Showed it to me.*

Q- *What was that order?*

A- *It has been repeated here in Court. I can't recollect the exact phraseology , it was to about this effect: "Benteen, come on, big village, bring packs" and then a postscript "bring packs" and signed "W. W. Cooke." He had not time to put his official designation as adjutant."*[386]

The only point that Reno could raise that he felt was significant regarding the order was that Lieutenant Cooke did not have the time to put his official designation of adjutant on it. His answer reeked of smug indifference and overt disobedience to a direct written order, from his commanding officer, which he dismissed with total nonchalance. Lee failed to ask Reno:

• Why he did not order Benteen to proceed and to comply with Custer's orders?

• Did Reno countermand Custer's written orders and if so, why?

• If Reno did not countermand Custer's written orders, why Reno allowed Benteen to not comply with them?

After these two questions, Recorder began interrogating Reno on other topics and did not return to this issue during his direct interrogation. Gilbert then cross examined Reno and on redirect the following day, Recorder Lee finally propounded the issue. The answers Lee received from Reno were smug, indifferent and inane:

Q- *You read the order that Captain Benteen received from General Custer?*

A- *Yes*

Q- *You omitted two words in repeating it. I would like you to state the exact words.*

A- *I do not remember the exact phraseology. As near as I can remember it was; "Benteen: come on, big village, big thing, bring packs. P.S. Bring packs."*

Q- *Do you remember the words "be quick"?*

A- *Yes, I do now that you called my attention to it.*

Q- *Would you, as an officer, regard that as a direction that he would bring them within easier reach to put them in a defensible position?*

A- *I think the latter supposition would be correct.*

Q- *Then how did that portion strike you if you reflect upon it?*

A- *It did not make any great impression on me at the time because I was absorbed in getting those packs together, and did not intend to move until I had done so.*

Q- *From the number of Indians you saw around you and your estimate of the number that were there, did it occur to you at the time that, with only 225 men, he might need someone to "be quick"?*

A- *It never occurred to me at all. 225 men could hold off quite number of Indians if they are properly disposed.*

---

[386]Nichols, *The Reno Court of Inquiry,* 566.

Q- *What number of Indians do you refer to?*

A- *The number that I saw.*[387]

Returning to his inept questioning of Reno, Lee elicited from Reno that the order said "be quick" but made no attempt to question him about having Benteen to comply with this. Reno, again with smug indifference, stated the order made no impression on him because he "was absorbed in getting those packs together." This is a blatant lie as Reno and Benteen have both previously testified that Reno was shown the order when Benteen arrived on the hill. This was between 30 minutes and one hour before the packs arrived. Lee failed to seize upon this lie and question Reno as to how he could be absorbed with an event that had not yet occurred?

Lee continuing in his inept manner, had Reno testify that he felt comfortable that Custer with 225 men could handle all the Indians Reno had seen. Lee failed miserably again, by not asking Reno how he expected Custer to handle all the Indians Reno had seen, if Reno could not handle them with 181 men. Lee failed to inquire how 49 additional men would make such a significant difference and if 49 more men could make such a significant difference would not have Benteen's 125 added to Custer's force made an even more significant difference?

When asked at the Inquiry if he ever asked Reno for permission to go to Custer in compliance with his orders, Benteen replied;

- "Not at all. I supposed General

Custer was able to take care of himself."[388]

Lee was not any better with Benteen. He got Benteen to show total indifference to a written order from his commanding officer and obviating himself from not following it by dismissing it with the curt "I supposed General Custer was able to take care of himself." Benteen's answer carried the stench of revenge for Custer having left Major Elliott to fend for himself eleven years prior. Where were these questions from Lee:

- Sir you had received a written direct order from your commanding officer, were you not under a duty to obey it?
- Why didn't you obey it?"

The historic version of the hilltop, at that moment, conveyed the image of Benteen, single handed, rallying all the troops. This is as far fetched as the image of Custer, standing alone with saber in hand, waiting on Last Stand Hill, to be the last one killed. It is incredulous to conceive of French, Weir, McDougall, and the other officers standing around, doing nothing to rally the troops, while the one man show called "Benteen" restored order and morale. This is nothing more than self serving propaganda generated by Benteen in the years following the battle.

There was nothing that prevented Benteen from then fully complying with Custer's written orders, to come quick and bring the packs, except the

---

[387]Ibid., 581-582.
[388]Ibid., 407.

194

technicality that he was under Reno's immediate command, which Reno was not exercising. When Benteen arrived, Reno was out of control, Reno had disobeyed his orders, he begged or ordered Benteen to assist him. Benteen helped in rallying Reno's troops and putting the combined command in order. At this point, he should have insisted that Reno allow him to move forward and attempt to comply with the written orders he had received. While Benteen had been involved in rallying Reno's command, the packs had come up.

McDougall's observations are appropriate here

> *"...the reason why Benteen did not assert himself before this, namely, when it appeared to everyone that all should go to support of Custer, was that Benteen hesitated to go on and join Custer, having come up with Reno, who might set up the technical claim that he was the commanding officer of both battalions. Reno and Benteen had not been on friendly terms and Benteen would not wish to stir up trouble."*[389]

Benteen continued to malinger by placating Reno, effectively drying Reno's tears and soothing his shattered spirit. Benteen allowed Reno to disappear from the hill for thirty to forty five minutes to look for Hodgson's body. Reno, by so doing, effectively abandoned his command. Benteen by allowing this to occur and doing nothing to put a stop to it was culpable as well. Benteen took advantage of

Reno's absence to malinger longer and delay in complying with his commanding officer's written order.

That Benteen had to stay and help rally Reno's troops, as he had come under Reno's immediate command and Reno asked him to do so, can be accepted. This was a proper request as it tended to resolve a greater immediate need. The remaining time he spent on the hill doing nothing, covering for and being Reno's yes man, is both inexcusable and unforgivable.

While the Court of Inquiry's purpose was to examine Reno's conduct, Benteen knew that his actions were under question as well. It is without a doubt that when Benteen testified he colored and distorted the truth to preserve and protect his reputation and image. A prime example of Benteen's revision to historic fact, as he knew them, was his testimony in regard to Custer's route to Last Stand Hill, whether there was an action at Medicine Tail Ford, and did Custer attempt to cross the river?

Benteen's testimony at the Reno Court of Inquiry, responding to questions if he examined Custer's route, trail and how close Custer came to the river, was:[390]

> *"I did, but I think now I was mistaken. The route I supposed he had gone to that ford was down through a canyon-like ravine or coulee. But I think now that he went around to the right of the second divide and did not go to the ford 'B' at all."*

---

[389]Hammer, *Custer in 76*, 71.
[390]Nichols, *The Reno Court of Inquiry*, 417-418.

"On the morning of General Terry's arrival I asked permission to saddle up my company and go over the battlefield of General Custer. I did so and followed down the gorge, thinking that was the route taken by General Custer on the 25th of June. Now I am satisfied that was not his route but it was all cut up by horse tracks and pony tracks so that it could not be told from any other trail. That was the same gorge the Indians rushed up when we arrived almost opposite to it when we made our advance down the river. That gorge was 50 to 60 or probably 100 yards wide, the bottom was irregular and cut up with ravines."

"I went over it carefully with a view to determine in my own mind how the fight was fought. I arrived at the conclusion then, as I have now, that it was a rout, a panic, till the last man was killed. That there was no line formed, there was no line on the battlefield. You can take a handful of corn and scatter it over the floor and make just such lines, there were none. The only approach to a line was there were 5 or 6 horses at equal distances like skirmishers. Ahead of those 5 or 6 horses there were 5 or 6 men at about the same distances showing that the horses were killed and the riders jumped off and were all heading to get where General Custer was. That was the only approach to a line on the

field. There were more than 20 killed there to the right . There were 4 or 5 at one place all within the space of 20 or 30 yards. That was the condition all over the field and in the [gorge]."

This was a most convenient readjustment of his memory, he now felt that Custer went from the river to Last Stand Hill directly and without purpose. That no lines were formed, it was a rout, a panic, no semblance of any organization or defense formed. Custer went from the river to the ridge, he was attacked and a panic ensued. Benteen now claimed that Custer made no attempt to ford the river and attack the village, in fact it was now his opinion that Custer did not even descend Medicine Tail Coulee.

How convenient for Benteen to have carefully rethought everything he saw and reach these new conclusions. Any indication of an attempted crossing at Ford B and a defensive stand on Calhoun Ridge would show there was an engagement for which Benteen could have arrived, on time. Thus, there could be legitimate questions raised regarding the propriety of his apparent dawdling, in defiance of written orders. A slaughter that was the result of a rout and a panic, showed that Benteen's compliance with written orders and timely arrival would not have mattered at all and just increased the number of Army dead. The conclusion to be reached from this was, thankfully, Benteen acted prudently and aided Reno and dawdled and malingered to avoid compliance with Custer's written orders as he saved the lives of his battalion from certain death with Custer.

Benteen's lies at the Court of Inquiry stood the test of time, until, unfortunately, for Benteen, his own words surfaced, in 1954, that proved his testimony at the Inquiry to be blatant lies. In May, 1954, Anita Benteen-Mitchell, a grand daughter of Benteen, when cleaning out an old trunk found a map drawn by Benteen, immediately after the battle. The map was sent by Benteen to his wife, accompanied by a letter Benteen had written on July 4, 1876. It was profusely annotated in his own hand. The map clearly shows an attempt to cross at Ford B and evidence of fighting on the two Ridges. The map is reproduced in Graham's *Abstract of the Reno Court of Inquiry*. Within the text of the letter was this description of an attempted crossing at Medicine Tail Ford and the subsequent action:

"Whether the Indians allowed Custer's column to cross at all, is a mooted question, but I am of the opinion that nearly - if not all of the five companies got into the village - but were driven out immediately - flying in great disorder and crossing by two instead of the one ford by which they entered. 'E' going by the left and 'F, I, and L' by the same one they crossed. What became of 'C' Co no one knows - they must have charged there below the village, gotten away - or have been killed in the bluffs on the village side of stream - as very few of 'C' Co. Horses are found. Jack Sturgis

and Porter's clothes were found in the Village. After the Indians had driven them across, it was a regular buffalo hunt for them and not a man escaped."[391]

Who is one to believe? Benteen number one, was writing to his wife nine days after the battle. He was describing to her the carnage he had seen days before, with no self serving interest. His motivation for the letter was to reassure her that he was alright, to inform her what happened during the battle and what became of men she knew. Or, do we believe Benteen number two, testifying at a Court of Inquiry, two and a half years after the battle, knowing that certain of his actions were subject to question, his performance less than adequate, and his image was in severe need of damage control.

It is quite obvious, based on the circumstances surrounding the preparation of the letter and the testimony at the Inquiry, that Benteen's testimony at the Inquiry was lie after blatant lie. Benteen's attempt at revisionist history was clearly a damage control effort to preserve his reputation and bolster his self-image.

Another enigma is the contents and meaning of the order itself: If Custer only wanted additional troops then it was properly sent to Benteen, but why did he ask Benteen to bring the packs up, as well.

If Custer wanted the pack train in addition to Benteen's battalion, then

---

[391]Graham, *The Custer Myth*, 297.

the order should have been sent to Captain McDougall, commanding officer of the pack train, as well. Why then was it sent only to Benteen? Why wasn't Martin given orders to deliver the order to both Benteen and McDougall?

The answer is quite simple, when Custer ascended Weir Point, he was able to visualize the morass and he saw the pack train arriving while Benteen was leaving. It appears that Custer wanted both Benteen's men, the extra ammunition and extra men assigned to handle the packs as well as the pack train guard. Custer must have assumed that the two groups had become one merged force and Benteen had assumed command, as Benteen out ranked McDougall. Hence, Custer sent the order to the commanding officer of what he believed to be a merged force.

Custer did not want the physical packs. He wanted the extra 25,000 rounds of ammunition and the extra men guarding and working the pack train, all 120 of them. When those men would be combined with Benteen's 125 and Custer's 229, it would have given Custer a fighting force of 474 fighting men to contain and fight the Indians. This would have been a formidable group, which probably could have held their own, even against the number of Indians opposing them. Of course this scenario did not come to fruition as Benteen had parted from the pack train when the order arrived and he utilized semantics to avoid compliance, and obviate any need for him to inform

McDougall of the orders.

In response to an order which directed him to quickly come forward and join in an apparent battle against a large enemy force, Benteen decided to dawdle for nearly one and a half hours before he was shamed by a subordinate officer to attempt compliance. He first dawdled, then he avoided compliance by utilizing semantics, and then he hid behind the orders of a deranged Reno. Finally, succumbing to the pressure of Captain Weir and his unilateral act of riding to the sound of the guns alone, did Benteen act. By this time, Custer's fight was over, and Benteen's advance became meaningless. His attempt to reach the battle scene occurred long after the last stand debacle.

Benteen's most aggressive act was to assume titular command of the siege position from the sniveling Reno, but this was after all the damage was done. He sustained Reno's order to Captain Weir, denying Weir permission to go to Custer's aid. Weir at least had the fortitude to go forward, on his own, in search of Custer. Weir 's act of courage forced Benteen and Reno to mount their command and attempt to fulfill their duty to report to their commanding officer, General Custer. Unfortunately, this was a case of too little, too late.

A chronology of Benteen's inactions and actions would be:

3:00 PM - Boston Custer rides with the Benteen Column

3:15 PM - Boston Custer leaves to join his brother

3:30 PM - Benteen leaves Morass as Pack Train arrives

4:00 PM - Private Martin delivers Custer's Order, Benteen hears gunfire

4:10 PM - Benteen reaches siege hill

4:15 PM - Heavy firing is heard in Custer's direction

4:20 PM - Lt. Hare returns from the pack train with two mules of ammunition

4:25 PM - Volley firing is heard in Custer's direction

4:40 PM - McDougall arrives with the rest of the pack train

4:50 PM - Weir asks permission to ride to the sound of the guns

4:55 PM - Reno denies Weir permission to go, Benteen concurs

5:00 PM - Weir leaves without orders, Edgerly follows with D Troop

5:10 PM - The last heavy firing is heard in Custer's direction

5:25 PM - Benteen leaves with Companies H, K, M to join the Weir Advance

5:40 PM - Reno leaves to join Weir Advance

5:52 PM - Companies A, B, G and pack train leave to join with the Weir Advance

6:02 PM - Companies A, B, D, G, H, M and pack train return to siege hill

6:10 PM - Company K returns to siege hill

On July 4, 1876 an enlisted man's petition was circulated among the troops of the 7th Cavalry asking that Reno be appointed commanding officer and Benteen be promoted to Major. While there is no direct evidence linking Benteen to its preparation and circulation, the petition appears to be the devious work of Captain Benteen's First Sergeant Joseph Mc Curry, with Benteen's blessings.

On Nov 2, 1954,[392] the FBI issued a report after an extensive examination of the petition and the regiment's muster roll and payroll records. Among the conclusions they reached were:

79 signatures were PROBABLE forgeries

17 signatures were of soldiers who signed for their pay with witnessed x's. {they couldn't sign a receipt for their pay but they could sign the petition}

8 signatures could not be compared to any known writing sample for the individual

The document is believed to have been prepared by H troop's First Sergeant Joseph McCurry, a strong Benteen supporter. It was alleged that many of the signatures bore a striking resemblance to McCurry's handwriting. Benteen was believed to be not involved in its production, but did not

---

[392]du Bois, *Kick the Dead Lion*, 85-89.

prevent it being produced. It appears that the malingerer Benteen wanted to pick the meat off the carcass of the 7th Cavalry's officer corps before the bodies of Custer's dead had turned cold in their graves.

Captain Benteen was Custer's Judas and betrayer! He had the time and ability to join the battle. Private Martin delivered Custer's last order, to Benteen, in adequate time for Benteen to reach Custer. The order read "Come on. Big village. Be quick. Bring packs. signed W. W. Cooke P.S. Bring packs." When the order was received Benteen had the means to know exactly where Custer was and how to get to him. All he needed to do was have Private Martin lead the way back to Custer.

Benteen was not that far from the pack train that he could not have sent a message back to McDougall to come forward with the ammunition and the extra men, as quickly as possible. McDougall could have followed Benteen's trail to Custer, and they were both under written orders to join Custer. Benteen was still sulking over the Mathey incident of the night before and was in no hurry to join Custer. He availed himself of semantics and did not relay the order to McDougall. He then allowed himself to come under Reno's command, at a time when Reno was out of control, and utilized this situation to add still further delay before making an attempt to comply with a written order from his commanding officer. When he was finally shamed into moving by Captain Weir it was too late for Custer and his command.

Benteen had hated Custer since the Battle of Washita. He had previously written and published a very uncomplimentary article about Custer, for which Custer first threatened to horse whip him and then backed down. Benteen was under a direct written order to come quick and join in the battle. Instead he wasted time, and then moved forward slowly. He failed to relay the order to McDougall though part of it pertained to McDougall. Benteen wasted just enough time to allow a late arrival to the battle, after the outcome was decided. He acquiesced to the sniveling Reno on the hill. Later, he assumed titular command of a defense against a siege, from an enemy neither proficient at, nor desirous of engaging in such a method of warfare.

In essence, Benteen was a prime contributor to the debacle by being a non-participant. His alleged contributions and achievements were first extolled by his mouth alone. When the battle was examined his contribution to the outcome was achieved not from his actions but from his inactions and his failure to act timely at a moment when prompt action was dearly required.

CHAPTER 21
Reno's Performance

Major Marcus Reno had his difficulties, both with his superiors and subalterns. Reno was not only reticent to obey Custer's orders, he had difficulty obeying General Terry's and Colonel Gibbon's as well. He blatantly disobeyed Terry's orders, on his June 10 to June 20, 1876, scout of the Powder River area. Not only did he fail to obey orders when he did follow the trail, he then failed to follow it far enough to discover the location of the Indians, making the scout purposeless. Some believe that if he followed the trail he could have found the Indians, pursued the advantage of surprise that he had and attacked with a good likelihood of defeating the warriors. He failed by breaking off the hunt, when he nearly came in contact with the Indians and returned to Terry with no positive results.

The futility of his scout is summed up by Godfrey in his diary, "Col. Reno's scout did not give any definite results. He went up the Powder River and over to the Tongue and thence to the Rosebud. He did not see any Indians or game but reports a camp about three weeks old of about 350 lodges."[393] General Terry was even more blase about Reno's disobedience and dismissed with this entry in his diary, "Sent Hughes to meet Reno. Hughes returned at ....Reno gave him no reason for his disobedience of Orders."[394]

Subsequent to the battle of Little Bighorn, Reno had his problems with Colonel Gibbon as well, culminating with Gibbon placing Reno under arrest on July 24, 1876.[395] Godfrey described this incident,

"Col Reno got a copy of charges against him. It all comes from Col R sending out some scouts as videttes Saturday eve after we got into camp. I presume however Col Reno's manner has as much to do with the results, as his manner is rather aggressive & he protested against the scouts being taken from the Reg't."[396]

---

[393]Godfrey, *The Field Diary of Edward Settle Godfrey*, 8.

[394]Terry, *The Field Diary of General Alfred H. Terry*, 23.

[395]Koury, *Diaries of the Little Bighorn*, 12.

[396]Godfrey, *The Field Diary of Edward Settle Godfrey*, 27.

Reno then proceeded to have more problems with General Terry, as noted by Godfrey on August 15, 1876,

"Walker says he has been detailed as personal Aid de Camp on the staff of Genl Terry, apparently for the purpose of carrying orders to Commdg. off. of the 7ᵗʰ Cav. Maj. Reno has been playing 'ass' right along and is so taken up with his own importance that he thinks he can 'snip' everybody and comment on the orders he receives from Genl Terry's Hdqurs. And insult his staff, so there is not any one with the personal staff on speaking terms."[397]

By August 16, 1876, Terry's frustration with Reno was so great, he verbalized his displeasure with Reno to his staff. Godfrey noted this in his diary,

"I understand that he has said if he had not so much respect for the officers of the Regt. He would put some other field officer on duty with the Regt. It seems that Reno's self important rudeness makes him unbearable."[398]

When examining Reno's performance at the Battle of the Little Bighorn, one must take into consideration the fact that Reno, at this period of time, was having difficulty with all his superiors and most underlings. He was constantly and consistently disobedient of General Terry's Orders, he was disobedient and disrespectful to Colonel Gibbon. As a result, he was placed under arrest by Colonel Gibbon. Reno was generally "snippy" to General Terry's staff,

forcing Terry to appoint an officer to act as his aid for the expressed purpose of dealing with Reno. That Reno was disobedient of Custer was not an isolated event, but a personality defect that Reno succumbed to with all people in authority above him, at that time. This was compounded by a severe drinking problem, a total lack of experience with Indian fighting, having never previously fired a shot at an Indian prior to the Little Bighorn, and a latent tendency to become a coward when his leadership was most needed.

Major Reno's cowardice was exacerbated by his propensity for drinking to excess. It is well established by survivors of the battle that Reno prematurely dismounted his troops before there was any Indian resistance in his front. In analyzing Reno's compliance to the orders given to him by Custer, the starting point is Reno's description of the order and his subsequent actions:[399]

"Gen. Custer directs you to take as rapid a gait as you think prudent and charge the village afterward and you will be supported by the whole outfit"

"We were then at a gallop and I was about 40 paces in advance. I could see a disposition on the part of Indians to lead us on, and that idea was confirmed when on advancing a little further I could see the Indians coming out of a ravine where they evidently had hid themselves."

---

[397]Ibid., 36.
[398]Ibid., 37.
[399]Nichols, *The Reno Court of Inquiry*, 561-562.

"I think [the], as I saw it, it was 8 [00] or 900 yards in front of me, and on what we called the foot hills on the left bank of the river. There were straggling parties of Indians making around to my rear. I said to myself that I could not successfully make an offensive charge. Their numbers had thrown me on the defensive."

"It was stretched along the bank of the river to my front and right. There were times going down that I could not see the village."

"I dismounted by telling the company officers. Lieutenant Hodgson gave the order to Company "G" and I gave it to "H" [meant M] and "A." I gave the order to dismount and prepare to fight on foot and their horses would be sheltered in this point of timber."

"I had an [idea] of the number of Indians from the trails in the first place, and I saw distinctly with my own eyes 5 [00] or 600 Indians. All the evidence through the bottom and over the trails showed there were Indians there. The dust on the trail I followed must have been from 4 to 6 inches deep, and there were several trails showing that numbers of animals had gone there."

There seems to be little dispute that Reno was ordered to charge the village, and he would receive support from Custer.

Girard[400]

"The General hallooed over to Major Reno and beckoned to him with his finger and the Major rode over and he told Major Reno: 'You will take your battalion and try and overtake and bring them to battle and I will support you.' And as the Major was going off he said, 'And take the scouts with you.' He gave him orders to take the scouts along and that is how I heard it..."

"I joined Major Reno."

"No, sir, I simply heard the order given and I knew where my duty was. With the scouts"

"Yes, sir, I should judge it was about noon."

"...and we came to a little knoll, and the road went around it, and as we went around the little knoll we lost sight of General Custer's command."

Reno described the receipt of the order to him as:
"I moved forward to the head of the column and shortly after Lt. Cook came to me and said, 'Gen. Custer directs you to take as rapid a gait as you think prudent and charge the village afterward and you will be supported by the whole outfit."

Reno did not comply with either the letter or spirit of this order. He was given no latitude to stop and

---

[400]Ibid., 86-87.

deploy skirmishers. He failed to advance and attack the enemy in his front. He failed, at any time in the valley, to engage the enemy or act in an offensive manner.

Reno was at direct odds with William O. Taylor who said he looked back and saw Reno drinking, while Reno says that he, Reno, was on the front line. Reno claimed to have seen 500 to 600 Indians in a ravine a half mile or more in his front. He gave no indication that he was engaged in any way by these Indians, and stated that he gave the order to dismount and fight on foot prior to meeting any Indian resistance to his charge. Participants of the charge confirm these actions:

Culbertson[401]

"They were circling in our front. They were 5[00] to 600 yards in our front just before we halted."

"There were, then in our front, 200 to 250 riding back and forth, and some crossed the bluffs on our left."

"They were firing at us as we were about 500 yards from them."

De Rudio[402]

"Some bullets had whistled past before."

"I heard several shots."

"As soon as the line was deployed as skirmishers some Indians began to come out of the dust and started on their right and our left on the high bluffs. They came all around and pretty soon after came on our flanks. The skirmish line advanced 75 or 100 yards during that fire."

Girard[403]

"The scouts were to my left and called my attention to the fact that all the Indians were coming up the valley. I called Major Reno's attention to the fact that the Indians were all coming up the valley. I halted there a little time. I thought it was of importance enough that General Custer should know it, and I rode back towards Custer's command. At this knoll I met Colonel Cooke and he asked me where I was going. I told him I had come back to report to him that the Indians were coming back up the valley to meet us, and he says, 'All right, I'll go back and report.' And he wheeled around and went toward Major Reno's [General Custer's] command."

"While the skirmish line was being drawn up, the Indians were coming up. They were distant, as well as I could judge from where I stood, about one thousand yards from the left flank of the skirmish line, and in front, not directly in a line with it.. We fired a few shots at the first Indians that came up."

[401]Ibid., 367.
[402]Ibid., 313-314.
[403]Ibid., 87-88.

Hare[404]

"Shortly after, the command moved down the valley to within a short distance of the timber and it was there dismounted and a skirmish line was thrown out. Up to the time the command was dismounted there were probably fifty or more Indians riding up and down in front and firing . As soon as the skirmish line was dismounted, four or five hundred came out of a coulee which was about four hundred yards in front of us. These Indians moved down in the left and rear."

Herendeen[405]

"I did not see any and I was in front. The Indians were sitting still on their horses, seemed to be awaiting our approach, and did not move till we were near to where the command dismounted, then they commenced making up and skirmishing out."

Moylan[406]

"They were so numerous that I supposed Major Reno thought it was more force than he could probably attack mounted, consequently he dismounted his command. At that time his command had reached this point of timber and the command was given to halt and dismount to fight on foot."

Porter[407]

"I saw a few Indians. I saw a great many ponies. They seemed to be driving the ponies down the river. I didn't see many Indians."

"As soon as they got to the woods they dismounted and formed skirmish lines and went into action then. I was right there where I could see them."

Varnum[408]

"We went on down possibly two miles and the line halted and dismounted. I was not present and didn't hear any of the orders and don't know what orders were given."

Wallace[409]

The Indians when the order was given were apparently running from us. There was a big dust; but as we moved on the dust cleared away and the Indians were coming back.

"After moving some distance the third company was brought to the left of the line and the command moved in that way until near the timber. There the command was halted, the men dismounted and prepared to fight on foot, the horses going in the timber, and the three companies then deployed as skirmishers with the right in the timber and the left towards the bluff. The skirmish line only took up a few hundred yards."

If there were Indians in Reno's

---

[404]Ibid., 227.
[405]Ibid., 252.
[406]Ibid., 216.
[407]Ibid., 189.
[408]Ibid., 141.
[409]Ibid., 22.

front they ranged from 50 to 250 warriors, essentially even odds for Reno's command of 181 men. Reno ordered the dismount without being engaged, with little to no heavy firing and apparently with no resistance as yet in his front. Reno ordered the dismount in the face of an attack by 40 to 50 Indians with perhaps 400 to 500 in reserve and there was very light firing, with no resistance before the halt. Reno omits discussion of the pony herd entirely, it is quite probable that what he saw was a few Indians and a pony herd. Perhaps 50 Indians and 500 ponies were the overwhelming force that made Reno stop and go to the skirmish line before he met any resistance or was fired at.

All of the above participants in their testimony at the Court of Inquiry gave essentially the same testimony. There was no resistance, perhaps a few hundred Indians in their front. They stopped and deployed to a skirmish line more than 500 yards from the enemy before few if any shots were fired at them. He failed by not maintaining his defensive position in the timber. Support does not have to come from the rear, a flank attack supplies as much as if not more support than a following attack. He did not wait a sufficient period of time for support to materialize. He demonstrated extreme cowardice when he broke and ran, abandoning his command.

When discussing Reno and his cowardly acts, much focus has been placed on his failure to complete the charge on the village and the rout from the valley. Other issues include Reno's refusal to go to Custer's aid and the question of what was Reno doing cowering on the hill for two days when no longer engaged by the Indians. After the arrival of Benteen and McDougall with the supply train, Reno was in command of seven-twelfths of the vaunted Seventh Cavalry. He was blatantly aware of the order to Benteen to come quickly and bring the packs. His forces approximated 350 cavalry soldiers, horses for most, a reserve supply of 25,000 rounds of ammunition, plenty of food and little water. This was a formidable fighting force in its own right, and it was largely unscarred by battle.

One of the points raised by Custer antagonists is that there were just too many Indians for any action to be of assistance to Custer and that there was just no time to effect a relief action. When Weir moved out on his own and achieved Weir Point, around 6 PM, he noticed "firings directed at the ground" perhaps indicating the end of the battle. Almost immediately after he reached the point, the Indians diverted from the Custer Field and headed towards the Weir/Reno/Benteen force which retreated back to Reno Hill. We also know that Reno reached the hill, the first time, around 4 PM, thus there was a two hour window where Reno did nothing, and Custer withered and died on the vine.

Custer began his actions approximately 4 PM, about the same time Reno reached the hill. DeRudio, who was trapped in the timber, claimed to have heard heavy firing downstream almost as Reno departed. McDougall arrived with the packs between 4:20 PM and 4:40 PM. About this time, Custer had probably suffered a bloody nose, but his battalion should have been relatively intact, I and L on Calhoun Hill, C and F on Last Stand Hill and E entrenched in Deep Ravine. Reno was in command of about 350 men at this time. If he left 100 men with the packs, other than the ammunition, in a well fortified position on the hill, and immediately moved out, with 250 of the best men - Benteen's battalion and McDougall's troop and Mathey's men, what could have happened, and how long would it have taken him to accomplish it?

> *"The distance from where the running Reno halted and kept the seven troops and reserve ammunition, to the extreme right of Custer's command was about four miles. A cavalry horse walked that distance in fifty-eight minutes. At a smart trot or gallop, as a cavalryman goes into action, fifteen minutes would have brought the whole command into the engagement and the result might have been entirely different. This we proved on that same ground by actual test of moving our horses over it, and timing them by the watch."*[410]

Reno needed to provide support, he did not have to go charging into the Custer debacle to add his men to what became the Custer dead. Reno, by merely moving forward with 250 men and assuming a strong position on Weir Point, would have become the support Custer would have required

to survive with the majority of his command. The Indians would have found themselves between two strong forces of cavalry totaling 400-450 men, well within cooperating distance and visualization of each other.

The Indians would have withdrawn, fighting a rear guard action while the village scattered and fled towards the mountains to west. The cavalry would have then united and advanced to the village, capturing much in the way of sustenance of life and perhaps could have claimed a mild, though awkward, victory.

Reno began his charge with approximately 151 officers and men plus approximately 30 scouts. When all fighting ended he had suffered less than 40 killed. Benteen's column contained 129 officers and men, and they had yet to fire a shot or suffer a casualty. McDougall commanded the pack train which included 113 officers and men plus additional civilians. The pack train was guarded by Troop B in its entirety, and in addition Custer had previously detached one sergeant and six troopers from each troop to manage and care for the respective company's supplies. There were numerous civilian herders and packers accompanying the pack train, as well. Thus, Reno's combined forces of combat, worthy soldiers and civilians, exceeded 350 well armed and equipped men.

It should be noted that Reno was rescued by General Terry and Colonel Gibbon whose column consisted of 300

---

[410]Miles, *The Personal Reflections of Nelson Miles*, 290.

infantry and 150 cavalry. The Terry/ Gibbon column was not much larger in manpower and not nearly as mobile as Reno's.

Indians were not modern fighters. They were not siege fighters or attackers and did not function as units, instead they acted as individuals in battle. The Indian warrior was most concerned in "counting coup" which was the showing of an act of bravery in battle. Such acts normally consisted of tapping a living opponent with a stick, a dead opponent would count also, but it was a lesser act of bravery. Normally the Indians allowed coups for up to three different coup taps on an opponent by three different warriors, with bravery points being awarded in a descending order. Indians did not feel it to be brave to kill an opponent at long range with a rifle or pistol, they did however feel it to be brave to cut the reins on an opponent's horse. Such mentality could hardly put forward a siege for two days against a well equipped modern army, unless the commander of the modern army wanted to be under siege and wait for help.

When Terry relieved Reno, the Reno combined force had plenty of ammunition left. The Reno force had sufficient ammunition to do as it desired, including breaking the siege and retreating. Or, if Reno desired to do a brave deed, they could have broken the siege and gone to reinforce Custer who they believed to be pinned down somewhere else in a predicament similar to theirs. Reno and Benteen of course had chosen the very safe alternative of waiting for help to find

them instead of taking the dangerous alternative of extricating themselves from the siege and then going to find Custer.

Various veteran soldiers have told of a certain incident that occurred between Gibbon and Reno after the arrival of Gibbon and his soldiers at Reno's hill position on the morning of June 27. Gibbon twitted Reno in this way: "I have seen many dead soldiers and dead soldier's horses in this vicinity, but I have not seen many dead Indians or dead ponies." This sort of twitting is said to have been repeated until General Terry suggested that some other topic of conversation would be better.[411]

To a man, all officers and enlisted men of Reno's combined column, asked as a first question to the rescuers, "Where is Custer?" The mere stating of the question is proof positive of Reno's cowardice. As second in command Reno was under a duty to break the siege and find his commanding officer who it could well be assumed was in trouble. Custer had promised to support Reno, his failure to do so was an indication of trouble. Reno knew the size of the Indian force and how outnumbered Custer must be. Reno was in command of seven-twelfths of the regiment, he had the superior force, it was his duty to go forward and aid his commander. Instead he chose to hide on the hill, behind his liquor bottle mourning the death of Lieutenant Hodgson, and waited for help to find him. Fortunately for Reno, all the

---

[411]Marquis, *Keep The Last Bullet For Yourself*, 169.

other officers present had conforming lapses of memory at his Court of Inquiry as they collusively decided to protect not Reno's but the Regiment's good name.

Reno, Benteen and Wallace claimed not to have heard any volleys or firing coming from downstream. Though Benteen did state he heard 15 to 20 shots coming from the center of the village, in the vicinity of Medicine Tail Ford.

BENTEEN[412]

"That was the firing I tried to describe I heard after my arrival there, 15 or 20 shots that seemed to have come from about ford "B" about the central part of the village. The village was in two divisions and at the ford "B" was about the place where I heard the shots, and all I heard that were not in sight were from that direction. I have heard, as a matter of course, officers disputing amongst themselves about hearing volleys. I heard no volleys."

RENO[413]

"If I had heard the firing, as they represent the firing, volley firing, I should have known he was engaged while I was on the hill but I heard no such firing."

WALLACE[414]

"The command could not have been seen from owing to intervening points. Whether their firing could have been heard I don't know. I did not hear any;

though others will testify that they did. I heard scattering shots in the bottom on the left but no heavy firing. It was apparently in the village; it did not sound like fighting. Whether the Indians were firing for their own amusement or not I don't know. It did not sound like fighting."

Their credibility is certainly subject to question, as all other witnesses at the Court of Inquiry testified that they heard volleys or firing downstream in the direction where Custer had gone. McDougall called Reno's attention to the firing downstream, and all Reno was concerned with was Lieutenant Hodgson's death and later could not recall hearing any firing. Varnum borrowed Wallace's rifle and when he handed it back to him, he mentioned the firing downstream, but Wallace could not recall hearing any firing. Benteen did not hear any volleys but heard light firing. Eight officers, including the near deaf Godfrey, heard firing coming from Custer's direction, but Wallace and Reno could not recall hearing any. The preponderance of testimony hearing firing severely challenges Reno's contention that he could hear no firing coming from downstream.

De RUDIO[415]

"Soon after he left the timber and reached the hill, the firing

---

[412] Ibid., 408.
[413] Ibid., 590.
[414] Ibid., 35.
[415] Ibid., 316.

commenced on the other side of the village. I heard immense volleys of firing and more than half the Indians around Major Reno left. Part of them went on the highest bluffs and part went down the river. Some of them picketed their ponies under the bluff and lay down flat, watching Major Reno."

EDGERLY[416]

"Shortly after I got to the hill, almost immediately, I heard firing and remarked heavy firing, by volleys, down the creek. Captain Weir came to me and said General Custer was engaged and we ought to go down. I said I thought so too."

GODFREY[417]

"I can't recollect the time exactly, except that it was after Lieutenant Hare had returned from going after the packs that we heard firing from below. I heard two very distinct volleys; still, they sounded a long distance off. Then we heard scattering shots afterwards, not very heavy."

"Lieutenant Hare and myself were together and I called his attention to it. I don't remember as there was any conversation between us."

HARE[418]

"It was just after Captain Benteen came up with his command. My attention was called to it by Captain Godfrey. He asked if I heard that volley. I said yes, I heard two distinct volleys. That was just

before I started for the pack train."

MOYLAN[419]

"I simply called McDougall's attention to it and asked him what he thought it was. He said he supposed it was General Custer firing at the other end of the Village."

"It was evidently volley firing, but very faint."

McDOUGALL[420]

"It was just two volleys. I told Major Reno about it and he said, 'Captain, I just lost your lieutenant, he is lying down there.' Then I left Major Reno and went to my company and threw out a skirmish line."

"I think it was quarter to four or four o'clock in the afternoon." "The firing was down the Little Bighorn from him and as I was going toward Major Reno, the firing was on my right."

"He was about four or four and one half miles from the firing and I was about the same. The sound could resound through the hills I heard was 4 to 4 ½ miles away. No, It was a dull sound, just two volleys. I thought it was some of the command. I thought it must be General Custer and the Indians."

---

[416]Ibid., 444.
[417]Ibid., 483.
[418]Ibid., 290.
[419]Ibid., 236.
[420]Ibid., 529-531.

"Only once, as soon as I arrived with the pack train."

VARNUM[421]

"Abut the time, or probably a few minutes after Benteen came up, I heard firing from away down stream and spoke of it to Lieutenant Wallace. I don't recollect any except that one time."

"I had borrowed a rifle of Lieutenant Wallace and fired a couple of shots at long range and as I handed the rifle back to him I heard the firing and said, 'Jesus Christ, Wallace, hear that! And that!' Those were my words."

"It was not like volley firing but a heavy fire, a sort of crash, crash. I heard it only for a few minutes."

"It must have pertained to Custer's command at the other end of the Indian village. It was from that end of the village where General Custer's body was afterwards found."

" I thought he was having a warm time down there, a very hot fire evidently."

Reno disobeyed his orders, deployed to a skirmish line when ordered to charge, abandoned the field of battle in an uncontrolled and cowardly state, causing nearly forty men to be needlessly killed. He reached the top of the hill in a complete state of disarray with his command out of control. Captain Henry B. Freeman of the 7th Infantry,

who was part of Gibbon's column, described Reno's rout from the valley as a stampede.[422] Captain Walter Clifford also of the 7th Infantry, described Reno's exit from the Valley with "The retreat was a mad race to a place of safety."[423] Benteen's actions calmed the situation, allowed Reno's troops to rally and regroup. However, his good efforts were minimized by Reno's failure to rally himself and move forward in a timely manner.

The unity of the surviving Officers came more from a desire to protect what remained of the Regiment's good name and not from a desire to reward Reno for his bravery and heroic leadership. The Court of Inquiry held in 1879 saw thru this and made its beliefs public with its conclusion as stated by its head Colonel Wesley Merritt:

"While subordinates in some instances did more for the safety of the command by brilliant displays of courage than did Major Reno, there was nothing in his conduct which requires animadversion from this Court."[424]

That the conspiracy was suspected, by the Court of Inquiry, was inferred by a private statement made by Colonel Merritt afterwards:

"Well, the officers wouldn't tell us anything, and we could do nothing more than damn Reno

---

[421]Ibid., 160.
[422]Freeman, *The Freeman Journal*, 64.
[423]Koury, *Diaries of the Little Bighorn*, 47.
[424]Sarf, *The Little Bighorn Campaign*, 193.
[425]Ibid., 193.

with faint praise."[425]

That Colonel Wesley Merritt was the head of the Court of Inquiry added a fitting irony to the debacle, as Merritt was Custer's rescuer at Trevelyan Station, Custer's first, last stand.

On June 25, 1876, fate dealt Major Marcus Reno an unenviable hand to play out. He was chosen by his commanding officer to lead a charge of 181 men against an enemy village containing over 10,000 inhabitants. Though Reno had the advantage of tactical surprise, and Indian testimony states he could have ridden through the village at will, he assumed a defensive stance, dismounted and deployed a skirmish line. His performance to this point was timid, cautious, substandard, indecisive and disobedient. Reno then lost all semblance of command and control for three reasons:

During the stand in the timbers, he was near Bloody Knife when the latter was fatally wounded in the head. Unfortunately for Reno and the men under his command, the blood and gore expelled when the shot impacted on Bloody Knife, landed mostly on Reno's face. This probably would have been sufficient to unnerve the most gallant, but in Reno's case it was the point of no return from which he could no longer effectively command his troops.

Reno's Adjutant, Lt. Benjamin Hodgson, was killed during the retreat across the river. This so bothered the distraught Reno, that during the most important time on siege hill, from shortly after the arrival of the survivors of Reno's Battalion to their departure to attempt to aid Custer,

Reno was obsessed with finding and burying Hodgson's body. The obsession delayed the departure of the troops and effectively denied the troops a commander for the interval. The critical chronology was:[426]

4:15 PM	Reno leaves in search of Hodgson's body
4:55 PM	Reno returns from search for Hodgson's body
5:02 PM	Reno orders Varnum to bury Hodgson's body
5:21 PM	Varnum leaves to bury Hodgson's body
5.22 PM	Benteen leaves to join Weir's advance
5:40 PM	Reno leaves to join Weir advance

Reno wasted the most critical hour and twenty-five minutes of the battle placating his obsession with finding and burying Lieutenant Hodgson's body. It was within this time frame, and only within this time frame, that any effective effort could have been mounted by Reno's command to aid or relieve Custer, or to divert the Indians' attention from Custer.

Reno's final nemesis was his alcohol dependence. It is far too late to determine exactly how drunk he was and how much it affected his ability to command. It is thoroughly documented in Chapter Nine that he consumed a quart of whiskey in the interval from when he first forded the river to when he reached the timber,

─────────────────────

[426]Gray, *Custer's Last Command*, 310.

perhaps forty five minutes. It is well known that Reno was a drinker and alcohol dependent. Reno had with the pack train a personal cask of whiskey from which he continually refilled his flask or returned to, for a brief period of imbibing. Private John Burkman, who was Custer's former orderly, accused Reno of drinking during the siege, but his accusations were dismissed as those of a trouble maker and a member of the Custer clan. The most damning statement authenticating this fact comes from General Godfrey who wrote on September 11, 1928, to Thomas B. Marquis: "I never made the statement quoted in the alleged interview. The whole statement is a lie. There were no whiskey kegs with the command. The only persons I have heard of having whiskey were Major Reno and Fred Girard, Ree interpreter. Varnum has said that Girard gave him a drink from a flask while in the valley."[427] After the 1879 Court of Inquiry Captain Benteen later confessed that the court: "knew there was something kept back by me, but they didn't know how to dig it out by questioning, as I gave them no chance to do so; and Reno's attorney was posted thereon."[428]

The gore from Bloody Knife and the remorse for Lieutenant Hodgson could only be erased and relieved, in Reno, by the comfort provided by alcohol. Reno had whiskey with him during the battle and consumed it freely. He may not have been drunk but he certainly was drinking and probably impaired. The smell of liquor was noticed on his breath by all officers including the outspoken

Benteen and Lieutenant Edgerly.

Reno because of his complete breakdown and Benteen because of his hatred for Custer, each in his own way, for his own reasons, never would have moved the remnants of the Regiment forward, in search of Custer, were it not for the independent act of bravery by Captain Thomas Weir. It was Weir who, independently, moved forward to the sound of the guns followed by his lone troop to attempt to aid his commander. Then, and only then, did the coward Reno and the betrayer Benteen feel compelled to move forward, but of course only to save their own reputations.

It is quite conceivable that Custer in death accomplished what he could not do in life and Reno would not do, cause the Sioux to break off the engagement and leave the battlefield. The Sioux broke off the siege and abandoned the battlefield before the Terry/Gibbon column arrived. Most Native American accounts of the battle indicate that the Sioux broke camp and moved late in the afternoon of June 26, 1876. They left behind a few warriors to continue harrying the besieged soldiers, but the entire camp moved towards the Shining Mountains. Conversely, Reno could have quit the battlefield at any time he chose after the afternoon of June 26, 1876, and sought out Custer instead of waiting for help to find him.

[427]Marquis, *Keep the Last Bullet for Yourself*, 120-121.
[428]Sarf, *The Little Bighorn Campaign*, 193.

213

There were six driving motivations for the move:

- The stench of the dead was blowing towards the village and was highly offensive to the Indians who had an extremely sensitive sense of smell.

- It was an established Plains Indian custom to end a battle when more than half of the enemy were killed and allow the survivors to go home.

- The Sioux had decided that they had won a great victory and any further hostilities would only tarnish the victory by killing more of their warriors. It was time to end the battle, and they did.

- The valley no longer had the resources to sustain the mass of humanity and horses the Indians had in the valley.

- The Sioux were getting scouting reports of another column of soldiers approaching from the west who were getting very close to their camp.

- They no longer wanted to expose their women and children to further risk.

An unbiased evaluation of Reno's performance was written by General Edward J Mc Clernand.[429]

"It was said that as Reno emptied his revolvers, he threw them away. A fine example to set for his men!... Had Reno shown a bolder spirit in the timber and greater confidence in his leader, he might at this moment from that position have changed the fortunes of the day; at least he might have saved Custer's command from annihilation without incurring his own. He left the woods at the worst possible time both for himself and Custer, even though the latter had not moved to his immediate support he should have known his chief would strike soon. It was not in the nature of the man to turn his back to the foe, and a diversion on any part of the field would have contributed to his lieutenant's relief. A short distance through the woods from the old bed of the river would have enabled Reno to fully see the village into which a withering fire might have been poured, while many of its defenders were confronting Custer, and with a most demoralizing effect.

...Reno having lost his hat, had a handkerchief tied around his head, and was plainly excited... Not having supported his Chief in the valley, every rule of warfare dictated that Reno should strike hard when gained the top of the bluffs. He now had half the regiment with him, and McDougall's troop coming on; in all seven troops against Custer's five. His own battalion was, it is true, badly shaken, but neither Benteen nor McDougall had been engaged... Reno stood still.

...Reno's front was practically cleared of the enemy. Among the officers on the bluff the question of what's the matter with Custer, that

---

[429]McClernand, *On Time For Disaster*, 71-88.

he don't send word what shall we do,' was being asked. If Custer could have heard and replied we may imagine his saying, 'I was counting on aggressive and helpful action from Reno, and but a short time ago Benteen was ordered to come on, to be quick, and to bring the packs. The extra ammunition, as you know, is on the packs. You hear heavy firing in the direction I disappeared. You must know I am fighting. You know it is my rule to act quickly and vigorously in battle. You are my subordinates. Why do you not observe the spirit of my instructions and act?'...it was evident a fight was on, for neither Custer nor the Indians would be wasting ammunition by shooting at a mark, and yet Reno with six troops and another approaching stood still, thus ignoring the well known military axiom to march to the sound of the guns.

Benteen's battalion was directed to divide its ammunition with Reno's. In view of the little firing Reno had done this may not have been necessary, but the thought, at least, should have impressed that officer with the significance of Custer's last order, to bring the packs and be quick. Was it not possible that Custer might need additional ammunition? Heavy firing was heard down river, if not when the distribution was made, at least soon after."

[Quoting Godfrey]

"...I have but little doubt now that these volleys were fired by Custer's orders as a sign of distress and to indicate where he

was..."

[Talking of Herendeen's group exodus from the timber]

"...As they were leaving the timber they repulsed an attack made by five Indians, who fired upon them, but the mere fact that they were able to leave their cover, ford the river, and ascend the bluffs (dismounted, for they had lost their horses) is quite good evidence that there was no serious opposition confronting Reno.

"...It was said that as Reno's battalion moved down the valley from the ford where it first crossed, the Indians commenced driving the loose ponies down stream. This seems logical. I was told the rapidly moving herds raised a great cloud of dust and it occurred to me then that Custer doubtless saw, from the high bluffs to the east of the river, this dust and the fleeing ponies, and was further confirmed in his opinion that the Indians would not stand for a stiff fight. It is possible that this sight caused Custer to be less cautious than he would otherwise have been in widely separating his own and Reno's battalions, and it may in part explain his apparent indifference in notifying his lieutenant that his support would be given, not in his immediate vicinity, but at a considerable distance, out of sight, near the middle of the village, and on the opposite side of the river.

"...The firing last mentioned ceased, and Reno was now to pay dearly for not joining his chief

while the latter was fighting, for through clouds of dust the Indians converged toward the hesitating commander and once more, due entirely to his own inactivity, he was to fight without Custer's support.

"...The hasty withdrawal and the close pursuit, if it had been unchecked, might have brought disaster to the entire command but fortunately Godfrey properly appraised the situation, and dismounting his one troop of Reno's seven, he opened fire, compelling the enemy to halt and take cover... Reno was now to have a taste of what his indecision or worse, had forced upon the smaller detachment under his chief...

"...The opposing Indians broke as soon as the charging line started. Benteen's attitude revived temporarily the old aggressiveness of his subordinate officers and men, but when they had advanced about one hundred yards Reno called out 'get back men, back,' and back they came.

"...The writer does not feel called upon to discuss the question of Reno's personal courage, but only to weigh his qualifications for an independent command. It is not unlikely that under the immediate supervision of Custer he would have performed his duties as a subordinate in a way that would not have invited comment, but the courage to follow is one thing and that to lead something very different. The first may dispense with all idea of responsibility for the movement

about to be attempted, while the latter must assume it, and also demands a courage of convictions that is not to be shaken by the thought of the lives about to be sacrificed, or by the suggestions, always ready, of associates that it might be well to delay, to side step as we say. It was in leadership that Custer's lieutenant seems to have failed, and that he had so failed and that Benteen was the man who stood between utter destruction and such safety as was found, was heard on all sides from his subordinates when Terry arrived. Many of the criticisms heard were severe. Later, before the Court of Inquiry that followed, many were toned down."

General Nelson A. Miles critiqued Reno's performance as follows:[430]

"...Captain Benteen halted his men and helped to rally the battalion of Major Reno. In that vicinity the two commands remained the entire day and night. One commander had received positive and repeated orders from Custer to attack the enemy; the other had received Custer's last and equally positive order to 'Come On', 'Be Quick', and 'Bring Packs' containing the reserve ammunition. The courier who brought Custer's last order was the best possible guide to be had to lead the way to Custer's position if any direction was needed; but the sound of the rifle shots and the volleys down the river indicated exactly where the troops and ammunition were required and

---

[430]Miles, *Personal Reflections of General Nelson A Miles*, 208-210.

should have gone.

"Under the rules governing all military forces, whenever two commands come together the senior officer is responsible for the whole. And the senior officer should give the necessary orders. Major Reno was therefore the responsible commander at that point.

"...Weir with his troops moved a short distance along... and seeing smoke and dust and a great commotion in the valley, reported that he could go no further. That may have been a time when one troop under a gallant officer might not have been able to go where seven troops could and ought to have gone. One of the scouts, Herendeen, and thirteen men who were with Reno, and who were left in the timber from which Reno retreated, after the Indians had gone down the valley, walked across the plain, forded the river, and rejoined their command on the hill. These two movements indicate that there were no Indians in this vicinity during the time that the firing was going on that is mentioned by Godfrey..."

Continuing on Miles added the following comments:[431]

"When asked what would have been the result if Reno had not retreated, the Indians frankly said that if he had not run, they would have fled. They were also asked what the consequences would have been if Reno with the seven troops had followed the Uncpapas and Ogallala when they turned and went down to the assistance of the

Indians in the village, and they candidly admitted that they would have been between two fires. In other words the battle was lost twice, not by the action of Custer, however, for his command fought gallantly as long as it lasted, and he had given proper and judicious orders to the other commands.

It is not expected that five troops could have whipped that body of Indians, neither is it believed that that body of Indians could have whipped twelve troops of the Seventh Cavalry under Custer's command, or if his orders had been properly executed. The fact that Custer's five troops had been annihilated, the Indians who came back and engaged the seven troops were repulsed and that they failed to dislodge these troops, is proof that the force was amply strong, if it had only acted in full concert. No commanding officer can win victories with seven twelfths of his command remaining out of the engagement when within sound of his rifle shots."

Walter Camp, after studying the battle for numerous years and interviewing hundreds of its participants, described Reno's behavior and the possibility of him drinking in the following manner:

"That something abnormal was the matter with Reno could hardly be denied, and the facts and testimony bearing on it are as follows:

[1.] Reno offered to give Dr. Porter his gun.

---

[431]Ibid., 289-290.

[2] *Gerard Saw Reno drinking in the valley.*

[3] *Reliable man says Reno was dazed.*

[4] *Reno's disgraceful negligence of command when retreating out of timber.*

[5] *His queer actions on bluff, borrowing a revolver to shoot at Indians a thousand yards away.*

[6] *Bewildered action in sending [Varnum] to rescue Hodgson's body.*

[7] *Being drunk at 9 p.m., according to sworn testimony of Churchill and Frett and the fact that he did not deny striking Frett, and threatening to shoot him.*

Even if Reno was not under the influence of liquor in the valley, the fact that he became intoxicated later in the day in the presence of such a trying ordeal, is an even worse indictment of his character and shows that he was utterly unfit to wear a uniform in the service of his country.[432]

Major Marcus B. Reno proved the axiom that the Courage to Follow is one thing, the courage to Lead is something very different.[433] Reno's failure to vigorously pursue the charge or hold the position in the timber and then finally lose all control, break and lead a rout out of the timber is what ultimately led to Custer's defeat. Reno failed to allow sufficient time for the promised support to manifest itself. Custer attempted to ford and attack at Medicine Tail Ford, but was driven back by an overwhelming foe. This overwhelming foe existed because the other half of his force had abandoned the field of battle and failed and refused to engage. By refusing to attempt to join Custer when there was no enemy in his front, Reno allowed the Indians to mass their entire efforts against Custer alone. **Thus, it is the coward Reno who by abandoning the field of battle and refusing to engage the enemy, failed to support Custer. His refusal to fight brought shame upon him and his regiment and he bears the brunt of the blame for the debacle at the Little Bighorn.**

General Jesse M. Lee who was the Recorder [or Prosecutor] at the Reno Court of Inquiry, told Walter Camp on October 27, 1912 that:

"...Gen. [Wesley] Merritt, who drew up the conclusions of the Reno court of Inquiry, said to him when the decision of the Court was announced:

'We have politely cursed him (Reno) and whitewashed it over.'"[434]

---

[432]Hardorff, *On The Little Bighorn With Walter Camp*, 235-236.

[433]McClernand, *On Time For Disaster*, 88.

[434]Hardorff, *On The Little Bighorn With Walter Camp*, 191.

EPILOGUE

Headquarters Military Division of the Missouri

Chicago, Illinois   July 9, 1876

Mrs. George A. Custer

Fort Lincoln, via Bismarck D. T.

I take this opportunity to convey to you and the ladies of the 7ᵗʰ Cavalry who have been so deeply bereaved by the terrible loss you have sustained, my sincere sympathy and condolence. And while conscious that nothing I can say will assuage your great sorrow, I can at least share in the grief you all feel. My acquaintance with General Custer and the officers who fell with him was most intimate, both officially and personally, and in a long service with them they sustained the high character now so justly appreciated by the Army and the country, for their gallantry and devotion to duty.

(Signed) P. H. Sheridan

Lieut. General[435]

---

[435]Transcribed from the original "Copy Telegram" delivered to Mrs. Annie Yates, in the author's collection.

With the foregoing telegram the Army's period of mourning officially ended and the guilt shifting and coverup commenced. The work of Major George Elliott in September, 1876 was the Army's initial attempt to rewrite history and the effort culminated with the Reno Court of Inquiry, in 1879. The Army's efforts at coverup and whitewash were blatant and well demonstrated by the decision of the Reno Court of Inquiry. The last paragraph of that decision was the final mockery, by Army, of the events of June 25, 1876.

"The conduct of the officers throughout was excellent, and while subordinates in some instances did more for the safety of the command by brilliant displays of courage than did Major Reno, there was nothing in his conduct which requires the animadversion from this court."[436]

General Wesley Merritt's opinion of the decision has been stated at the end of Chapter 21. While Merritt, a member of that court, was a bit more straight forward than the written decision, he was far from fully honest.

Today's government no longer knows the whereabouts of the original handwritten transcript of the Reno Court of Inquiry. All that remains of this significant event for the researcher is a microfilm version which is missing both pages and pieces of pages. The microfilm that the government maintains is a 35 mm positive image version, for which very few readers and printers exist today.

President Grant's term was coming to an end and his administration was scandal ridden. He did not want yet another blot on his presidency, in the form of blame for the Custer massacre. He had his doctrine of Manifest Destiny to defend. He had to convince western settlers, lumber, mining, cattle and railroad interests that the Army could protect them, and the West was a safe place to live and conduct business. Surely, the blame for the debacle could be neither the Administration's, the Army's nor the surviving officers, it had to fall to the dead commander, Lieutenant Colonel George Armstrong Custer. Grant was well aware that a dead commander was powerless to defend his actions against spurious accusations. The Grant administration took the safe approach, followed the path of least resistance and put all the blame for the day's events on Custer.

Sherman and Sheridan could not publicly admit that their Grand Plan was sheer folly, from the moment they conceived it. They could not publicly state that they arrogantly put three columns into the field, believing any one of them would be invincible against the intended foe, yet not one of them was up to the tasks asked of them.

They could not let the public know that one of their columns, under General Crook, suffered a minor defeat or perhaps fought to a draw with the enemy and then abandoned the field, under the pretense of refitting and did not return until it was well too late.

---

[436]Nichols, *The Reno Court of Inquiry*, 629.

Nor could it be divulged that the second column, under colonel Gibbon, refused to engage the enemy, though it sat opposite them for ten days, and this same column was essentially unfit for battle on June 25, 1876.

The public could not be allowed to know that General Terry, commanding the third column, had no clue as to where the enemy was, was oblivious as to the strength of the enemy and formulated a plan of battle that was so loose and undefined that it constituted no plan at all. That this general, General Terry, for want of any plan of action of his own, told his field commander, "...do what you think is best when you strike the trail."

Lastly, they could ill afford to let the public know that when the field commander of the third column, Lt. Colonel Custer, did find and engage the enemy, his two main subalterns, Major Reno and Captain Benteen, commanding nearly sixty percent of the regiment refused to fight and further refused to ride to the sound of the guns, even when there was no enemy or resistance in their front.

None of this could be allowed to reach the public domain, for the public would no longer have any confidence in the Army's ability to maintain their safety. The answer was simple, the choice was obvious: the debacle was Custer's fault because he failed to obey orders and follow the plan, as drawn up by his commanding general.

The surviving officers of the 7th Cavalry were coerced into agreeing with the Army's public pronouncements regarding the battle and not permitted to publicly disagree. What form of coercion could exact such unanimous cooperation. Simply the intimation that if you did not go along with the request, you would finish out your career in some obscure post without any hope of ever again being promoted. Cooperation meant a continued career in the Army, dissent meant your career was over.

The surviving officers had another dilemma with which to cope: their performance in the battle was so poor and the results so disastrous that they could not let either the families of the deceased or the public know how and why their loved ones died. There was an unwritten code of silence among these officers that they would say nothing of the truth as long as Mrs. Custer lived, and then they could tell all. Unfortunately, Mrs. Custer lived for 57 years after the battle and outlived all the surviving officers, except Charles Varnum. By the time bits and pieces of the truth started to resurface, it was too little too late. The Grant Administration, The Army and the Reno Court of Inquiry had so tarnished Custer's reputation that he went from the boy icon of the Civil War to the hated manifestation of all that was wrong in the dealings of the Whites and Indians.

Libby Custer did her best to champion her dead husband's cause by writing three books and doing all she could to keep his good memory alive. In 1892, then Captain Edward Settle Godfrey had his infamous version of the battle published in *Century Magazine*, wherein he succeeded in erasing from public view all remaining known facts pertaining to the sequence of events of the battle. Godfrey accomplished this by completely misunderstanding and misinterpreting what was told to him by Gall at the 1886 Tenth Anniversary Re-Union at the battlefield. Godfrey did not realize that when Gall told him Custer never got to the river, Gall arrived at the battle scene after Custer departed from the river. Therefore, Gall had no knowledge that Custer had been to the river and retreated from it, never to return again. Using Godfrey's erasures as a base, the history revisionists had a ball. Writing commenced, creating alleged versions of the battle, totally unsupported by any facts. The true events were still available, all one had to do was examine the pre 1879 writings of the participants, especially their post battle letters to loved ones back home, but nobody did or wanted to.

When historians finally realized there was yet another version of the battle that had been untapped, the Indian version, they started interviewing the surviving Indian participants. Unfortunately, these interviews were rarely time sequenced, hardly ever conducted one on one in the same language, distorted by interpreters, embellished upon by the interviewers, distorted by interviewees who gave the answers they thought the interviewer wanted, and a never ending assortment of leading and loaded questions, the answers to which were destined to prove the interviewer's preconceived notions of what occurred. These interviews when viewed either singly or collectively, in an attempt to determine the events of June 25, 1876, produced a result similar to that of

trying to solve a jig saw puzzle, with the pieces face down.

Walter Mason Camp spent nearly his entire life conducting hundreds of interviews of people who were in any way remotely related to the battle. He compiled voluminous notes and letters during the process. Unfortunately, he died before he could ever write a book on his beloved topic. His papers were disseminated to numerous libraries, schools and other repositories across the country, forever destroying the thoroughness of his work. It was not until recently that some of his writings and notes started to become publicly available, reactivating the long lost information.

The Northern Plains Tribes never again came together to form a village or gathering as large as the one on the Little Big Horn in the summer of 1876. They did not learn the lesson of the battle, that if they banded together and stood and fought they could give the white soldiers all they could ask for and more. After the battle, they did what the Army feared most, they scattered and fled in different directions. The worst fear of the Army became its best ally in the Sioux Wars of 1876 to 1877. One by one the small bands were either defeated by troops, or driven by starvation and lack of sustenance onto reservations. Railroads forevermore prevented the roaming of the Buffalo and the nomadic Plains Indians. White hunters lusting for buffalo hides and tongues, a very profitable delicacy in the east, all but made the Buffalo extinct. The Plains Wars, which for the Indians had its zenith at the Little

Big Horn reached its dismal conclusion at Wounded Knee in 1891, and the way of the Plains Tribes passed into history, rendered extinct by progress and Manifest Destiny.

In 1984, a fire on the battlefield denuded much of the land and it came under the scrutiny of archeologists. While their endeavors unearthed many new artifacts and gave us new hypotheses based on their findings, they overlooked what was no longer there, and did not adequately adjust their findings for 125 years of natural events including floods, fires, rains, snow, erosion, rusting and souvenir hunters. Much of what was left on the battlefield, was removed, ruined or moved by these events, within 25 years of the battle, forever eliminating much of their synergy with the actual events. Simply because there are no relics in a specific area, does not mean that an event did not take place there. Simply put, no modern archeological study can create a better description of what took place at the battle than the writings of the people who saw the field, littered with bodies of dead soldiers and horses and other debris of the battle, in the days immediately following the battle.

The Army, through its arrogant plan predicated on invincibility, failed itself, the public and George Armstrong Custer on June 25, 1876. It blatantly contrived to distort and change records, suppress the truth, coerce the surviving officers from relating what actually occurred, and whitewash the entire sordid mess by placing the blame on the deceased Custer. Their efforts were thwarted by Mrs. Custer for 57 years following the battle. With her passing, history entered the age of blatant revisionism, and the name Custer became a synonym for evil as it pertains to White and Indian dealings in the old west.

The betrayer, Benteen, became more morose and sullen with the passage of time, if that can be imagined. He ironically became a Major of the 9th Cavalry, in 1882, as this was the position he originally turned down for his Captaincy in the 7th Cavalry. He too fell victim to alcohol abuse. He was Court Martialed and suspended from the Army, for drunk and disorderly conduct in 1884. Much like Macbeth who was bothered by the ghost of his murdered brother, Benteen, later in life appeared unable to get the blood of the 230 abandoned comrades off his hands. He recessed further and further into a fantasy world where he continually embellished upon his ever growing self importance and bravery at the Battle of the Little Big Horn, until he died in 1898.

The coward Reno became the butt of many Sutler's Store jokes as to his bravery leading him to get involved in numerous fights. He was detested by his commanders and underlings, alike. He was eventually Court Martialed by the Army for drunkenness and acts of perversion on November 24, 1879 and dismissed from the service on April 1, 1880. He died of cancer of tongue and mouth in 1889, most likely a result of his excessive consumption of alcohol.

This tome has attempted to correct most of the erroneous concepts pertaining to the Battle of the Little Big Horn that the public has been led to believe. Blame has been properly placed and long overdue criticism given to many who rightly deserved it, but have long been protected by either the Army "whitewash" or Anti-Custer revisionism. This vindication of Lieutenant Colonel George Armstong Custer has been overdue for 125 years. On June 25, 1876, Colonel Custer and 260 of the men under his command died, victims of Arrogance, Betrayal and Cowardice, the perpetrators of which have now been unmasked.

ADDENDUM
The Lt. W. Philo Clark Report

During 1877, the Army victories over the hostile tribes increased, and more and more bands surrendered to the will of the Government and the reservation way of life. In the Spring of 1877, Lt. W. Philo Clark, who was the Army's expert in sign language, was given the task of debriefing and interviewing many of the Chiefs, including Crazy Horse, significant warriors and prominent members of the surrendering tribes. These interviews were conducted at Camp Robinson, Red Cloud and Spotted Tail Agencies over a period of several months, culminating with his report dated September 14, 1877.

This most significant document is believed to have achieved a status of being virtually lost. It is uncertain if it was ever published in its entirety. It is solely available today from the National Archives as part of their microfilm document program. Attached to the report was a map prepared by Clark of the Battle of the Little Big Horn. This map is derived from a sketch made by one of the Indians interviewed by Clark, and it contains extremely important information which has heretofore been lost to history for over 130 years.

The map and the accompanying report provide new and significant insights into this battle. They lend strong support to the theory that Custer attempted to ford the river and attack at Medicine Tail Coulee, but that he was repulsed by the Sioux. The Report shows that the Indian non-combatants were initially hidden in the Squaw Creek area and the timber southwest of Last Stand Hill, on the west side of the river. Custer had to have seen non combatants moving about the village heading to these locations, and he attempted to pursue and capture them. The map shows Custer made a second attempt to ford the river and attack the village at "Ford C,"[437] and from this failed attempt he retreated to Last Stand

---

[437]This ford has been given several different designations on the many maps that have been prepared on this topic, typically it is referred to as eithr C, D1, or D. Mark Kellogg's body was found on the east side of the river near this ford.

Hill to meet his ultimate fate.

Following the Report is an endorsement by Lt. General Philip H. Sheridan giving both his analysis of the Report and his views and opinions of what transpired during the Battle of the Little Big Horn. Sheridan in part takes issue with Clark, but more directly he is critical of the general source, i.e. the Indian informant who he believes is unreliable and merely saying what Clark and others want to hear.

He refers to another version of the Battle, one rendered by Chief Red Horse, as being a better version. The Red Horse narrative which was attached to the endorsement is no longer attached in the microfilm version. There is available a version of the battle from Chief Red Horse, obtained five years later, by Dr. Charles E. McChesney. The Red Horse second narrative was given in sign language to Dr. McChesney. As the original narrative was an integral part of Sheridan's comments and endorsements, the subsequent McChesney narrative is included herein as a substitute, in its entirety, in lieu of the text of the original Red Horse narrative, the current whereabouts of which are unknown.[438]

"Five little grasses ago Sioux had pitched tepees near Red Cloud Tepees when scout reported white soldiers were moving on trail. So I, Red Horse, with many Cutthroats took down tepee and moved from Good River. Many Sioux warriors then moved to Greasy Grass Creek for war council. I, Red Horse, chief of Sioux, pitched my tepee in midst of Sioux tepees. Sitting Bull's warriors pitched tepees highest up river under bluff. One hot day around noon Sioux scout mounted horse to look for soldiers at Red Cloud Tepees. When Sioux scout had ridden short distance from tepee, he saw cloud of dust rising. He turned back and said, 'I think many buffalo are moving near.' I, Red Horse, and four women were short distance away digging turnips. Suddenly, one woman pointed to cloud of dust rising. I saw white man soldiers moving where Sioux had many tepees. Women and I ran back to camp. When I, Red Horse, arrived, Sioux scout told me to hurry to council tepee. But we Sioux could not talk. We saw White Man Soldiers moving on trail. Straightway we ran out of council tepee in all directions. Then we Sioux mounted horses and took guns to fight White Man Soldiers. Women and children mounted horses to flee. White Man Soldiers forded Greasy Grass Creek farther up than Sioux had crossed and fought Sitting Bull's tribe. Suddenly White Man Soldiers charged among us set fire to many tepees. Sioux charge White Man Soldiers and drove them into confusion across Greasy Grass Creek. Creek was so rapid that many white man soldiers drowned. White Man Soldiers stopped on hill.

---

[438]*"Chief Red Horse Tells About Custer,"* edited by Jessie Brewer McGaw.

Sioux surrounded them. Sioux scout rode up and said, 'Different White man soldiers may make women and children prisoners.' Like whirlwind word spread and Sioux heard. We Sioux left White Man Soldiers on Hill and hurried to save women and children. Sioux feared White Man Soldiers on Hill would charge Sioux in rear. When White Man Soldiers on Hill did not charge, Sioux thought they had no cartridges. On level ground by creek I, Red Horse, saw different White Man Soldiers moving on trail. In front of soldiers, White Man Soldier Chief was riding horse with feet like snow. White Man Soldier Chief had long hair, big brimmed hat, and deerskin clothes. White Man Soldier chief had divided soldiers. One band was charging many tepees. I, Red Horse, Sioux Chief, spoke: 'Sioux warriors, watch White Man Soldiers on Hill. Do not let them join different White Man Soldiers.' Immediately all brave Sioux ran short distance, separated, surrounded soldiers, and charged to save women and children. Brave different White Man Soldiers fought hand to hand and stopped five charges. Different White Man Soldiers shot guns not many times. We Sioux charged in the midst of white man soldiers. They scattered in confusion. Different White Man Soldiers became foolish. Many threw away guns and raised hands, saying, 'Sioux, make us prisoners.' By custom,

Sioux did not take one prisoner. Sioux killed all Different White Man Soldiers. None were left alive. I heard Sioux say: 'White Man Soldier Chief saved many white man soldiers by turning his horse and covering retreat.' I saw White Man Soldier Chief fighting, but after fight did not see him dead. I was told he was killed by warrior of Knife Tribe, who took horse. Sioux for long time have fought bravest of various people. I, Red Horse, believe White Man Soldier Chief was bravest of all."

Not surprisingly so, Red Horse's version contains different thoughts on how the battle was fought from the composite obtained by Lt. Clark. Both versions do make a strong case that Custer was threatening the noncombatants and the Sioux fought to protect them. Both Red Horse and Clark's report talk of Custer fighting in two places before reaching Last Stand Hill. Red Horse states one band was charging tepees and another was threatening the noncombatants. Clark talks of Custer being repulsed at Medicine Tail Coulee, moving across the ridge and then following the trail to Ford C. Earlier Clark talks of the women and children who fled Reno's charge, hiding in Squaw Creek and the Timber on the west side of the river just southwest of Last Stand Hill. These two versions correlate well, a failed charge at Medicine Tail Coulee could equate to the band charging tepees, while a withdrawal across the ridge and then down the trail to Ford C could well be the second band which threatened the women and children.

The Report and its accompanying Map are the first attempt, performed in mid 1877, at reconstruction of the events that occurred from the Indian point of view and was prepared in a matter of fact style, by an unbiased observer of an event in history. The Red Horse narrative is perhaps an untainted Indian version as Dr. McChesney not only recorded Red Horse's words, he recorded the signs Red Horse used to create the words. Thus, there is little likelihood that Red Horse's words could have been misinterpreted or distorted over time. These documents contain such major revelations about this battle in what could aptly be described as "fresh or new writings" that it was felt to be worthwhile to reproduce the entire text of both, herein.

Camp Robinson, Neb

Sept. 14, 1877

Adjutant General
Department Platte

Sir:

In compliance with the verbal instructions of the Dept Commander I have the honor to submit the following report of the late Sioux War based upon facts gleaned from statements made to me by Indians who have surrendered at Red Cloud and Spotted Tail agencies during the past eight months and information obtained from Interpreters and friendly Indians it has been a very difficult matter to get accurate information in regard to the different engagements. Not only as the Indians from Crazy Horse down have been extremely reticent, but some of the battles were on as extensive a scale that no one Indian could possibly be conversant with all the actual details. Especially difficult has it been to ascertain the number of killed and wounded in the Rosebud and the Little Horn fights, where so many bands participated, I am confident however that as the Indian accounts it is the most reliable that could be obtained.

The small number of killed is due to the fact that an Indian has a wonderful faculty of protecting himself and unless he is shot through the brain, heart or back there is no certainty at all about his dying for since I have seen many Indians here who have been shot in all manner of ways through the body and still enjoying excellent health. I have been convinced that of all animals they are superior in point of tenacity of life, magnificent horsemen and fine shots - doing about as good execution on the backs of their thorough trained speedy and hardy Ponies as on the ground, accustomed from their earliest youth to take advantage of every knoll, rock, tree, trift of grass and every aid topography of the country affords to secure game and their education completed and perfected by constant warfare with other tribes and the whites, each warrior becomes as adept in their way of fighting needing no orders, to promptly seize, finish and hold any opportunity for success, or in retreating, protecting themselves from harm. Each tribe is organized by accident or pleasure into several different bands. Each band having a Chief, but his powers and authority are in a great measure limited by the will and wishes of his people.

Great prominence has been given Crazy Horse and Sitting Bull in this war, the good fighting strategy and subsequent number by retreats being attributed to them, whereas they are really not entitled to more credit or censure than many others so far as plans and order were concerned, but they headed two of the worst bands on the plains, and were the two fiercest leaders the Sioux nation has produced for years. Constantly in the northern country these bands had renegades from all Agencies as well as some of the strongest men from a spiritual stand point that the Sioux as a nation possess today. These latter worked from conviction and held fast to their Non Treaty ideas, the impression seems to have obtained that the Arapahoes participated with the Sioux and Cheyennes in this war, this is a mistake as they remained quietly at their Agency till they went out as our allies when they performed excellent service. In March 1876 about sixty lodges of Cheyennes under "Old Bear" and fourteen of Sioux under "He Dog" were encamped on Powder River, they knew that the troops were in their vicinity, and on the evening of March 16 a party of young bucks was sent out to scout the country

and ascertain their whereabouts. It was a bitter cold night and the scouts went into camp, in the morning they discovered a trail which they followed it led them to the ashes of their own lodges. Genl Crook's Cavalry under Colonel Reynolds by a long and terrible trying night march completely surprised the village on the morning of March 17 captured and partially burnt it. This village was particularly rich in bead work, buffalo robes, furs, dried meats, fine skin lodges, in fact everything that goes to make Indians wealthy and comfortable. The first charge upon the lodges swept everything before it, men, women and children rushed frantically from comfortable tepees. (Many cutting their way out with knives) to the adjacent ravines and rocky bluffs, but a rally was soon made and from behind rocks and other shelter they fired on the troops which soon abandoned the village and retired.

This was a complete surprise yet nearly every Indian as he rushed from his lodge took his gun and cartridges with him, this presence of mind or instinct never seems to fail this warlike and savage race. About one thousand ponies were captured, but the Indians recovered nearly all of them that night. There was one Sioux, one Cheyenne and one Squaw killed in this fight which was erroneously called Crazy Horse's as that Chief and Sitting Bull were camped at this time on the Little Missouri and did not know that a fight had taken place till some time after. The Indians gathered up what they could and started for Crazy Horses' Camp which they soon afterwards found, suffering greatly en route however. Soon after this, Indians commenced going out from agencies here and on the Missouri River, well armed with plenty of ammunition thoroughly equipped for field service. Nearly every tribe or band of the Sioux Nation was well represented. They kept themselves thoroughly posted in regard to the movement of troops in the Department of Dakota, and as forces advanced into their country they harassed and annoyed them by firing into their camps and trying to steal stock, and kept a sharp watch on all small parties. While Genl Crook's forces were encamped on Goose Creek in June '76 a small party was sent out under Lieut Sibley, which made an almost miraculous escape.

The Indians discovered it soon after it left camp but the spirited resistance offered where they attempted to capture it - one Indian being killed and some wounded and the prompt action taken in abandoning the horses in some brush as well as the favorable topography of the country saved the party. The escape was so cunningly conducted that it was not suspected and the horses were not taken out of the brush till the next morning.

On June 17th the Indians were camped on a small tributary of the Little Big Horn about eighteen miles above the place where Gen. Custer's Troops found them on the 25th.

They had at this time about 1200 standing lodges and 400 wickyups or brush shelters and numbered about 3500 fighting men. Gen Crooks forces left their Camp on Goose Creek early on the morning of June 16th and started for the Rosebud where the Indian village had been, but a few days before, soon after the troops left camp the Indians knew of the movement, and nearly all of their available fighting men started out to meet them. The Ogallalas, Minneconjous, Sans Arcs, Uncpapas, Cheyennes, Yanktoris, Yanktonais, Blackfeet and Brules were all represented. On the morning of the 17th the Crows were first discovered and in chasing them the engagement was precipitated, as it was intended that the fight should take place a little further down the Rosebud; The Indian tactics of carrying everything before them with a grand rush or wild charge was tried and failed. They were repulsed but though driven back they vanished only to reappear at some other point of the line and in this way the engagement was kept up some three hours. Failing however in their efforts to stampede the troops a retreat was made down the Rosebud canon for the purpose of decoying the white soldiers into an ambush, where if they had been followed in all human probability, Genl Crook's forces would have suffered the same fate that befell Genl Custer's Troops a few day's later.

In this fight eight Indians were

killed (two Cheyennes, two Uncpapas, one Sans Arc, one Minneconjous, and two Ogallalas) and a large number wounded. Some few remained behind to watch the troops and the rest returned that night to their village which in a day or two they moved down the Little Horn to the point where General Custer found it. The enclosed map is a fair copy of a rude sketch made for me by an Indian with a pencil on the floor of my room in giving me a description of the Custer massacre. He attempted to erase it with his moccasin but enough was left behind to allow me to retrace it, which I did and then copied it on paper.

Though the Indians knew that the troops were in their vicinity and though their scouts had seen them on this very morning yet they marched at such a rapid rate that a comparative surprise was made, and the Indians in the village first saw them at the point "A" and knew that the white solders were upon them. The right hand bank of the Stream is a specimen of bad lands rough precipitous, cut into ravines and nearly impossible to cross the river except at the regular fords B, C, & D. On account of the peculiar topography of the ground but a small portion of the village could be seen from the point "A." A grassy flat led back from the river on the left hand bank for about two miles terminating in bluffs and ridges with a dry creek bottom or ravine at "G." As soon as the troops were seen on the bluffs at the point "A" the old

men, women and children were hustled into the thick timber below "D" and ravine "G." The village was about three miles and a half in length and its widest part about two miles.

The Uncpapas, Ogallalas, Minneconjous, Cheyennes and Sans Arc were each camped in a circular or crescent shape forming the outer circumference of the village. The Brules, Santees, Blackfeet, Yanktoris and Yanktonias, having their lodges with the other bands or between them. The white forces separated at "A", one column going down and crossing the river at "B." The other turning to the right of the ridge with the evident intentions of striking the village in the centre, this however was impossible from the nature of the ground and crossing fill the trails leading down to the ford "D" were reached.

The first column under Col. Reno after crossing were thrown out as skirmishers "E - F" the Indians rushed out and formed line opposite them. Especially strong against the flank "F", doubled it up and forced the troops across the river at a very difficult ford "C" not however without suffering great lofs. After driving Col. Reno's forces acrofs the river most of the Indians left his immediate front and went down to join those who were fighting General Custer's column, which came down and made an attempt to crofs at the mouth of the little stream at "K" finding it impossible turned up the ridge, then turned again as the trails leading down to the ford "D" were reached. The Indians had massed in the ravines and timber and opened such a terrific fire from all sides that the troops gave way. The Indians rushed in and made it a hand to hand conflict. The troops attempted to rally once or twice but literally over whelmed with numbers and in few moments not one was left alive to tell the story.

The temporary respite gave Col. Reno time to gather his forces on a sort of bluff, at "M" and partially entrench himself.

The Indians believing that they had him anyway in a measure abandoned the attack for the night, and besides they had a large number of dead and wounded on their hands to care for. If Col Reno had attempted to succor Genl Custer and forces he would most surely have met their fate.

The next day the approach of Genl Terry's column was discovered and as General Custer had fallen upon them so much more quickly than they anticipated they hurriedly broke camp leaving much of their camp equipage behind them.

The timely arrival of this force saved Col Reno's party. In this fight about 40 Indians were killed and very large number wounded. They say the white soldiers fought bravely and desperately and give instances of personal gallantry which created admiration and respect even in their savage hearts. But it is impossible to positively identify the individuals from their imperfect descriptions. I am convinced however that none were take prisoner

and subjected to torture as has been represented.

The Indians say that many of dead soldiers carbines were found with shells stuck fast in the chambers rendering them entirely useless for the time being.

This fight brought Crazy Horse more prominently before all the Indians than anyone else. He rode with greatest daring up and down in front of Col Reno's skirmish line, and as soon as these troops were driven across the river, he went at once to Genl Custer's front and there became the leading spirit. Before this he had a great reputation, in it he gained a greater prestige than any other Indian in the camp.

Sitting Bull seems not to have marked his conduct on this day with any special fierceness though of course he was a leader where the fighting was the hardest.

They moved over the mountains to Tongue River thence to Powder and from there to the Little Missouri, here to subsist they separated a little and on the 9th of Sept. a small village of some forty lodges was struck by Col Miles near Slim Buttes. The main camp was on the Little Missouri about twenty miles away - and in the afternoon those who had been in the small village having gone to the main camp, they returned with all the available young bucks to annihilate the small force that had commenced the fight, but instead of this they found an army opposed to them, and as they knew that quite a number of captives had fallen into our hands, *this taken in connection with the warm reception they met, cause them to desist and also refrain from firing into the troops afterwards. Nine Indians were killed in this fight. Four bucks, four squaws and one child, and some twenty men, women and children captured, about 200 ponies some secured in the first charge by our cavalry.*

The village had several thousand pounds of dried meat, some little flour, quite a quantity of dried berries all of which fell in our hands and as Genl Crook's forces were reduced to rations of horse meat, made a most desirable and necessary acquisition to the subsistence Department. The lodges, robes, blankets, saddles, cooking utensils, in fact all that the camp contained except what could be used to subsist our troops was thoroughly destroyed.

About this time many Indians left the hostile camp and returned to their Agencies some went in to get a fresh supply of ammunition and obtain information, but the most of them had become tired of war. The camp separated on account of the Scarcity of game, Sitting Bull with some three hundred lodges crossed over the Yellowstone, and soon after had his council and fight with Genl Miles' forces. One Indian was killed in this fight an Uncapapa. After this council some lodges recrossed to this side of the Yellowstone and the rest went north some going as far as the British Possessions.

Crazy Horse went to the Rosebud Country and while en route at the mouth of Clear Fork of Powder river the Cheyennes left and crossed over into the Big Horn Valley. The Cheyennes numbering one hundred and eighty lodges finally reached the head waters of the north fork of Powder River on Bates Creek and here on November 25th Genl Crook Cavalry with three hundred and forty Indian Scouts all under command of Col R. J. MacKenzie 4' Cavalry completely surprised them, captured and destroyed their entire village with nearly all it contained, secured six hundred ponies killed fourteen bucks and two squaws wounded many more and left them in bitterly cold weather on the top of the Big Horn mountains without shelter with few blankets, scarcely any saddles nothing to eat but their few remaining ponies and what game they could find and kill. Under these trying circumstances they started to rejoin Crazy Horse who was supposed by them to be on the Rosebud, but that Chief had moved his band down Tongue river near the mouth of Beaver creek. The Cheyennes suffered terribly en route; infants died of cold at their mother's breasts, fourteen men, women and children were badly frozen. This blow inflicted in part by their own people, one hundred and fifty Sioux, Cheyennes and Arapahoes scouts having been enlisted at these Agencies and acting as our allies in the fight created consternation in the minds of all the hostiles. Every Indian who now came to their camp from the Agencies they suspected as a spy and the surprise at Slim Buttes and on Bates Creek kept them in a constant state of suspense and fear of a like disaster. Soon after the Cheyennes joined Crazy Horse, they all moved by short marches up Tongue river and on January 5th 1877 were camped a few miles above the Canon by which that river breaks through Wolf mountains. There were in this camp at the time about 500 lodges. Gen Miles' forces consisting of Infantry and a few Crow Scouts had been seen crossing up river and were met at the mouth of this Canon and a portion of Indians engaged him. They were to fall back and the troops were to be entrapped in this Canon. The plan did not succeed however as the troops did not follow and the ambush prepared for them failed.

If the troops had followed in all human probability they would have been all killed. In this fight three Indians were killed two Sioux and one Cheyenne and some wounded.

The day previous 8 Cheyenne Squaws who were away from the main village cutting up game and did not know of the approach of the Soldiers were captured by the Crow Scouts.

Soon after this Engagement the camp broke up as they could not subsist on the game in the immediate vicinity.

Sitting Bull had returned to this side of the Yellowstone and was camped with about 50 lodges at the mouth of Little Powder river about one hundred and fifty more lodges of Sans Arc, Minneconjous and Uncpapa joined him and he went north.

All the hostiles this side of the Yellowstone through efforts made at the different Agencies surrendered with the exception of about fifty lodges of Minneconjous, Uncpapas and Cheyennes under Lame Deer who declined to accept the terms offered. He moved to a branch of the Rosebud where on May 25. 77. he was completely surprised by Genl Miles' cavalry his entire village captured and destroyed with nearly all it contained and also suffered a loss of some four hundred ponies. Lame Deer, his son and six other Indians were killed and many wounded. The remnants of the band fled to the vicinity of Slim Buttes and have since committed some depredations near the Black Hills and mouth of the Tongue river.

They are headed at present by Fast Bull. Some twenty of the Cheyennes who were with the band at the time of the fight surrendered at this Agency soon after it took place, and some sixty of the Sioux have come into Spotted Tail.

The rest with the exception of some five lodges of Uncpapas who have gone north remained out till Sept. 9th when they surrendered at Spotted Tail Agency.

I have not been able to find a Indian who was in Lieut Baldwin's fight, but I am told that it was with the Uncpapas and that three Indians were killed and seven captured.

I am Sir

very respectfully
your obedient servant
(sgd) W. P. Clark

1 Lieut, 2nd Cavalry
Headquarters Dept of the Platte
Asst Adjt General's Office
Omaha, Neb Sept. 19,
1877
Official copy respectfully forwarded to the Asst Adjt Genl of U.S.A. Headquarters Mil. Div of the Mo. Chicago, Ill for the information of the Lieut Genl Commanding.

In absence of Brig Genl Crook

(sgd) R. Williams
Asst Adjt Genl

Endorsement
Headqrs. Mil Dis of the Mo
Chicago, Oct 31, 1877

Respectfully forwarded for the information of the General of the Army

There is much interesting information in this report, and Lieut Clark's description of the capabilities of the Indians for offensive warfare is very accurate; but the narratives of the Indians should be received with a considerable degree of allowance and some doubt, as Indians generally make their descriptions to conform to what they think are the wishes of those who interview them. For instance, the statement that the Indians surrendered at Red Cloud and Spotted Tail agencies through the influence of Spotted Tail, is entirely too much of an assumption.

Spotted Tail went out to induce them to come in, but only when they were on the eve of coming in themselves.

They surrendered mainly on account of the permanent occupation of their country by the military at Tongue River and on the Big-Horn, and from the effects of the hard blow given them by Colonel MacKenzie last fall, and the constant pursuit by Col. Miles with troops stationed at Tongue river during the winter, spring and summer.

The general features of the enclosed topographical sketch of Custer's battle field are correct, but I doubt if the Indian who made it was in the fight as he puts the main attack on Col Custer's party upon the wrong side of the ridge.

As to number of Indians killed, accounts greatly differ.

There certainly were enough Indians there to defeat the 7ᵗʰ Cavalry divided as it was into three parts, and to totally annihilate any one of these three detachments in the open field as was found in the destruction of one of them and its gallant commander.

The reasons given why Major Reno should have remained where he was driven, on the top of the bluff that he afterwards fortified and held are very good, but here are reasons no less strong. For instance, he could not abandon his wounded who would have been slain by the enemy, and further more, he had no knowledge of the whereabouts of Col. Custer, nor of the straits he was in, and it is natural to presume that he supposed Col. Custer would return to his support, when he discovered the superiority in numbers of the Indians, in order that the regiment might be re-unified.

The history of the Battle of the Little Big Horn can now be told in a few words. The Indians were actually surprised, and in the confusion arising from the surprise and the attempt of the women and children to get out of the way, Col. Custer was led to believe that the Indians were retreating and would escape him. Furthermore, from the point he left Maj. Reno, he could only see a small portion of the Indian encampment and had no just conception of its size, consequently he did not wait to close up his regiment and attack with its full strength, but, ordering Maj. Reno to attack the village at its upper end, he started directly down the stream on the further side of the bluffs which concealed the Sioux from his vision and hid him from the Indians, with five companies of the 7th Cavalry. Upon reaching a trail that led down to the river opposite about the middle of the village, he followed it down nearly to the stream, and then without even attempting to cross (for no bodies of men or horses were found upon either side of the stream near this ford) he went back for a few hundred yards, and started directly up the line of the fatal ridge, where his body and the bodies of his command were afterwards found, with the evident intentions of going to the lower end of the village, and crossing and attacking the Indians there. It was up this ridge that he was completely surrounded and his command annihilated.

There are no indications whatever that he attempted to go back and rejoin Maj Reno. Had he done this, after reaching this ford above named, Capt Benteen having in the mean time joined Maj Reno, he would have had his whole regiment together, and would have held his own at least, and possibly defeated the Indians.

If the Indians had really known that he was coming, they would have gone out to meet him, as they did to meet Genl Crook only eight days before, in order to let their women and children and the village get out of the way. Again, if Col. Custer had waited until his regiment was closed up, and crossed it at the point Major Reno did, and had made his attack in the level valley, posting some of his men in the woods, all the Indians there would not have defeated him. I do not attribute Colonel Custer's action to either recklessness or want of judgement, but to a misapprehension of the situation and to a super abundance of courage.

I enclose herewith a statement of the battle of the Little Big - Horn made to the commanding officer at Cheyenne Agency by Red Horse, a Sioux Indian who evidently took part in the action and whose statement of the number killed and wounded Indians is greatly in excess of that named by Lieut. Clark's informant.

(Sgd) P. H. Sheridan
Lieut General
Commanding Official
R. C. Dr
A.A.G.

TABLE OF EXHIBITS

NUMBER	DESCRIPTION
1	June 2, 1876, a telegram from Merritt to Sheridan [1 PAGE]
2	June 2, 1876, a telegram from Captain W.H. Jordan Capt 9th Infantry Camp Robinson to Major E.F. Townsend 9th Infantry commanding Fort Laramie, W. T. [2 PAGES]
3	June 2, 1876, a telegram from Major E.F. Townsend to Lieut Gen Sheridan [1 PAGE]
4	June 4, 1876, a telegram from Capt Poland 9th Infantry, to Assistant Adjutant General Department of Dakota, Saint Paul Minn. [5 PAGES]
5	June 7, 1876, a telegram from Merritt to Sheridan [1 PAGE]
6	June 8, 1876, a telegram from R. Williams Fort Robinson to Sheridan [1 PAGE]
7	June 15, 1876, a telegram from Crook to Sheridan
8	June 19, 1876, a telegram from General Alfred Terry by Ruggles Assistant Adjutant General to Adjutant General Division of Missouri Chicago
9	June 23, 1876, a telegram from Crook to Sheridan [1 PAGE]
10	June 23, 1876, a telegram from Crook to Sheridan [3 PAGES]
11	Seventh Cavalry Roster Reconciliation
12	Original Maguire Map circa July 2, 1876
13	Original W. Philo Clark Map circa September 14, 1877
14	Map of Custer Battlefield - Compiled and drawn by Russell White Bear
15	Custer Battlefield Preservation Committee Map, circa 2001.
16	Treaty of 1868 - Fort Laramie. [3 PAGES]
17 to 22	Author prepared, time sequenced, Maps of Custer Battlefield. [6 PAGES]

Block No. 1.

THE WESTERN UNION TELEGRAPH COMPANY.

No._____

The rules of this Company require that all messages received for transmission shall be written on the message blanks of the Company, under and subject to the conditions printed thereon, which conditions have been agreed to by the sender of the following message.

A. R. BREWER, Secretary.   WILLIAM ORTON, Prest.

1853

Dated,_____

To_____

Rec'd at cor. Lasalle and Washington Sts., CHICAGO, Ills.

June 2 187

to Shoydan the post Commander here has sent to the post Commander at Robinson for all information as to Indians who have left agencies up to this time I will await instructions from headquarters here

Merritt
36 9 Collect
fort rate

Russell Brothers' Print, 17 Rose Street, N. Y.

Exhibit 1

Head Qrs. Camp Robinson Neb.
June 2. 1876,

Major E.F. Townsend
9ᵗʰ Infantry
Commanding Fort Laramie W.T.

Major:

I have the honor to acknowledge the receipt of your communication of the 29ᵗʰ ultimo asking for information as to the number of indians that have left Red Cloud and Spotted Tail Agencies. In reply thereto I would report that I can give no definite information on the subject but from the result of inquiries made at the Agency and elsewhere and from my own knowledge I believe that at least 2000 indians (1500 Sioux and 500 Cheyennes) men women and children, have left the Agency here in the North, since the 10ᵗʰ ultimo, containing a-

Exhibit 2

-mong the number at least 500 Warriors, I would report further that the Agent here claims that 12000 Indians men women and children belong to his Agency.

I will report relative to the number of Indians that have left Spotted Tail Agency as soon as practicable

I am Major

Very respectfully

Your Obedient Servant

(Sgd) Wm N. Jordan

Captain 9 Infantry

Comdg Post,

Official copy, for file

M. V. Sheridan

Lieut Col & A.D.C

Exhibit 2

THE WESTERN UNION TELEGRAPH COMPANY.

No. 7 H

The rules of this Company require that all messages received for transmission shall be written on the message blanks of the Company, under and subject to the conditions printed thereon, which conditions have been agreed to by the sender of the following message.

A. R. BREWER, Secretary.   WILLIAM ORTON, Prest.

1155

Dated Fort Laramie Wy 2   Rec'd at cor. Lasalle and Washington Sts., CHICAGO, Ills.

To Lieut Genl Sheridan Military Headquarters June 2 1876
Chicago Ill

The following is the disposition of troops with regard to protection of routes to Black Hills two Companies of infantry at Sidney two companies of infantry + one of cavalry at Laramie four companies of infantry at Robinson + one Company of infantry + one of cavalry at Sheridan there are two Companies of infantry enroute to this post + the Company of cavalry at Sheridan has been ordered to change stations with a Company of Infantry from robinson the two companies enroute here one to take stations on the black Hill road one at the head of sage brush Creek sixty two miles from here the other at the East end of red Canon about fifty miles from the above + forty miles from Custer also a company of Infantry is ordered from robinson to take station at the Laramie road Crossing of the running water the cavalry is to scout the roads the Company at this post + the Company at Robinson alternating it is safe to say that a great many Indians have left the red Cloud agency it is said there are not four hundred warriors remaining there some families have gone it is hard to tell how many as the Indian agents are themselves but poorly Informed + are interested in understating the number the Indians now on reservation are bitter against all who took part in last winters expedition + there was no chance of Crooks Inducing any of them to go with him this time Captain Egan whose reports you have seen is positive that from seven hundred to a thousand warriors have left the two agencies he also says some have gone from missouri river agencies it would be well. If two more companies of Infantry could be sent here one for service at Robinson the black Hills road cavalry would answer better I dont know what for protection of the sidney road

Exhibit 3

Headquarters U. S. Military Station
Standing Rock, D. T. June 4, 1876.

To the
 Assistant Adjutant General
  Department of Dakota.
   Saint Paul, Minn.

Sir:

An indian recently arrived from Cheyenne
Indian Agency reports that a large war party,
composing indians from Spotted Tails' and Cheyenne River Indian Agencies, left the latter place
with the avowed intention of going to Fort Berthold
Agency to attack the Rees.

One of the party came into this agency last
night, probably to obtain reinforcements. He reports
the war party seven days out and at some dis-
-tance below Standing Rock awaiting other rein-

Exhibit 4

forcements from Cheyenne.

The above information I have communicated by scout to the Commanding Officers of Forts Rice Abraham Lincoln and Stevenson D.T.

I learn from reliable authority to-day, that "Kill Eagle" a prominent chief of the Blackfeet Sioux at this Agency who lately left with twenty (20) lodges, osten-sibly to hunt, has certainly joined the hostile Sitting Bull.

Many of the Young men belonging to this Agency have left the agency. Some on the pretext of hunting game, who are now probably with Sitting Bull. The principal chiefs remain here, and did they receive an adequate and proper supply of food, would I think continue here; disposed upon every consideration to keep the peace, But notwithstanding that the agent has officially reported and estimated for rations for over 7000 indians at this agency and he is required by U.S. statutes to issue to and subsist the

Exhibit 4

number actually present, and that there has
not been to exceed a monthly average of 4500
the rations are so diminished as to cause partial
distress and dissatisfaction.

The following memorandum of issues
June 3d was prepared on the statement of one
of the most reliable indians at this agency.

A diminished quantity of flour and corn, a
little coffee, usual quantity of beans, but the
Corn is not ground, and beef has not been
issued for three weeks.

Bacon has not been issued for three months
Pork   „   „   „   three months
Sugar and Tobacco „   „   „   two weeks
The Corn is not available as food, yet an
engineer and miller and mill are, but not
used.

Exhibit 4

Other items go to show that there is, besides the deliberate falsehoods uttered by this agent in his official report to the Commissioner of Indian Affairs as to the products of Indian labor &c, last year, either gross maladministration or inefficiency, or both — as the supplies sent here for food certainly should be ample for 4500 indians.

Last year these indians starved for one month.

In consideration of the organized expeditions against the hostiles — their relatives — should these agency indians generally join the hostile camp it ought to be charitably attributed to the want of food two years in succession which they have been compelled to suffer, and which if issued to them, would keep them, as no other bond or attraction can, at these Reservation homes. with confidence in the promises of Great Father.

Very respectfully

Exhibit 4

Your Obedient Servant

(Sgd.) J. S. Poland

Captain 6ᵗʰ Infantry, Comdg.

Headquarters Department of Dakota

Saint Paul, Minn., June 9, 1876

Official Copy respectfully forwarded to Head-

-quarters Military Division of the Missouri for

the information of the Lieutenant General.

(Sgd.) Geo. D. Ruggles.

Assistant Adjutant General

In the absence of the Department Comdr.

Official Copy for file

M. V. Sheridan

Lieut Col & A.D.C.

Exhibit 4

THE WESTERN UNION TELEGRAPH COMPANY.

No. 9om   The rules of this Company require that all messages received for transmission shall be written on the message blanks of the Company, under and subject to the conditions printed thereon, which conditions have been agreed to by the sender of the following message.

A. R. BREWER, Secretary.   WILLIAM ORTON, Prest.   10 55 Am

Dated Camp Robinson Via Ft Laramie   Recd at cor. Lasalle and Washington Sts., CHICAGO Ills.

To Lieut Gen P H Sheridan   June 7th 1876

Military Hdquarters
Chicago Ill

Have just arrived and have opportunity to send despatch by Courier Have seen Indian agent and talked with Captain Jourdan. It is thought that from fifteen hundred to two thousand Indians have left the reservation Since tenth of May a large proportion of those who have gone are warriors The agent is inclined to underestimate those who have gone I made proposition for him to call for certain young men I would name to show themselves when he admitted reluctantly that Red Cloud had informed him that some of his and other principal families had gone but that they were absent to recover stock stolen by northern Indians Some of the Sons of principal Chiefs are absent The Indians here are not friendly in their feelings in fact they are generally hostile The feeling at Spotted Tail is better though some Indians have left there I will be able to send more definite information when I return to Laramie

Merritt

168 Collect Govt

Exhibit 5

THE WESTERN UNION

No. 34 om

The rules require that all messages received for transmission shall be written on the message blanks of the Company, under and subject to the conditions printed thereon, which conditions have been agreed to by the sender of the following message.

A. R. BREWER, Secretary.   WILLIAM ORTON, Prest.

Dated *Omaha Feb 8*

Rec'd at cor. Lasalle and Washington Sts.
CHICAGO, Ills.
June 8 1876

Assistant Adjutant General
Headqrs Mil Div Mo
Chicago Ill

Commanding officer at Laramie reports "Hand" Indian courier from Red Cloud brings report that just before he left an Indian arrived from the mouth of Tongue river Found there twelve hundred and seventy three 1273 lodges under Sitting Bull Crazy Horse & others on their way to Powder River to fight Gen Crook On his return he met some band that saw May seventeenth they told him that they had met Custers troops and had fought them all day Many killed on both sides No result reported. This occurred about eight days ago. He also reports Spotted Tail at Laramie yesterday who says his people are at home and will not go out and that many have left Red Cloud and other agencies on the Missouri River

R Williams
Asst Adjt General

146 paid 292
Govt rate.

Exhibit 6

THE WESTERN UNION TELEGRAPH COMPANY

No. 66m Govt

The rules of this Company require that all messages received for transmission shall be written on the message blanks of the Company, and under and subject to the conditions printed thereon, which conditions have been agreed to by the sender of the following message.

A. R. BREWER, Secretary.

WILLIAM ORTON, Prest.

755 95

Dated Camp South Fork Tongue River sent Via Ft Fetterman 11 15   Rec'd at cor. Lasalle and Washington Sts.,
CHICAGO, Ills.

To Lieut Gen Sheridan Chicago

June 15   1876

Have been waiting in this vicinity three days for Indian Scouts am daily expecting them my guards went for them to return but have heard nothing of them yet night before last Indians made demonstration on our camp firing a good many shots at long range and retiring as troops sent to dislodge from their actions I think their main Camp is on little Rosebud or Tongue river and probably attack to cover movements of the main body will you please direct such disposition and movement of the fifth cavalry as circumstances require it being impossible for me to know what is necessary in time to direct movements.

Crook
Brig Genl

123 Collect Govt rate

8 Extra wrds

β

RFC

tel to adj June 16

Exhibit 7

THE WESTERN UNION TELEGRAPH COMPANY.

No. 42

The rules of the Company require that all messages received for transmission shall be written on the message blanks of the Company, under and subject to the conditions printed thereon, which conditions have been agreed to by the sender of the following message.

A. R. BREWER, Secretary.

WILLIAM ORTON, Prest.

4730

Dated, St Paul Minn 19   Rec'd at cor. Lasalle and Washington Sts. CHICAGO, Ills.

To Adjutant General Division Missouri Chicago June 19 1876

The following just received — Camp at Junct of Powder And
Yellowstone Rivers June twelfth eighteen seventy six Reached Powder
River at a point twenty four miles above here late
on the seventh Inst No Indians East of Powders Reno
With six Companies seventh Cavalry is now well up the
River on his way to the forks whence he will cross to
Come down Mizpah Creek & thence by Pumpkin Creek to
Tongue river where I Expect to meet him with the rest of the
Cavalry fresh supplies — I intend then if nothing new is
developed to send Custer with nine Companies of his regiment
up the Tongue & thence across to and down the Rosebud
While the rest of the seventh & will join Gibbons who will
move up the Rose Bud Have met Gibbon & Concerted
movements with him — Troops and animals in fine
Condition signed alfred H Terry Brigadier General

Ruggles

Assistant adjutant General

162 paid 324 Govt

Exhibit 8

3 4 8

THE WESTERN UNION TELEGRAPH COMPANY.

No. *7 om*

The rules of this Company require that all messages received for transmission shall be written on the message blanks of the Company, and are subject to the conditions printed thereon which conditions have been agreed to by the sender of the following message.

L. BREWER, Secretary.   WILLIAM ORTON, Prest.

12.25 *pd*

Dated, *Omaha Neb 23*

Rec'd at cor. Lasalle and Washington Sts., CHICAGO, Ills.

June 23 1876

Assistant Adjutant
General

Headquarters Mil Div Mo
Chicago Ill

The following despatch received
Camp South Fork Tongue River
June 19th
via Fort Fetterman June 23rd

"We had a sharp fight on Rosebud
Creek Mont Morning seventeenth instant
lasting several hours Our loss nine
men killed and twenty one wounded
Capt. Henry Third Cavalry only officer
hurt He is severely wounded in
the face. We won the fight
and camped on the field the
Indians made the attack and had
a force they no doubt believed
sufficient to whip the command
(signed) Nickerson ADC

Hawkins
Asst Genl

Exhibit 9

252

THE WESTERN UNION TELEGRAPH COMPANY.

The rules of this Company require that all messages received for transmission shall be written on the message blanks of the Company, under and subject to the conditions printed thereon, which conditions have been agreed to by the sender of the following message.

A. R. BREWER, Secretary.   WILLIAM ORTON, Pres.

Dated, Camp on South of _____ Rec'd at Lasalle and Washington Sts.,
Yea Ft Fetterman 23   Chicago Ill. June 23 1876

To Lt Gen Sheridan   Chicago Ill

Returned to Camp today haveing
Marched as indicted in my
last telegram when about forty
Miles from here on Rosebud
creek Mont Morning seventeenth
inst Scouts reports indeans in
vicinity & within a few minutes
we were attacked in force the
fight lasting several hours we
were near the mouth of a deep
canyon through which the creek
ran the sides ware very steep covered
with pine & apparently impregnable
the village supposed to be at the
end about Eight miles off they displayed
strong force at all points occupy
many of such covered places

Exhibit 10

THE WESTERN UNION TELEGRAPH COMPANY.

No.

The rules of this Company require that all messages received for transmission shall be written on the message blanks of the Company, under and subject to the conditions printed thereon, which conditions have been agreed to by the sender of the following message.

A. R. BREWER, Secretary.

WILLIAM ORTON, Prest.

Dated,

To

Rec'd at cor. Lasalle and Washington Sts., CHICAGO, Ills.

187

that it is impossible to correctly
estimate their numbers the attack
however showed that they anticipated
that they were strong enough to
thoroughly defeat the command during
the engagement I tried to throw a
strong force through the canyon but
I was obliged to use it elsewhere
'efore it had gotten to the supposed
location of the village the command
finally drove the indians back in
great confusion following them several
miles the scouts killing a good
many during the retreat our casualties
were nine men killed & fifteen wounded
of third cavalry two (2) wounded
second cavalry three men wounded fourth
infantry and capt Henry third cavalry
several wounded in the face it is
impossible to correctly estimate the loss
of the indians many being killed in
the ... others being gotten off before

Exhibit 10

THE WESTERN UNION TELEGRAPH COMPANY.

No.

The rules of this Company require that all messages received for transmission shall be written on the message blanks of the Company, under and subject to the conditions printed thereon, which conditions have been agreed to by the sender of the following message.

A. R. BREWER, Secretary.

WILLIAM ORTON, Prest.

Rec'd at cor. Lasalle and Washington Sts., CHICAGO, Ills.

Dated,

To

187 6

We got possession of that part of the field 13 thirteen dead bodies being left we remained on the field that night & having nothing but what each man carried himself we were obliged to return to the train to properly care for our wounded who were transported here on mule litters & die now comfortable all doing well I expect to find those indians in rough places all the time & so have ordered five (5) companies of infantry and shall not probably make any extended movement until they arrive officers and men behaved with marked gallantry during the engagement

Crook. Brig genl.

349 Collect govt Rate.

Exhibit 10

SEVENTH CAVALRY ROSTER RECONCILIATION

UNIT	ROSTER OFF	ENL	CIV	DETACHED OFF	ENL	CIV	AVAILABLE OFF	ENL	CIV	KILLED OFF	ENL	CIV	SURVIVORS ON HILL OFF	ENL	CIV	FAUGHT OFF	ENL	CIV	PACKS OFF	ENL	CIV	ON HILL OFF	ENL	CIV
STAFF	7	21		4	19		3	2	0	2	2		1	0	0	1								
ATCHD	4	2		1	2		3	0	0	2			1	0	0	1								
A	3	55			10		3	45	0	1	9		2	36	0	2	34			2				
B	3	71		1	29		2	42	0	1	2		1	40	0				1	40				
C	3	66			16		3	50	0	3	35		0	15	0					8			7	
D	3	64		1	17		2	47	0		3		2	44	0	2	44							
E	3	61		1	12		2	49	0	1	37		1	12	0	1	2			8			2	
F	3	68		2	20		1	48	0	1	36		0	12	0		1			9			2	
G	3	66		1	24		2	42	0	1	13		1	29	0	1	26			3				
H	3	55		1	11		2	44	0		4		2	41	0	2	39			1			1	
I	3	65		1	19		2	46	0	2	36		0	10	0					9			1	
K	3	69		1	30		2	39	0		5		2	34	0	2	31			3				
L	4	67		3	10		1	57	0	1	44		0	13	0					12			1	
M	3	63			7		3	56	0	1	12		2	44	0	2	44							
REGIMENT	48	793	0	17	226	0	31	567	0	16	238	0	15	330	0	14	221	0	1	95	0	0	14	0
CIVILIANS		21					0	0	21			8	0	0	13		2			11				
NA SCOUTS		51				18	0	0	33			2	0	0	31		17			2				12
TOTAL	48	793	72	17	226	18	31	567	54	16	238	10	15	330	44	14	221	19	1	95	13	0	14	12

UNIT	ROSTER OFF	ENL	CIV	DETACHED OFF	ENL	CIV	AVAILABLE OFF	ENL	CIV	KILLED OFF	ENL	CIV	SURVIVORS ON HILL OFF	ENL	CIV			
STAFF	6	21		4	19		2	2	0	2	2	[CUSTER, COOKE. SHARROW, VOSS]						
ATCHD	2	2		1	2		1	0	0	1	[LORD]							
C	3	58			16		3	42	0	3	35			7			7 NOTE-B	
E	2	51		1	12		1	39	0	1	37			2			2 NOTE-B	
F	3	58		2	20		1	38	0	1	36			2			2 NOTE-B	
I	3	56		1	19		2	37	0	2	36			1			1 NOTE-B	
L	4	55		3	10		1	45	0	1	44			1			1 NOTE-B	
A	1						1	0	0	1	[SMITH]							
G		1					0	1	0	1	[DOSE]							
H		1					0	1	0									
K		2					0	2	0	2	[HUGHES, CALLAHAN]			1			1 NOTE-B	
M	1						1	0	0	1	[STURGIS]							
CIVILIANS			4				0	0	4	4	[B. CUSTER,REED,BOUYER, KELLOGG]							
NA SCOUTS			6				0	0	6				0	0	6		6 NOTE-A	
CUSTER	25	305	10	12	98	0	13	207	10	13	193	4	0	14	6	0 0 6	0 0 0	0 14 0
PERCENT							41.9	36.5	18.5									

UNIT	ROSTER OFF	ENL	CIV	DETACHED OFF	ENL	CIV	AVAILABLE OFF	ENL	CIV	KILLED OFF	ENL	CIV	SURVIVORS OFF	ENL	CIV	FAUGHT OFF	ENL	CIV
STAFF	1						1	0	0				1	0	0 [1]	1		
ATCHD	2						2	0	0 [1]	1			1	0	0 [2]	1		
A	1	53			10		1	43	0		9		2	34	0	2	34	
G	3	62		1	24		3	38	0 [2]	1	12		1	26	0	1	26	
M	1	63			7		1	56	0		12		1	44	0	1	44	
A	1			[V...			1	0	0				0	0	0			
B	1			[H...			1	0	0 [3]	1			0	0	0			
E	1	2		[D...			1	2	0				1	2	0 [3]	1	2	
F		1					0	1	0				0	1	0 [4]		1	
K	1			[H...			1	0	0									
CIVILIANS			5				0	0	5 [4]			3	0	0	2 [5]		2	
NA SCOUTS			44			18	0	0	25 [5]			2	0	0	23	11 NOTE-C	NOTE	12
RENO	12	181	49	1	41	18	11	140	30	3	33	5	7	107	25	7 107 13	0 0 0	0 0 12
PERCENT							35.5	24.7	55.6									

[1-DeWOLF]   [1-RENO]
[2-MACINTOSH]   [2-PORTER]
[3-HODGSON]   [3-De RUDIO, MEDICS ABBOTTS & SHIELDS]
[4-BLOODY KNIFE,DORMAN,REYNOLDS]   [4-DAVERN]
[5-BOB TAILED BULL, LITTLE BRAVE]   [5-GIRARD, HERENDEEN]

UNIT	ROSTER OFF	ENL	CIV	DETACHED OFF	ENL	CIV	AVAILABLE OFF	ENL	CIV	KILLED	SURVIVORS OFF	ENL	CIV	FAUGHT OFF	ENL	CIV
D	3	64		1	17		2	47	0	3	2	44	0	2	44	
H	3	53		1	11		2	42	0	4	2	39	0	2	39	
K	2	64		1	30		1	34	0	3	2	31	0	2	31	
BENTEEN	8	181	0	3	58	0	5	123	0	0 10 0	6	114	0	6 114 0	0 0 0	0 0 0
PERCENT							16.1	21.7	0.0							

UNIT	ROSTER OFF	ENL	CIV	DETACHED OFF	ENL	CIV	AVAILABLE OFF	ENL	CIV	KILLED	SURVIVORS OFF	ENL	CIV	FAUGHT OFF	ENL	CIV	PACKS
B	2	71		1	29		1	42	0	2	1	40	0				1 40
C		8					0	8	0		0	8	0				8
E		8					0	8	0		0	8	0				8
F		9					0	9	0		0	9	0				9
I		9					0	9	0		0	9	0				9
L		12					0	12	0		0	12	0				12
A		2					0	2	0		0	2	0				2
G		3					0	3	0		0	3	0				3
M	1			[M...			1	0	0		1	0	0	1 [MATHEY]			1
H		1					0	1	0		0	1	0				1
D							0	0	0		0	0	0				
K		3					0	3	0		0	3	0				3
CIVILIANS			12				0	0	12	[MANI] 1	0	0	11				11 NOTE-E
NA SCOUT			1				0	0	2		0	0	2	[GOOD FACE, WHITE SWAN]			2
PACKS	3	126	13	1	29	0	2	97	14	0 2 1	2	95	13	1 0 0	1 95 13	0 0 0	
PERCENT							6.5	17.1	25.9								

TOTAL	48	793	72	17	226	18	31	567	54	16	238	10	15	330	44	14	221	19	1 95 13	0 14 12
VARIANCE	0	0	0	0	0	0	0	0	0	0	0	0	0	0	0	0 0 0			0 0 0	0 0 0

Exhibit 11

Note A SIX NATIVE AMERICAN SCOUTS WHO WERE RELEASED BY CUSTER

William "Billy" Cross	Claimed to have left GAC before fight met weir as he advanced
Curly-Crow	Released by GAC
Goes Ahead-Crow	Released by GAC
Hairy Mocasin-Crow	Released by GAC
Half Yellow Face-Crow	Released by GAC
White Man Runs Him-Crow	Released by GAC

Note B FOURTEEN FROM CUSTER'S WING WHO WOUND UP ON RENO HILL OR ELSWHERE

C	Daniel Knipe	Claimed to be a messenger
C	John Fitzgerald }	Per P Thompson turned to rear 2 miles after Lone Teepee
C	John Brennan }	Per John McGuire > W.M. Camp-They did not care to go with Custer
C	Morris M Farrar	Per Hammer straggled and joined Reno on hill
C	Peter Thompson	Horse quit-joined Reno-Awarded Medal of Honor-Water Carrier
C	James Watson	Per Hammer-horse quit at or near Thompson's wound up on Hill
C	Nathan Short	Either messenger, survivor or deserter-found near Rosebud
E	William Shields	Fought on hilltop-wounded-may have been medic for Dr. Porter
E	William Reese	Fought on hilltop
F	Bernard Lyons	Fought on hilltop
F	John W Sweeney	Fought on hilltop
H	John Martin	Orderly returned with message
I	Gustave Korn	Horse bolted at river, fought on hilltop
L	Philip McHugh	Fought on hilltop

Note C THIRTEEN NATIVE AMERICAN SCOUTS WHO CROSSED THE RIVER WITH RENO AND ATTACKED

Black Calf-Ree
Foolish Bear-Ree
Forked Horn-Ree
Goose-Ree
William Jackson-Pik
Little Sioux-Ree
One Feather-Ree
Red Bear-Ree
Strikes the Bear-Ree
Strikes Two-Ree
Young Hawk-Ree
Young Hawk-Ree
Good Face-Crow
White Swan-Crow

Note D TWELVE NATIVE AMERICAN SCOUTS WHO REFUSED TO CROSS THE RIVER WITH RENO

Bear Came Out-Dakota
Bear Running in Time-Dakota
Bull-Ree
Bull in The Water-Ree
Bush-Ree
Round Wooden Cloud-Dakota
Rushing Bull-Ree
Soldier-Ree
Stab-Ree
Strikes The Lodge-Ree
White Cloud-Dakota
White Eagle-Ree

Note E ELEVEN CIVILIAN PACKERS WHO FOUGHT WITH PACK TRAIN

William Alexander-Packer
Benjamin Franklin Churchill-Packer
George Edwards-Teamster
Moses E Flint-Packer
John Frett-Packer
John Lainplough-Packer
William Lawless-Packer
Chris Loeser-Packer
Harry McBratney-Packer
Edward L. Moore-Packer
John C Wagoner-Chief Packer

Exhibit 11

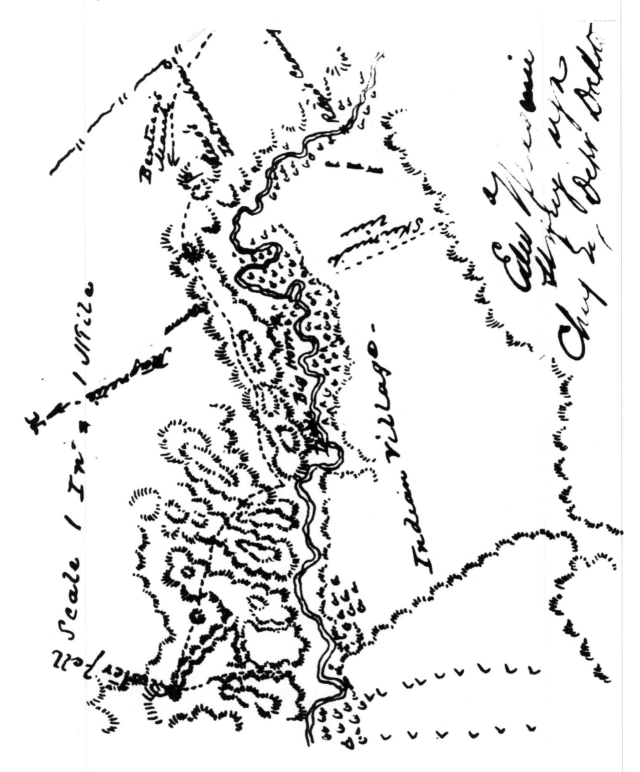

THE MAGUIRE MAP
Exhibit 12

THE MAGUIRE MAP

This version of the "Maguire Map" is the earliest known version and it predates all previously believed "first maps." It has never before been either published or used by a historian as a research tool in studying the battle. The authenticity of the map has been attested to by Mr. Douglas C. McChristian, on March 20, 1991, in his then position of Chief Historian for the Custer Battlefield National Monument. Mr. McChristian said in part; "I think it is safe to presume he prepared it "on the ground" immediately after the battle. "...I do not know exactly how the map found its way into Smith's possession. However, considering that he and Maguire were fellow-staff officers, it may be that Maguire either presented the map to Smith as a memento after more detailed versions were prepared, or that Smith "liberated" it from the files. W. Kent King, in his <u>Massacre: The Custer Coverup</u>, presents several versions of this map, but none are exactly like the one you have. By comparing the one King labels "First Battlefield Map" you will readily see that it has a few refinements not shown on your map, thus making yours the more primitive. I have personally examined this map and am comfortable in saying that I believe it is the earliest one known of the Little Big Horn Battlefield."

This version of the Maguire Map, when viewed in conjunction with the Philo Clark Map and the Russell White Bear all self corroborate each other and show that Custer made a strong move towards the river, reached the river and was driven back to Last Stand Hill where he met his demise.

THE PHILO CLARK MAP

W. Philo Clark was a 1ˢᵗ Lieutenant with U.S. 2ⁿᵈ Cavalry and was stationed at Fort Robinson in 1877. He was the Army's acknowledged expert in "Indian Sign Language" and was accordingly assigned the task of debriefing the prominent members of each band as they surrendered. It is believed among those that he interviewed was Crazy Horse. On September 14, 1877 he submitted his report to the Adjutant General of the Department of the Platte. Attached to the report was a map prepared by Clark of the Battle of the Little Big Horn. This map is derived from a sketch made by one of the Indians interviewed by Clark and it contains extremely important information which has heretofore been lost to history, for nearly 130 years.

The map and the accompanying report provide new and significant insights into this battle. In the report he states that the Indian village consisted of "1200 standing lodges, 400 wickyups and 3500 fighting men." They lend strong support to the theory that Custer attempted to ford the river and attack at Medicine Tail Coulee, but that he was repulsed by the Sioux. The Report shows that the Indian non-combatants were initially hidden in the Squaw Creek area and the timber southwest of Last Stand Hill, on the west side of the river. That Custer may have seen non combatants moving about the village heading to these locations and that he may have attempted to pursue them. The map shows Custer made a second attempt to ford the river and attack the village at "Ford C" and from this failed attempt he retreated to Last Stand Hill to meet his ultimate fate.

The Philo Clark Report and Map were the first prepared as a result of interviews with the actual Indians who fought Custer. The information contained in both the map and report was derived through direct, impartial interrogation, solely with the intent to gain knowledge, without the dilution of an interpreter or being colored by the beliefs of later interviewers with ulterior motives. Thus the report and map represent the closest documents surviving today that present the unaltered Indian version of the battle. The map is also drawn from a non-standard perspective as it shows the area as one would see it approaching from the north, the direction from which Terry and Gibbon came. When looking at the map, the village is on the right and the battlefield on the left as opposed to the more common view with the positions reversed.

The image of the map presented here is taken from the original map, nearly 10 inches by 13 3/4 inches, on silk paper, drawn by Lieutenant Clark, with ink colors, red, blue and black. It accompanied the copy of his report submitted to Army Headquarters Division of the Missouri and on its reverse side it bears the Army Documentary Stamp and number 5839 for the year 1877. It was acquired at public auction from a seller who described it as "an old map of the Custer battlefield, with meaningless writing on the back."

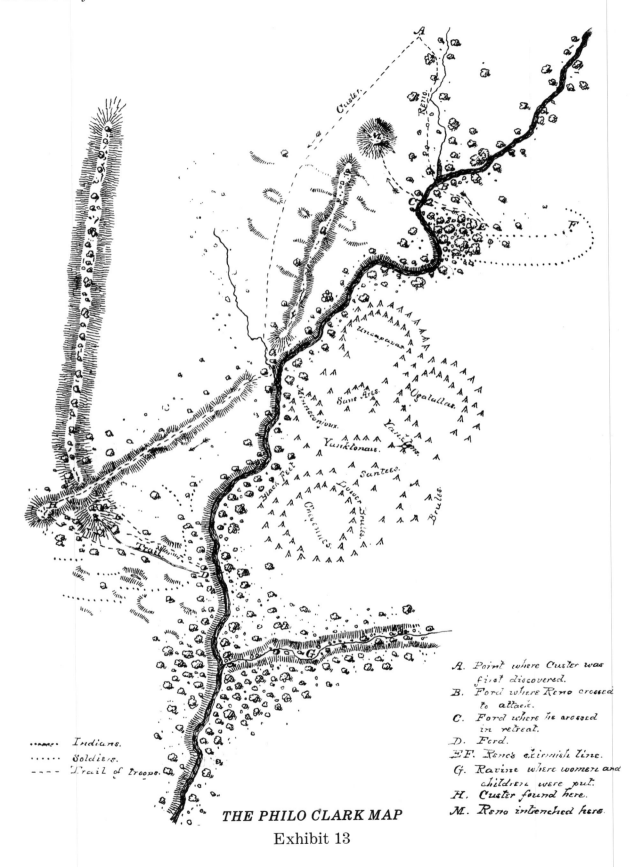

A. Point where Custer was
    first discovered.
B. Ford where Reno crossed
    to attack.
C. Ford where he crossed
    in retreat.
D. Ford.
EF. Reno's skirmish line.
G. Ravine where women and
    children were put.
H. Custer found here.
M. Reno intrenched here.

.... Indians.
...... Soldiers.
- - - - Trail of troops.

THE PHILO CLARK MAP
Exhibit 13

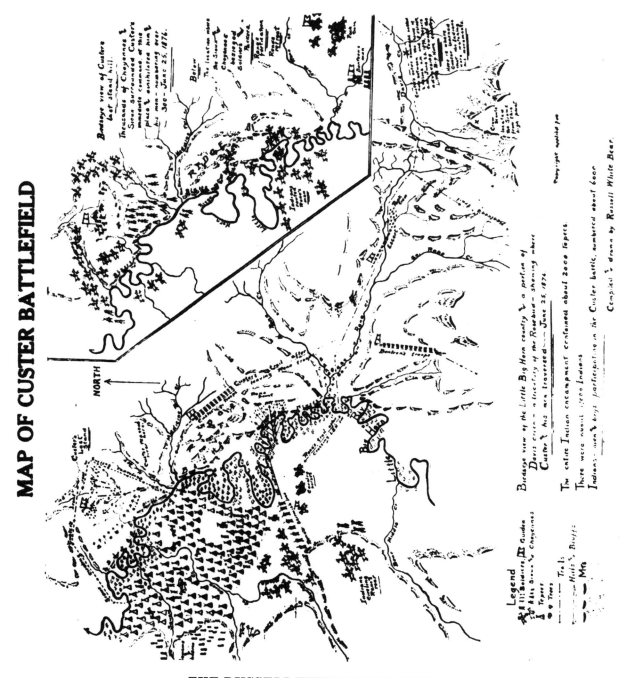

THE RUSSELL WHITE BEAR MAP

This is a hand drawn map of the battlefield by Russell White Bear, who was General Secretary of the Crow Tribe, in 1926, based upon information derived from primary Indian sources. It shows that Custer reached the river at Medicine Tail Coulee, that the village contained about 2,000 tepees with 17,000 inhabitants and 6,000 men and boys who participated in the fight against Custer. The Russell White Bear Map and the Philo Clark Map are the direct products of primary Indian accounts from the warriors who fought against Custer. Both maps are the product of primary statements and self corroborate each other as to the enormity of the village and the vast horde of warriors which Custer was forced to face on his own, when his subalterns refused to do their duty and march their columns forward towards the sound of the guns, in the midst of a battle.

Exhibit 14

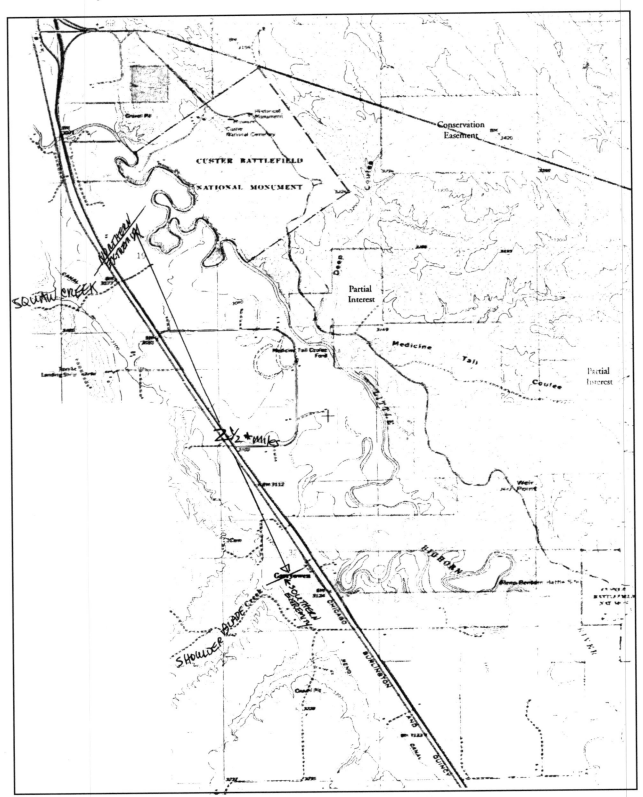

CUSTER BATTLEFIELD PRESERVATION COMMITTEE

Exhibit 15

Articles of a Treaty made and concluded by and between Lieutenant General William T Sherman, General William S Harney, General Alfred H Terry, General C C Augur, J B Henderson, Nathaniel G Taylor, John B Sanborn and Samuel F Tappan, duly appointed Commissioners on the part of the <u>United States</u> and the different Bands of the <u>Sioux Nation of Indians</u> by their Chiefs and Head men whose names are hereto subscribed, they being duly authorized to act in the premises

<u>Article 1</u>   From this day forward all war between the parties to this agreement shall forever cease. The Government of the United States desires peace and its honor is hereby pledged to keep it. The Indians desire peace and they now pledge their honor to maintain it.

If bad men among the whites or among other people, subject to the authority of the United States, shall commit any wrong upon the person or property of the Indians, the United States will, upon proof made to the Agent, and forwarded to the Commissioner of Indian Affairs at Washington City, proceed at once to cause the offender to be arrested and punished according to the laws of the United States, and also reimburse the injured person for the loss sustained.

If bad men among the Indians shall commit a wrong or depredation upon the person or property of any one, white, black or Indian, subject to the authority of the United States and at peace therewith, the Indians herein named, solemnly agree that they

Exhibit 16

263

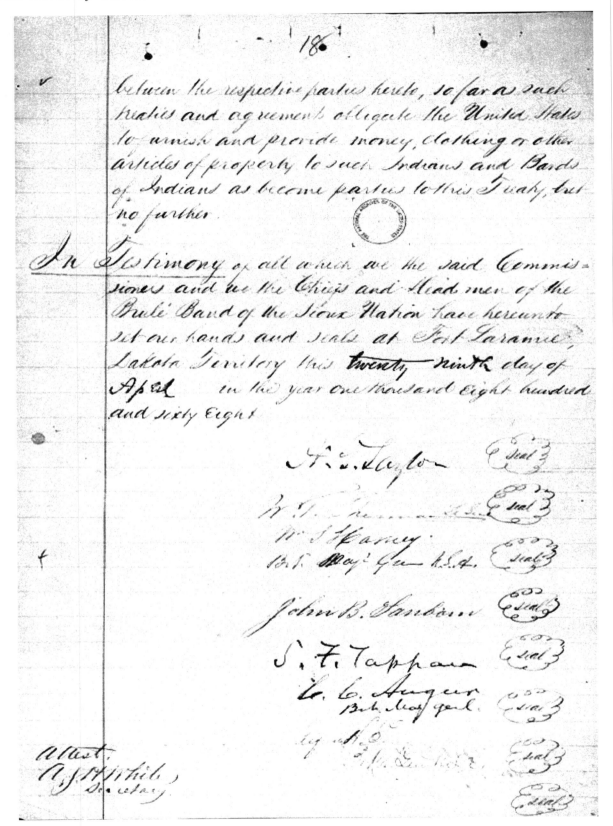

between the respective parties hereto, so far as such
treaties and agreements obligate the United States
to furnish and provide money, clothing or other
articles of property to such Indians and Bands
of Indians as become parties to this Treaty, but
no further.

In Testimony of all which we the said Commissioners and we the Chiefs and Head men of the
Brulé Band of the Sioux Nation have hereunto
set our hands and seals at Fort Laramie,
Dakota Territory this twenty ninth day of
April in the year one thousand eight hundred
and sixty eight

N. G. Taylor   [seal]

W. T. Sherman Lt.   [seal]

W. S. Harney.
Bvt. Maj. Gen. U.S.A.   [seal]

John B. Sanborn   [seal]

S. F. Tappan   [seal]

C. C. Augur   [seal]
Bvt. Maj. Genl.

                            [seal]

                            [seal]

Attest:
A. S. H. White,
Secretary.

Exhibit 16

Executed on the part of the Brule Band of Sioux, by the Chiefs and Headmen whose names are hereto annexed, they being thereunto duly authorized, at Fort Laramie D.T. the twenty ninth day of April in the year A.D. 1868.

Ma-za-om-Kaska,	his + mark	Iron Shell
Wah-Pat-Shah,	his + mark	Red Leaf
Hah-Sah-Pah,	his + mark	Black Horn
Zin-Tah-Gah-Lah-Wat,	his + mark	Spotted Tail
Zin-Tah-Wah,	his + mark	White Tail
Me-Wah-Tah-ete-Ho-Skah,	his + mark	Tall Mandan
She-Cha-Chat-Kah,	his + mark	Bad Left Hand
He-Mah-Ate-Pah,	his + mark	No Flesh
Tah-Tonka-Skah,	his + mark	White Bull
Con-Ra-Washta,	his + mark	Pretty Coon
~~Hah-Sah-Kah-Ata-She~~		
Tah-Cah-Cah-She-Chah,	his + mark	Bad Elk
Wa-Ha-Ho-Yah-Noh-He-Ta,	his + mark	Eagle Lance
Ma-To-Ha-He-Tah,	his + mark	Bear that looks behind
Bella-Tonka-Tonka,	his + mark	Big Partisan
Mah-To-Ho-Honka,	his + mark	Swift Bear
To-Wis-Ne,	his + mark	Cold Place
Ish-Tah-Skah,	his + mark	White Eyes
We-Tah-Loo-Yah	his + mark	Tall Bear
An-Hah-Hah Vah-She	his mark	Standing Elk
Kan-ta-ta-ka-yah,	his X mark	Day Hawk
Shunka Shaton		
Tahtanka Watkon	X mark	Sacred Bell
Maria Shatan	X mark	Hawk Cloud
Mashawou	X mark	Stands and Comes
West Spon Ka tou ka	his + mark	Big Dog

Ashton S. H. White
Secretary of Commission

Exhibit 16

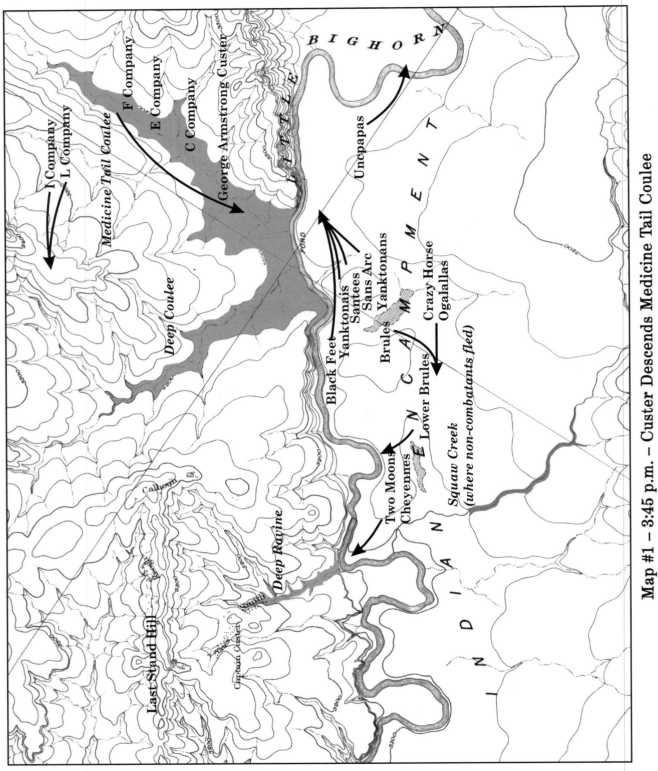

Map #1 – 3:45 p.m. – Custer Descends Medicine Tail Coulee

Exhibit 17

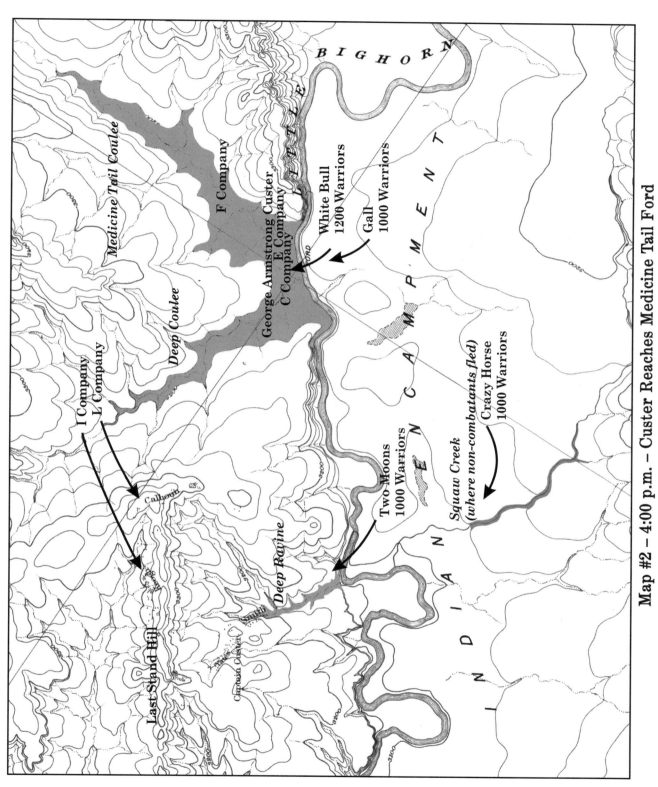

Map #2 – 4:00 p.m. – Custer Reaches Medicine Tail Ford

Exhibit 18

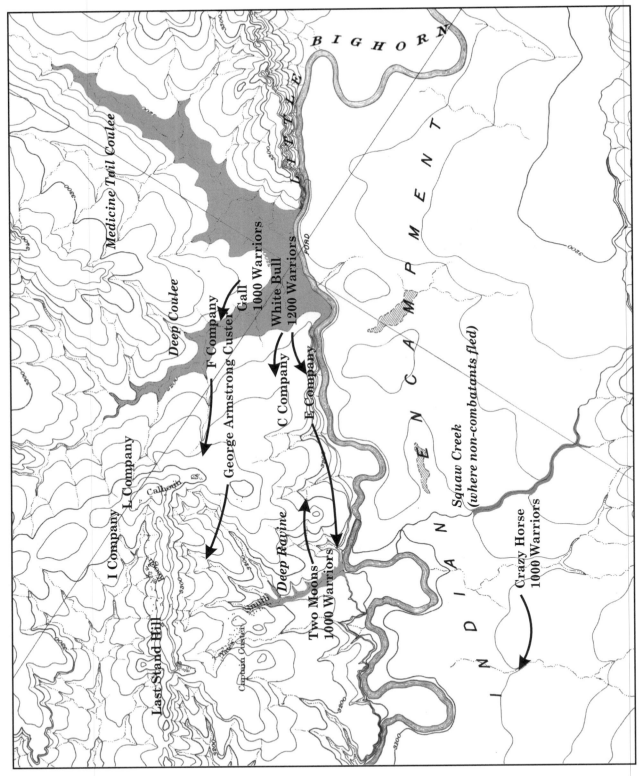

Map #3 – 4:15 p.m. – Custer Deploys on Calhoun Ridge

Exhibit 19

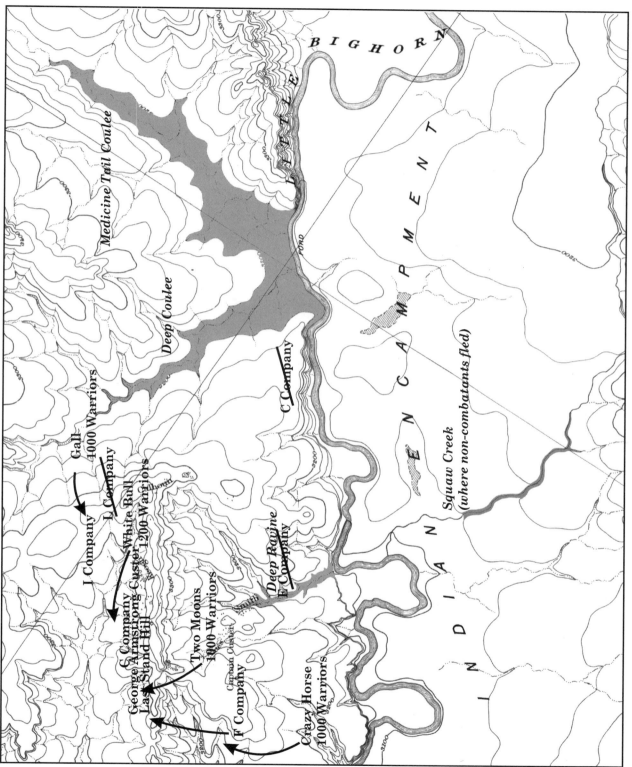

Map #4 – 4:30 p.m. – Calhoun Ridge Overrun; E Troop Falls

Exhibit 20

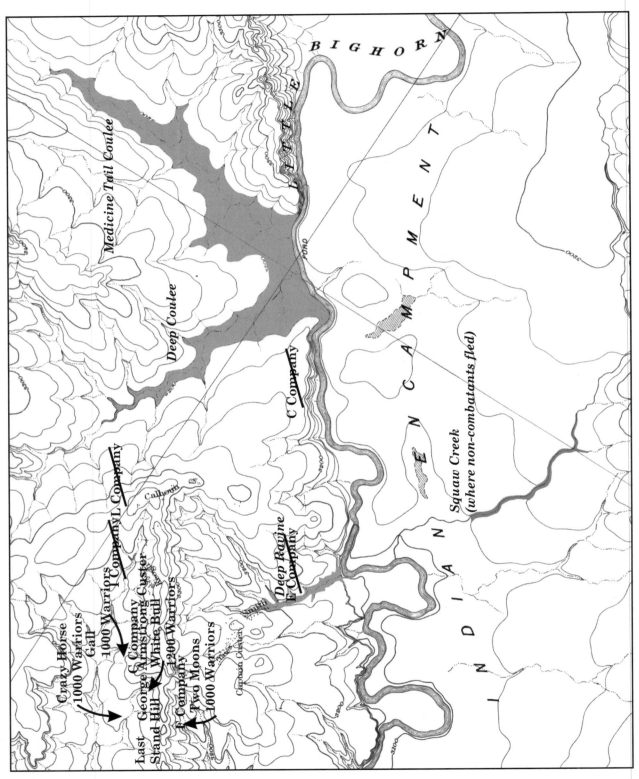

Map #5 – 4:45 p.m. – Last Stand Positions

Exhibit 21

Map #6 – 5:00 p.m. – Battle Over

Exhibit 22

BIBLIOGRAPHY

United States Government Publications

Adjutant General's Office. Official Army Register 1866. Washington: Adjutant General's Office, 1866.

Adjutant General's Office. Official Army Register 1867. Washington: Adjutant General's Office, 1867.

Adjutant General's Office. Official Army Register 1876. Washington: Adjutant General's Office, 1876.

Adjutant General's Office. Official Army Register 1877. Washington: Adjutant General's Office, 1877.

Annual Report of the Commissioner of Indian Affairs to the Secretary of the Interior for the Year 1876. Washington: Government Printing Office, 1876.

Message from the President of the United States to the Two Houses of Congress at the commencement of the 2nd Session 44th Congress, with the Reports of the Heads of Departments and selections from accompanying documents. Edited by: Ben, Perley Poore. Washington: Government Printing Office, 1876.

National Archives. Microfilm Records M 1495. Rolls 2. 3. & 4. October 1875 to December 1877.

Proceedings of the Senate sitting for the Trial of William W. Belknap, Late Secretary of War, on the Articles of Impeachment Exhibited by the House of Representatives. 44th Congress 1st Session. Washington: Government Printing Office, 1875.

Report of the Secretary of War. 2nd Session 44th Congress. Volume 1. 1876-1877. Washington: Government Printing Office, 1876.

Articles, Magazines and Maps

Brininstool, E. A. "With Col. Varnum at the Little Big Horn." *Hunter-Trader-Trapper Magazine.* Volume LIV Number 6. June and July 1927.

Bryan, William L. "Montana's Indians." Volume 4. Helena. *Montana Magazine.* 1985.

By Valor and Arms. The Journal of American Military History. Volume II, Number 2. "Custer Centennial Issue." Fort Collins. *Valor and Arms.* 1976

Chapman, Arthur. "Custer's Last Battle - A Fifty Year Mystery." *Liberty Magazine.* June 26,1926.

Fry, James B. "Comments by General Fry on the Custer Battle." *Century Magazine.* January 1892. Pages 385-387.

Garland, Hamlin. "General Custer's Last Fight. by Two Moons." *McClures Magazine.* September 1898.

Godfrey, Edward S. "Custer's Last Battle." *Century Magazine*. January 1892. Pages 358 - 384.

"Guns at the Little Bighorn." *Man at Arms Special Publication*. 1988.

King, Captain Charles. "Custer's Last Battle." *Harpers New Monthly Magazine*. Vol. LXXXI - No.483-37. Pages 370-387.

King, Captain Charles. "Map of Big Horn and Yellowstone Expedition of 1876." Denver. Clason Map Co.

McChristian, Douglas C. "Burying the Hatchet." *Montana The Magazine of Western History*. Volume 46 Number 2. Summer 1996.

The Galaxy. Vol XXI January, 1876 to June, 1876. New York. Sheldon. 1876.

The Galaxy. Vol XXII June, 1876 to January, 1877. New York. Sheldon. 1877.

Thompson, Peter. "His Story." *The Black Hills Trails*.

White Bull, Joseph, by Vestal. "The Battle of the Little Bighorn." *Blue Book Magazine*. 1933.

Booklets

Barry, D. F. *Indian Notes on the Custer Battle*. Baltimore: Baltimore. Wirth Brothers,1949.

Bates, Charles Francis. *Custer's Indian Battles*. Bronxville: Bates, 1936.

Bloch, *Outstanding Historical Events - The Massacre of General Custer and His Men in Montana, June 25, 1876*. Cleveland: Bloch and Company,1959.

Marquis, Thomas B. *Sketch Story of the Little Bighorn*. Scottsdale: Cactus Pony, 1933.

Marquis, Thomas B. *She Watched Custer's Last Battle*. Scottsdale: Cactus Pony, 1933.

Marquis, Thomas B. *Two Days after the Custer Battle*. Scottsdale: Cactus Pony, 1933.

Marquis, Thomas B. *Which Indian Killed Custer?* and *Custer Soldiers Not Buried*. Scottsdale: Cactus Pony, 1933.

Marquis, Thomas B. *Rain-in-the-Face and Curly, The Crow*. Scottsdale: Cactus Pony, 1934.

Marquis, Thomas B. *Sitting Bull and Gall, The Warrior*. Scottsdale: Cactus Pony, 1934.

Roe, Charles. *Custer's Last Battle*. New York: National Highway Association, 1927.

Ronshiem, Milton. *The Life of General Custer*. Cadiz: Reprinted from the Cadiz Republican, 1929.

Taunton, Francis B. *Custer's Field*. London: Johnson-Taunton Military Press, 1986.

Books

Anders, Frank L. *The Custer Trail*. Glendale: University of North Dakota, 1983.

Bad Heart Bull, Amos. *A Pictographic History of the Oglala Sioux*. Lincoln: University Nebraska Press, 1967.

Barnard, Sandy. *Digging into Custer's Last Stand.* Terre Haute: Ventana Graphics, 1998.

_____. *Ten Years With Custer. A 7ᵗʰ Cavalryman's Memoirs.* Terre Haute: Citizen Printing, 2001.

Barnett, Louise. *Touched by Fire.* New York: Henry Holt, 1996.

Bradley, James H. *The March of the Montana Column.* Norman: University of Oklahoma, 1961.

Brininstool, E. A. *A Trooper With Custer.* Columbus: The Hunter-Trader-Trapper Co, 1926.

_____. *The Custer Fight. Captain Benteen's Story.* Hollywood: Brininstool, 1940.

_____. *Troopers With Custer.* Harrisburg: Stackpole, 1952.

Brown, Dee. *Bury My Heart At Wounded Knee.* New York: Henry Holt, 1974.

Brown, Mark H. and Felton, W. R. *The Frontier Years.* New York: Henry Holt, 1955.

Callwell, C. E. *Small Wars.* Lincoln: Bison Books, 1996.

Carroll, John M. *Custer in Periodicals.* Ft. Collins: The Old Army Press, 1975.

_____. *Custer in Texas.* New York: Lewis and Liveright, 1975.

_____. *Roll Call on the Little Bighorn.* 28 June 1876. Mattituck: The Old Army Press, 1974.

_____. *The Custer Autograph Album.* College Station: Creative Publishing, 1994.

_____. *The Benteen Goldin Letters.* New York: Liveright, 1974.

_____. *The Cyclorama of Custer's Last Stand.* El Segundo: Upton and Sons, 1988.

_____. *The Battle of the Little Bighorn: The Federal View.* New Brunswick: Gary Owen Press, 1976.

_____. *The Battle of the Washita: The Federal View.* Bryan: Guidon Press, 1978.

_____. *The Two Battle of the Little Big Horn.* New York: Liveright, 1974.

_____. *They Rode with Custer.* Mattituck: The Mad Printers of Mattituck, 1993.

Chandler, Melbourne C. *Of Garryowen in Glory.* Annandale: The Turnpike Press, 1960.

Clark, George M. *Scalp Dance - The Edgerly Papers.* Oswego: Heritage Press, 1985.

Coffeen, Herbert A. *The Custer Battle Book.* New York: Carlton Press, 1964.

Coleman, Thomas W. *I Buried Custer.* College Station: Creative Publishing Company, 1979.

Connell, Evan S. *Son Of The Morningstar.* New York: Harper Collins, 1984.

Cox, Kurt Hamilton. *Custer and His Commands.* London: Greenhill Books, 1999.

Custer, George A. *My Life On The Plains.* New York: Sheldon, 1874.

Custer, Elizabeth B. *Boots And Saddles.* New York: Harper & Brothers, 1885.

_____. *Following the Guidon.* New York: Harper & Brothers, 1890.

_____. *Tenting on the Plains.* New York: Webster, 1887.

Darling, Roger. *A Sad and Terrible Blunder.* Vienna: Potomac Western, 1992.

_____. *Benteen's Scout.* El Segundo: Upton & Sons, 1987.

_____. *General Custer's Final Hours.* Vienna: Potomac Western, 1992.

Debarthe, Joe *Life and Adventures of Frank Grouard.* Sheridan: 1894.

Dippie, Brian W. *George A. Custer in Turf. Field and Farm.* Austin: University of Texas Press, 1980.

Dixon, Joseph K. *The Vanishing Race.* Garden City: Doubleday Page, 1913.

Donnelle, A. J. *Cyclorama of Custer's Last Stand.* New York: Promontory Press, 1966.

Donovan, Jim. *Custer and the Little Bighorn.* Stillwater: Voyageur Press, 2001.

Dowell, William Chipchase. *The Webley Story.* Kirkland: The Skyrac Press, 1987.

Du Mont, John S. *Custer Battle Guns.* Ft. Collins: Old Army Press, 1974.

_____. *Firearms in the Custer Battle.* Harrisburg: The Telegraph Press, 1953.

Du Bois Charles G. *Kick the Dead Lion.* El Segundo: Upton and Sons, 1987.

Dustin, Fred. *The Custer Tragedy.* Ann Arbor: Edwards Brothers, 1939.

Ellison, Douglas W. *Sole Survivor.* Aberdeen: North Plains Press, 1983.

Evans, David C. *Custer's Last Fight.* El Segundo: Upton and Sons, 1999.

Fox, Richard Allen. *Archaeology. History and Custer's Last Battle.* Norman: University of Oklahoma, 1993.

_____. *Archeological Insights into The Custer Battle.* Norman: The University of Oklahoma, 1989.

_____. *Archeological Perspectives Battle Little Bighorn.* Norman: University of Oklahoma Press, 1989.

Freeman, Henry B. *The Freeman Journal.* San Rafael: Presidio Press, 1977.

Frost, Lawrence A. *General Custer's Libbie.* Seattle: Superior Publishing, 1976.

_____. *General Custer's Photographers.* Monroe: Monroe County Library, 1986.

_____. *The Custer Album.* Seattle: Superior Publishing, 1964.

_____. *The Phil Sheridan Album.* Seattle: Superior Publishing, 1968.

Gibbon, John. *Adventures on the Western Frontier.* Bloomington: Indiana University Press, 1994.

_____. *Gibbon on the Sioux Campaign of 1876.* Bellevue: Old Army Press, 1970.

Godfrey, Edward S. *Custer's Last Battle:* Olympic Valley, Outbooks. 1976.

_____. *The Field Diary of Lt. Edward S. Godfrey.* Portland: Champoeg Press, 1957.

Graham, W. A. *The Custer Myth.* Harrisburg: Stackpole, 1953.

_____. *The Reno Court of Inquiry - Abstract.* Harrisburg: Telegraph Press, 1954.

_____. *The Story of the Little Big Horn.* New York: The Century Company, 1926.

Grant, Ulysses S. *Personal Memoirs of Ulysses S. Grant.* New York: Charles Webster, 1885.

Gray, John S. *Centennial Campaign.* Norman: University of Oklahoma, 1988.

_____. *Custer's Last Campaign.* Lincoln: University of Nebraska Press, 1991.

Greene, Jerome A. *Battles and Skirmishes of the Great Sioux War.* Norman: University of Oklahoma, 1993.

_____. *Evidence and the Custer Enigma.* Golden: Outbooks, Inc. 1985.

_____. *Yellowstone Command.* Lincoln: University of Nebraska Press, 1991.

Grinnell, George Bird. *Cheyenne Indians.* New York: Cooper Square Publishers, 1962.

_____. *The Fighting Cheyennes.* Norman: University of Oklahoma Press, 1958.

Hamersly, Thomas. *Complete Regular Army Register 1779 to 1879*. Washington: T. H. S. Hamersly. 1881.

Hammer, Kenneth A. *Custer in 76*. Norman: University of Oklahoma, 1990.

_____. *Men With Custer*. Hardin: Custer Battlefield Historical Museum Assoc., 1995.

Hancock, Winfield Scott. *Reminiscences of Winfield Scott Hancock*. New York: Charles Webster, 1887.

Hardoff, Richard G. *Camp. Custer and the Little Bighorn*. El Segundo: Upton and Sons, 1997.

_____. *Cheyenne Memories*. Lincoln: University of Nebraska, 1998.

_____. *Hokahey A Good Day to Die*. Spokane: Arthur H. Clark, 1993.

_____. *Lakota Recollections*. Lincoln: University of Nebraska, 1997.

_____. *Markers. Artifacts. and Indian Testimony*. Short Hills: Don Horn Publications, 1985

_____. *On The Little Bighorn With Walter Camp*. El Segundo: Upton, and Sons, 2002.

_____. *The Custer Battle Casualties*. El Segundo: Upton and Sons, 1989.

_____. *The Custer Battle Casualties - II*. El Segundo: Upton and Sons, 1999.

_____. *The Death of Crazy Horse*. Spokane: Arthur H. Clark, 1998.

Hart, John P. *Custer and His Times Book Four*. La Grange Park: Little Big Horn Associates, 2002.

Heleniak, Roman J. *Leadership During the Civil War*. Shippenberg: White Main Publishing, 1992.

Historical Society of Montana. Volume IV. Helena: Independent Publishing, 1903.

Hoig, Stan. *The Battle of Washita*. Garden City: Doubleday, 1976.

_____. *Tribal Wars of the Southern Plains*. Norman: University of Oklahoma, 1993.

Hook, Jason. *The Frontier Wars 1860 - 1890*. Oxford: Osprey, 1999.

Horn, W. Donald. *Witness for the Defense*. Short Hills: Horn Publications, 1981.

Hoxie, Frederick E. *Encyclopedia of North American Indians*. Boston, New York: Houghton Mifflin, 1996.

Hunt, Frazier and Robert. *Windolph, I Fought With Custer*. New York: Charles Schribner, 1947.

Hutchins, James S. *Boots and Saddles at the Little Bighorn*. Ft. Collins: Old Army Press, 1976.

Hutchins, James. S. *The Papers of Edward S. Curtis*. El Segundo: Upton and Sons, 2000.

Hutton, Paul Andrew. *The Custer Reader*. Lincoln: University of Nebraska, 1992.

Isham, Asa B. *Seventh Michigan Cavalry*. Huntington: Blue Acorn Press, 2000.

John Stands in Timber. *Cheyenne Memories*. Lincoln: University of Nebraska, 1972.

Kain, Robert C. *Little Big Horn*. North Hollywood: Beinfeld Publishing, 1975.

Kammen, Lefthand & Marshall. *Soldiers Falling Into Camp*. Encampment: Affiliated Writers of America, 1992.

Karr, Charles Lee. *Remington Handguns*. Harrisburg: The Telegraph Press, 1960.

Katcher, Philip D. *The American Indian Wars*. London: Osprey, 1977.

Katz, D. Mark. *Custer in Photographs*. Gettysburg: Yo-Mark Productions, 1985.

Kautz, August V. *Customs of Service for Officers of the Army.* Philadelphia: Lippincott, 1876.

Kidd, J. H. *Personal Recollections of A Cavalryman.* Grand Rapids: The Black Letter Press, 1969.

King, W. Kent. *Massacre The Custer Cover Up.* El Segundo: Upton and Sons, 1989.

Koury, Michael J. *Diaries of the Little Bighorn.* Bellevue: The Old Army Press, 1968.

Kuhlman, Charles. *Legend into History.* Mechanicsburg: Stackpole Books, 1994.

Leckie, William H. *The Buffalo Soldiers.* Norman: University of Oklahoma, 1967.

Libby, *The Arikara Narrative.* New York: Sol Lewis, 1973.

Linderman, Frank B. *Indian Why Stories.* New York: Charles Schribner, 1915.

Longacre, Edward G. *Custer and His Wolverines.* Pennsylvania: Combined Publishing, 1997.

Luce, Edward & Evelyn. *Custer Battlefield.* Washington: National Parks Service, 1957.

Magnussen, Daniel O. *Peter Thompson's Narrative of the Little Big Horn Campaign 1876.* Glendale: Arthur H: Clark, 1970.

Mangum, Neil C. *Battle of the Rosebud.* El Segundo: Upton and Sons, 1996.

Manion, John S. *General Terry's Last Statement to Custer.* El Segundo: Upton and Sons, 2000.

Marquis, Thomas B. *Custer, Cavalry and Crows.* Ft. Collins: Old Army Press, 1975.

_____. *Keep the Last Bullet for Yourself.* Algonac: Reference Publications, 1985.

_____. *Wooden Leg.* Lincoln: University of Nebraska, 1977.

Marshall, S. L. A. *Crimsoned Prairie.* New York: Da Capo, 1972.

McClellan, George B. *McClellan's Own Story.* New York: Charles Webster, 1887.

McClernand, Edward J. *Time for Disaster.* Lincoln: University of Nebraska, 1989.

McGaw, Jessie Brewer. *Chief Red Horse Tells About Custer.* New York: Elsevier/Dutton, 1981.

McLaughlin, James. *My Friend the Indian.* Boston - New York: Houghton Mifflin, 1910.

Merrington, Marguerite. *The Custer Story.* New York: Devin-Adair, 1950.

Michno, Gregory. *Lakota Noon.* Missoula: Mountain Press, 1997.

_____. *The Mystery of E Troop.* Missoula: Mountain Press, 1994.

Miles Nelson A. *The Indian Campaigns of Nelson A Miles.* Beverly: Sherman Miles, 1957.

_____. *The Personal Reflections of.* Chicago-New York: Werner Company, 1896.

Miller, David Humphreys. *Custer's Fall.* New York: Meridian, 1992.

Moeller, Bill and Jan, *Custer His Life His Adventures.* Wilsonville: Beautiful America, 1988.

Myatt, Frederick. *The Illustrated Encyclopedia of Pistols and Revolvers.* New York: Crescent Books, 1980.

N. A. H. S. *The Custer Battle Papers.*: Frontier, 1969.

National Custer Memorial Association. *The Teepee Book.* Sheridan: The Mills Company, 1926.

Neihardt, John G. *Black Elk Speaks.* Lincoln: University of Nebraska, 1961.

Nichols, Ronald H. *Reno Court of Inquiry.* Crow Agency: Custer Battlefield Historical & Museum Assoc, 1992.

Nightengale, Robert. *Little Big Horn.* Edina: Far West Publishing, 1996.

Northrop, Henry D. *Indian Horrors.*: J. R. Jones, 1891.

Overfield, Loyd J. II. *The Little Big Horn 1876.* Lincoln and London: University of Nebraska, 1990.

Panzieri, Peter. *Custer's Last Stand.* London: Osprey, 1995.

Pegler, Martin. *U.S. Cavalryman 1865-1890.* London: Osprey, 1993.

Pennington, Jack. *The Battle of the Little Bighorn.* El Segundo: Upton and Sons, 2001.

Perret, Bryan. *Last Stand - Famous Battles Against the Odds.* London: Arms and Armour, 1993.

Poyer, Joe. *The .45-70 Springfield.* Tustin: North Cape Publications, 1996.

Reusswig, William. *The Custer Fight.* New York: Hastings House, 1967.

Reynolds, Arlene. *The Civil War Memories of Elizabeth Bacon Custer.* Austin: University of Texas, 1994.

Reynolds, Quentin. *Custer's Last Stand.* New York: Random House, 1951.

Rickey, Don. *History of Custer Battlefield.* Ft. Collins: Old Army Press, 1998.

Roberts, Richard Anderson. *Custer's Last Battle.* Monroe: Monroe County Library System, 1978.

Roe, Charles Francis and Charles Francis Bates. *Custer Engages the Hostiles.*: Old Army Press, 1976.

Roe, Frances M. A. *Letters From An Officer's Wife 1871-1888.* New York and London: D. Appleton and Company, 1909.

Rosa, Joseph. *Guns of the American West.* New York: Crown Publishers, 1985.

Russell, Don. *Custer's Last.* Ft. Worth: Amon Carter Museum, 1968.

Russell, Jerry L. *1876 Facts About Custer.* Mason City: Savas, 1999.

Rutledge, Lee A. *Field Uniforms of the Indian War Army 1872-1886.* Tustin: North Cape Publications. 1997.

Sandoz, Mari. *Crazy Horse.* Lincoln and London: University of Nebraska, 1992.

Sarf, Wayne Michael. *The Little Bighorn Campaign.* Conshohocken: Combined Books, 1993.

Scott, Douglas D. *They Died with Custer.* Norman: University of Oklahoma, 1998.

Sheridan, Philip H. *Personal Memoirs of P.H. Sheridan.* New York: Charles Webster, 1888.

_____. *Record of Engagements with Hostile Indians.* Ft. Collins: Old Army Press, 1972.

Sherman, William T. *Memoirs of William T. Sherman.* New York: Charles Webster, 1890.

Sklenar, Larry. *To Hell With Honor.* Norman: The University of Oklahoma Press, 1999.

Stewart, Edgar I. *Custer's Luck.* Norman: University of Oklahoma, 1955.

Taylor, Colin F. *Native American Weapons.* London: Salamander Books, 2001.

Taylor, William O. *With Custer on the Little Big Horn.* New York: Viking, 1996.

Terrell, John Upton *Faint the Trumpet Sounds.* New York: David McKay, 1966.

Terry, Alfred H. *The Field Diary of Alfred H. Terry.* Bellevue: The Old Army Press, 1970.

Tillet, Leslie. *Wind on the Buffalo Grass.* New York: Thomas Crowell, 1976.

Upton, Emory. *Cavalry Tactics United States Army*. New York: D. Appleton and Company, 1876.

_____. *Infantry Tactics United States Army*. New York: D. Appleton and Company, 1876.

Upton, Richard. *The Custer Adventure*. Hardin: Custer Battlefield Historical & Museum Assoc., 1981.

Urwin, Gregory J. *Custer and His Times*. La Grange: Little Big Horn Associates, 1987.

Utley, Robert. M. *Cavalier In Buckskin*. Norman and London: University of Oklahoma Press, 1988.

_____. *Custer And the Great Controversy*. Pasadena: Westernlore Press, 1980.

_____. *Life in Custer's Cavalry*. New Haven and London: Yale University Press,. 1977.

_____. *The Frontier Regulars*. New York: Collier MacMillan, 1973.

_____. *Reno Court of Inquiry - Chicago Times Account*. Ft. Collins: Old Army Press, 1972.

Varnum, Charles A. *I Varnum*. Glendale: Arthur H. Clark, 1982.

Varnum, Charles A. *Custer's Chief of Scouts*. Lincoln and London: University of Nebraska, 1982.

Vietzen, Raymond C. *Archeology Around the Great Lakes*: Whitehorse, 1987.

Viola, Herman J. *Little Bighorn Remembered*. New York: Rivilo Books, 1999.

Walter, John. *The Guns That Won The West*. London: Greenhill Books, 1999.

Weibert, Don. *Four Days With Custer*. Ft. Collins: Citizen Printing, 1985.

_____. *Custer. Cases and Cartridges*. Billings: Weibert, 1989.

Weibert, Don and Henry. *Sixty Six Years in Custer's Shadow*. Billings: Falcon Press, 1985.

Wert, Jeffrey D. *Custer - The Controversial Life of*. New York: Touchstone, 1996.

_____. *The Personal Memoirs of P. H. Sheridan*. New York:: Da Capo, 1992.

Whittaker, Frederick. *A Complete Life of General George A Custer*. New York: Sheldon & Co., 1876.

Willert, James. *March of the Columns*. El Segundo: Upton and Sons, 1994.

_____. *Little Big Horn Diary*. La Mirada: James Willert, 1977.

Zupan, James. *Tools. Targets. and Troopers*. Mattituck and Bryan: Mattituck, 1985.

INDEX

(MOH = Medal of Honor; MTC = Medicine Tail Coulee)